The Value of Arts for Business

The traditional view of the relationship between business and the arts is very much a one-way affair: organisations may endorse, fund or publicise the arts but the arts have nothing to offer from a business perspective. *The Value of Arts for Business* challenges this view by showing how the arts, in the form of Arts-based Initiatives (ABIs), can be used to enhance value-creation capacity and boost business performance. The book introduces and explains three models that show how organisations can successfully implement and manage ABIs. First, the Arts Value Matrix enables managers to see how organisational value-drivers are affected by ABIs. Second, the Arts Benefits Constellation shows how to assess the benefits of using ABIs. Finally, the Arts Value Map shows how ABIs can be integrated and aligned with organisational strategy and operations. These models lay the foundations for a new research area exploring the links between the arts and business.

GIOVANNI SCHIUMA is Scientific Director of the Centre for Value Management and Professor of Innovation Management at the Università della Basilicata, Italy. He is also a visiting professor at the Institute for Manufacturing, University of Cambridge; a visiting fellow at the Cranfield School of Management; Adjunct Professor at Tampere University of Technology, Finland; and a co-editor of the international journal *Measuring Business Excellence*.

The Value of Arts
for Business

GIOVANNI SCHIUMA

CAMBRIDGE
UNIVERSITY PRESS

CAMBRIDGE
UNIVERSITY PRESS

Shaftesbury Road, Cambridge CB2 8EA, United Kingdom

One Liberty Plaza, 20th Floor, New York, NY 10006, USA

477 Williamstown Road, Port Melbourne, VIC 3207, Australia

314–321, 3rd Floor, Plot 3, Splendor Forum, Jasola District Centre, New Delhi – 110025, India

103 Penang Road, #05–06/07, Visioncrest Commercial, Singapore 238467

Cambridge University Press is part of Cambridge University Press & Assessment, a department of the University of Cambridge.

We share the University's mission to contribute to society through the pursuit of education, learning and research at the highest international levels of excellence.

www.cambridge.org
Information on this title: www.cambridge.org/9780521769518

First published 2011
Reprinted 2011

A catalogue record for this publication is available from the British Library

Library of Congress Cataloging-in-Publication data
Schiuma, Giovanni.
The value of arts for business / Giovanni Schiuma.
    p. cm.
Includes bibliographical references and index.
ISBN 978-0-521-76951-8
1. Creative ability in business.   2. Management.   3. Arts.   I. Title.
HD53.S358   2011
658 – DC22   2011003318

ISBN   978-0-521-76951-8   Hardback

To Gabriela for always supporting me in my path . . .

Contents

Figures

Boxes

Acknowledgements

The writing of this book has been like undertaking an intense and inspiring journey towards the desired destination. I was already prepared to put in the effort needed and I was feeling confident in the research that I have been carrying out in the last decade. However, it was while writing that I discovered the passion that needs to be put in a project like this in order to reach the final destination. I was lucky because along this journey I was not alone. Many people have contributed in different ways and at various stages to the writing of this book. I would like to first acknowledge Arts & Business for supporting the development of an early stage of the empirical research. Arts & Business helped me to identify some of the most important challenges to reconciling business and arts. This has stimulated the identification of the research issues inspiring my writing. I am also grateful for the support they provided in organising events with academics, executives and arts practitioners to discuss some of the draft research ideas presented in this book. Therefore, I would like to thank the extraordinary group of people from Arts & Business who have contributed to my research. My thanks to Gavin Buckley, Jane Chambers, Simon Cronshaw, Frances Gallagher, Jessica Garland, Linda Griffiths, Meghann Jones, Sebastian Paul, Joanne South and Chloe Theobald. I would also like to acknowledge Mark McGuinness who, in the first stage of the project, helped me in putting together the panel of artists and executives to be interviewed, and my colleagues Chris Bilton and Sheila Galloway who read and commented on the very first research idea behind this book.

Walking my path to developing the research, I have greatly benefited from the experience of the artists and managers who have offered their availability for interviews, taking part in discussion meetings and workshops, filling in questionnaires and reviewing many draft versions of the case studies. Their experiences and passion for the use of the arts in business have been a source of great value. I myself have discovered that working with the arts and artists involves a lot of passion which is contagious and sparks energy. I am thankful to the arts practitioners who have shared their passion for their work with me. Their energy has fuelled my curiosity, so I extend a big thank you to Sam Bond from tradesecrets; Paul Bourne from Menagerie Theatre Company; Duncan Bruce from The Brand Conspiracy; Geoff Church and Richard Hahlo from Dramatic Resources; Peter Feroze from The Creative Knowledge Company; Martin Gent from Spinach; Chris Higgins and Fiona Lesley from The MAP Consortium; Martin Holme from Spider and Givaudin; Piers Ibbotson from Directing Creativity; Tom Morley from Instant Teamwork; Tim Stockil from Ci: Creative Intelligence; Rob Colbert from Circus Space; Raphaële Bidault-Waddington from Laboratoire d'Ingénierie d'Idées; and Beth-Marie Norbury and Clare Titley from Welsh National Opera. I am also grateful to the executives who participated in the research. They are pioneers in the integration of the arts in management systems. I would like to thank Nick Wright from UBS; Stephen Bampfylde from Saxton Bampfylde Hever Plc; Natalie Bentley from Nestle UK; Tom Conway from Spinach; Rick Haythornthwaite from Star Capital Partners Ltd and The Southbank; Donald Hess from Hess Family Estates; Jonathan Michelmore from Nescafe Dolce Gusto; Annemarie Shillito from Experian; and Terry Willie from Hall & Partners. In addition, I am grateful to all the organisations appearing in the book.

A special thanks to the staff of Cambridge University Press. They provided their excellent support for the development of the editorial project. I especially thank Paula Parish who saw the book's potential and encouraged me with the original conception and with the overall development of it, and Philip Good who took care of the production process.

My deepest thanks to J C Spender, Daniela Carlucci, Daniela Castrataro, Antonio Lerro and Karim Moustaghfir for their feedback and the helpful, constructive review of the manuscript. A special thanks to my friend and 'art architect' Beth-Marie Norbury who has significantly helped me in refining the contents and writing of this book: her assistance and passionate support has been invaluable. I would like also to acknowledge Vito Epifania and all the staff from Altrimedia for their creative energy in designing the cover of this book.

I want to express my appreciation to all my colleagues who directly and indirectly in the past years have sparked and nourished the research ideas that are formalised here. This book is the result of the convergence of many efforts that I have shared with friends and colleagues. I am grateful to them for all the formal and informal artful conversations and discussions that have inspired my journey. A special thanks to Vito Albino for reasons that a 'captain' knows well.

My deepest thanks to my parents who have always believed in me and gave me the emotional energy needed to undertake any challenge.

To Gabriela, I express my deepest gratitude. She gave me the space and time to immerse myself in my journey. She tolerated my obsessive passion for writing and my countless weekends spent locked in my studio. To her, my deepest thanks for supporting me in whatever I do and for being my best friend.

Giovanni Schiuma

Foreword

What is the value of arts in business? What is the role of the arts in management? How can the arts contribute to develop organisations and boost business performance? Why do organisations need to absorb the arts in their working mechanisms and business models? These are some of the crucial questions that occupy the debate about the strategic relevance of the arts in business. Giovanni Schiuma provides answers to these fundamental issues and shows how the arts can enhance organisational value. In *The Value of Arts for Business* the author argues that the arts represent a new 'territory' to innovate management systems. Through the implementation of Arts-based Initiatives (ABIs), managers can both manage the organisational aesthetic and develop their people and infrastructure.

Arts & Business works to bridge the worlds of arts and business and to create a platform to support the growth of the business capacity for the arts. Fostering the creation of partnerships between arts and business, we have addressed a twofold goal. On the one hand we have transferred the mindset of business to the arts, in order to sustain the development of arts organisations through the deployment of business principles. On the other hand we advocate and facilitate the adoption of the arts in business, as a tool to help organisations face management challenges. This book explains the strategic relevance and contribution that the arts can offer for the development of twenty-first century organisations.

An important focus of our work with partners from arts and business has been to encourage business to look to the arts for solutions to some of the key challenges they face. We have fostered a wide spectrum of business engagement with the arts, creating new ventures, new types of relationships and new ways of doing business. One of the main problems we have dealt with has been the difficulty to systematically elucidate and assess the benefits that organisations can achieve by absorbing the arts in their working mechanisms and management systems. Although we have been working with many organisations, only a few businesses seem to have a clear understanding of what the arts can deliver in terms of their likely impact on performance improvements. On the other hand, arts organisations and artists still lack a thorough understanding of how they can contribute to the development of organisations and build sustainable partnerships producing mutual benefits.

The importance of clarifying how the arts can contribute to the development of organisations is even more crucial in today's complex business landscape. As organisations search for new solutions to engage and improve the working life of their people, face difficult management challenges, generate experience-based market value and spur resilience and innovativeness, the arts can help them to find new possible solutions to emergent business problems. This suggests that the relationships between the arts and business have to evolve beyond the more traditional arts-based training and professional interventions, sponsorship engagement and creation of art collections. Through this scholarly book, Giovanni Schiuma shows how the arts can have a positive impact on the enhancement of organisational value. In today's new economic age, the arts can represent a 'revolution' in innovating management practices, providing tools to manage organisational aesthetic experiences and properties. This book makes a significant contribution to strengthening the conceptual and managerial base for understanding the value of arts in business and how ABIs can impact on business performance. The proposed frameworks will help managers and arts-based organisations to better design, implement and assess ABIs that are fully incorporated into management systems.

Today, with so many management challenges and business problems that are radically changing the economic and competitive scenario, it is critical for organisations to identify new knowledge to inspire management innovations. I believe the arts can provide tools and techniques to transform business models. Understanding how the arts work to sustain and drive organisational value-creation is a crucial first step in adopting art forms as management tools. For this reason, *The Value of Arts for Business* is an authoritative research work that will help organisations to understand what the arts can do for them.

Colin Tweedy
Chief Executive, Arts & Business

Introduction

Organisations have, traditionally, considered the arts, at best, as something nice to have and to support for socio-cultural reasons, an acces-
sory with little impact on organisational value creation. *The Value of
Arts for Business* discloses the relevance of the arts as a means by which
management can enhance organisational value-creation capacity and
boost business performance. It will investigate why and how the arts,
in the form of Arts-based Initiatives (ABIs), can represent a powerful
management tool for developing employees and organisational infrastructure that can drive superior value creation.

Beginning with the definition of the principles of Scientific Management by Frederick Taylor (1911), management, in both theory and
practice, has been essentially focused in the design, implementation,
assessment and control of the rational and engineering characteristics
that drive the working mechanisms of organisations and the achievement of strategic objectives. The positivistic approach has dominated
the development of modern management, with its paraphernalia of
models, approaches and tools providing interpretative and normative
guidelines for management initiatives, both to affect the efficiency of
organisational processes and to drive business growth. The fundamental idea of the modern management paradigm has been that it
is possible to define and manage organisations essentially as an efficient system able to achieve, without inconvenience and/or unexpected
negative events, the targeted business objectives. In accordance with
this view, the arts have not had any role to play in management.
At best, they have been considered as a component of promotional
strategies, organisational social responsibility policies, training activities for employees and investment strategies based on the creation of art
collections.

In today's complex business landscape, as organisations are challenged by new and increasingly complex problems, the arts provide
a new 'territory' to inspire executives both to see their organisations

1

differently and to define innovative management systems. It is more and more difficult for organisations to plot a clear course to achieve the targeted value-creation objectives according to a specific business development vision. Organisations are continuously challenged to find new routes to accomplish their strategic business objectives and to deliver value to stakeholders. They have to become agile, intuitive, imaginative, flexible to change and innovative. This means that organisations have to be managed as 'living organisms' in which the people and the organisational aesthetic dimensions are recognised as fundamental factors to meet the complexity and turbulence of the new business age.

The new problem that management has to focus on and solve is not only the technical efficiency of the organisational processes, but also the dynamic adaptability and resilience of organisations. This problem requires a shift of attention from outputs and input–output ratios to outcomes and impacts, but most importantly a revaluation of the centrality of people in organisations.

The twenty-first century business landscape is scattered with ambiguities, uncertainties, a high pace of change, dynamism and unpredictability. In such a context, the success of an organisation is increasingly based on the creation of emotive and energetic organisations in which employees feel engaged, in control of themselves and aware of the situations around them, and experience happiness and wealth. In addition, in today's advanced mass-consumption economy, the evolution of consumer behaviours requires organisations to create intangible value. Products and services have to be able to let people undergo fulfilling experiences that involve their emotions. The arts can make a distinctive contribution to the creation and management of the emotive and energetic characteristics of organisations as well as to the development of organisational assets that incorporate intangible value. The managerial deployment of the arts allows managers to affect the organisational aesthetic dimensions. Through the arts it is possible to foster aesthetic experiences and manipulate the aesthetic properties of an organisation's infrastructure. This enables management to handle emotional and energetic mechanisms in organisations.

The use of the arts in management can be addressed by introducing the notion of Arts-based Initiatives (ABIs). An ABI is the planned managerial use of art forms to address management challenges and business problems with the aim of developing employees and infrastructure that affects the organisational value-creation capacity. Examples can range from the use of art forms to entertain organisations' employees and clients, to the deployment of arts to develop the 'soft competencies' of people in the organisation, and may include the exploitation of the arts to create intangible value to be incorporated into products or to transform and enhance an organisation's infrastructural assets such as, for instance, image, identity, reputation, culture and climate.

By deploying the arts, organisational aesthetic dimensions that evoke and mobilise people's emotions and energy can be stimulated. This does not mean that ABIs have no room for efficiency, on the contrary they significantly contribute to a system's productivity, but they do so by impacting on organisational dimensions that cannot be controlled analytically and rationally, and nevertheless play a fundamental role in explaining the success and the excellence of organisations. They are the emotive and energetic factors affecting the behaviours of employees and the characteristics of an organisation's infrastructure.

In order to investigate the role and relevance of the arts in management, the author adopts a utilitarian perspective, which recognises the need to integrate the traditional rational-based view of the organisation with the emotive-based perspective of organisational life and its components. The fundamental thesis is that organisational value-creation capacity depends on the integration of 'technical knowledge' with 'emotive knowledge', which denotes the content and characteristics of the knowing process related to human emotional traits. The arts provide approaches and tools to handle emotional and energetic dynamics within and around organisations.

The focus is not on a specific art form, but on the arts in general. While acknowledging that not all art forms are equal, the book's focus is on the deployment of artistic products and processes to activate and induce aesthetic dynamics that affect the emotive knowledge characterising employees and organisational infrastructure.

The Value of Arts for Business situates the arts in organisations among the management resources and sources for organisational development. Accordingly the central question of this book is: *What is the value of the arts for business?* This issue is explored by addressing other important questions such as: *Why do twenty-first century organisations need to use the arts as a management tool? How are organisations experimenting with the use of the arts to solve their business problems? How can we classify and analyse the managerial use of art forms in organisations? What are the organisational benefits of ABIs and why should organisations invest in them? How can ABIs support the achievement of business objectives and organisational growth? How can managers and arts-based providers manage ABIs with the aim of driving business performance improvements?*

The answer to these questions involved research across many disciplinary boundaries. For this reason, the conceptual pillars of *The Value of Arts for Business* are grounded in insights derived from different disciplines including psychology, sociology, neurobiology, neuroscience, organisation theory, human resources, strategic management, economics and philosophy. Travelling on the borders and intersecting different disciplines to draw useful implications and build hypotheses and thesis may be a bold journey, but it is rewarding and necessary in order to build new perspectives and frameworks that can help managers to shape organisations that better fit with the challenges of the new millennium. The answers to the newly emergent business problems increasingly lie at the intersection and convergence of the solutions developed in different scientific fields. The purpose in writing this book is to contribute to laying the foundations of a new research area by investigating the links between the arts and business, as well as defining models that can help organisations to deploy and integrate the arts in management systems. The book makes a twofold contribution. On the one hand, it provides the conceptual pillars that help us to understand how the arts can inspire managers to blend extant rational-based approaches with the emotive-based view of organisational life and activities, recognising the relevance of people's emotions and energy. On the other hand, it proposes managerial principles and frameworks to support managers in adopting the arts in organisations as an instrument to develop organisational assets and improve business performance.

The fundamental argument is that the adoption of the arts in management creates organisations that are more human and that take into account the human-based nature of business. Indeed, the arts bring with them the passion of life and contribute to transforming the organisation. They are able to engage employees in their daily work activities, to inspire executives to shape organisations as living organisms endowed with the capabilities to face today's business complexity and turbulence, and to make organisations more aware of the value propositions delivered to stakeholders.

The book consists of five chapters that build the conceptual and managerial pillars that will help the reader to understand the potential of the arts in business to create and deliver value. Chapter 1 defines the theoretical background, explaining why the arts matter in management. Starting from an analysis of today's management challenges, the importance of shifting from the modern management paradigm to the postmodern management perspective is discussed. It is clear that managers have to face a fundamental managerial mindshift that recognises the centrality of people in business. By interpreting organisations as techno-human systems, the relevance of aesthetics and emotions as factors affecting organisational life and components becomes apparent. Hence, the arts are introduced as a learning platform and a device or vector that affects organisational aesthetic dimensions and impacts on an organisation's value-creation capacity.

Chapter 2 investigates how the use of arts in business can be translated into action. The notion of ABIs is proposed as a conceptual category for an understanding of the content, forms and practical formats of the use of arts. Afterwards the working mechanisms of ABIs are analysed and the impact of aesthetic dynamics on people and organisational infrastructure is presented. The chapter ends with an exploration of the links between ABIs and emotional and energetic dynamics in organisations.

Chapter 3 takes a closer look at how ABIs can generate business benefits. The beneficiaries and the characteristics of the benefits of ABIs are illustrated. This defines the basis of the 'Arts Value Matrix' as a framework to map the value of ABIs and to point out how organisations have experimented with the use of the arts. The Arts Value Matrix is proposed as a model through which to perform both interpretative and normative analysis of the strategic reasons for the adoption of ABIs. It classifies the organisational value-drivers explaining the strategic benefits that ABIs can produce. This supports the definition of a further framework entitled 'the four value zones of the arts' that defines the fundamental strategic intents of the use of arts in management.

Chapter 4 explains the links between ABIs and business performance. In particular, it addresses the linkages between ABIs and organisational knowledge assets, highlighting the fact that the arts act as a trigger and a catalyst for the creation and management of emotive knowledge. Recognising that ABIs, first and foremost, impact on knowledge assets, the 'Arts Benefits Constellation' is presented as a framework to assess the impact of the use of the arts on organisational knowledge domains. The attention is focused on how ABIs promote business performance improvements by activating a cause-and-effect chain that impacts on knowledge assets, influencing organisational capabilities that in turn enhance the quality and productivity of business processes with a resulting achievement of operational and strategic performance objectives. To assess the business performance benefits generated through the ABIs, the 'Arts Value Map', based on mapping visualisation techniques, is proposed as a model.

Finally, Chapter 5 focuses on how to manage ABIs to make sure that they produce business performance improvements. Starting from the identification of the main arts-based strategic approaches that managers can put in place to deploy the arts in order to develop people and organisational infrastructure, the fundamental importance of integrating and aligning ABIs to organisational operations and strategy is discussed. ABIs can be adopted as a 'one-off' management action or can be fully integrated into the organisation's DNA. What matters is that they are designed to meet the specific organisation's wants and needs. In order to help organisations to adopt the arts, the management cycle of ABIs is presented as a closed-loop process based on five fundamental stages: plan, design, implementation, assessment and review. The chapter concludes by outlining some fundamental management implications for the successful implementation of ABIs.

Although the discipline of management has been populated with many different models and concepts that have supported business growth, one century on from the definition of the principles of Scientific Management, organisational management systems appear to be anchored in the rational-based perspective. However, the characteristics of the new business age force us to recognise that the quality and the productivity of organisational business models increasingly depend on emotional and energetic factors. My research over the past decade has investigated the key intangible assets driving value creation. I have discovered that people's emotions and energy are strategic factors for the improvement of business performance. My investigation of the role and relevance of the arts in management sheds light on how ABIs can be deployed both to humanise organisations, by harnessing the emotional and energetic dynamics that affect business activities, and to support the development of management innovations that can drive the creation of a new generation of management systems that are more suited to meet the challenges of the twenty-first century. This book is a research endeavour to disclose the power of the arts to manage those aesthetics and emotions that shape organisations and drive value creation.

1 | *Why arts matter in management*

Introduction

Without a doubt, the arts represent one of the most important knowledge domains for the expression of human feelings and values. They are the product of human civilisations and an essential instrument in shaping culture and society. Indeed, people's lives and communities are entrenched in the arts: they play a fundamental role in shaping and conveying human emotions and a community's values and culture (Guss, 1989). Through the arts people can express and communicate what matters most to them. Mankind's history is tied to the arts. The use of the arts has accompanied the evolution of organisations. Kings and queens, emperors, dictators, politicians and leaders have used the power of the arts to manipulate organisational reality at macro and micro levels, and to affect people's experiences and behaviours.

In acknowledging the importance of the arts in human life, it is worth reflecting on the role and relevance of the use of the arts in management. The arts as a cornerstone of human life provides a vehicle that can inspire and improve today's management discipline and practice (Adler, 2006; Darsø, 2004; Taylor and Ladkin, 2009). From an instrumental and a utilitarian point of view, the arts can support and drive the development of organisational value-creation capacity and in turn improve business performance. The arts represent a knowledge 'mine' – rich in ideas, techniques, artistic know-how, products and processes – that can be used to define and adopt innovative managerial models and techniques that are more suited to governing organisational value-creation in the twenty-first century business landscape (Austin and Devin, 2003; Nissley, 2010).

This chapter addresses two key questions: *What is the role of the arts in management?* and *Why is the adoption of the arts in today's organisations important?* The investigation of these questions requires a preliminary conceptual journey that involves the exploration of other critical issues. Today's business models and management systems are being challenged due to widespread changes in the current business climate and the growing demand for the transformation of management discipline and practice (Hamel, 2007, 2009; Mol and Birkinshaw, 2008). This poses questions such as: *How should management view twenty-first century organisations?* and *What strategic organisational traits need to be managed in order to improve business performance and drive sustainable value creation?* In addressing these issues, this chapter will address why the arts constitute a new 'territory' that can inspire managers to develop management innovation, frame new organisational and business models and draw on new approaches and instruments to tackle emergent business challenges.

The chapter begins by outlining the main macro forces that are reshaping the twenty-first century business landscape. These global trends are transforming the competitive environment and forcing organisations to develop new capabilities. They are challenging the validity of traditional management principles. In today's economic and competitive environment, organisational value-creation capacity is not only linked to the definition of efficient and consistent organisational systems, as traditionally postulated by modern management, but it is also increasingly tied to the establishment of adaptable and resilient systems that are able to meet changing market demands and the continuous emergent business problems. In the new business age, the practice of management has to evolve. From a conceptual point of view, this chapter will highlight the need to shift from the traditional modern management paradigm to a postmodern management paradigm. The fundamental underlying idea is that the creation of value in the new millennium is tied to the recognition of the relevance of people's experiences, emotions and energy in shaping and influencing the quality and performance of organisations. This is the basis for understanding why the arts matter in management and defines the conceptual background to explain how the arts can be adopted by organisations for management purposes.

The management challenges of the new business landscape

Today, managers are navigating a new business landscape and increasingly find themselves facing newly emergent challenges that create both opportunities and threats. Different and integrated macro forces, individually and in combination, are already shaping the twenty-first century business landscape. These forces are imprinting deep changes on the characteristics of the economic and competitive environment.

The global trends that are reshaping the new business age have been largely discussed in management literature (e.g., Friedman, 2005; Held *et al.*, 1999; Mau *et al.*, 2004; Meredith, 2007). However, their practical fallout for companies is now becoming evident. They highlight the need to develop new management systems that integrate traditional management approaches and tools with new methods for interpreting and solving business problems that fully take into account the human nature of business activities. In particular, nine main global trends can be identified and they call for the adoption of new management principles and models: intensification of web dynamics; social and sustainable development of business; acceleration of the pace of change; competitive anarchy; value networking; increasing growth and role of new competitive players; commoditisation of technical knowledge; exponential technology evolution; and development of an experienced-based economy. Below each macro trend is briefly introduced.

Intensification of web dynamics

Companies now operate in a 'flatter world' in which economies and production systems are increasingly interconnected and interdependent (Friedman, 2005). Increasing global interconnectedness and interdependence is reshaping global and local political, economic and cultural process dynamics (Held *et al.*, 1999; Mau *et al.*, 2004). As a result, in today's business world changes tend to ripple across industries and countries, much like a 'domino effect'. This is making the competitive arena more and more complex and unpredictable. In this context managers are challenged to make organisations more agile, resilient and capable of adaptation and transformation.

Social and sustainable development of business

There is increasing attention paid towards the role and responsibility of business in society (Post *et al.*, 2002). Nowadays the private sector plays a crucial role as a co-creator of society (Adler, 2006). Companies are being challenged to take into account the impact of their business activities on social and economic wellbeing, and they are equally charged with the prevention of environmental degradation. The environmental disaster of the oil spill in the Gulf of Mexico involving British Petroleum (BP) is an example of the role and responsibility that today's companies share in affecting environmental pollution as well as the wellbeing of communities. This means that companies increasingly need to address multiple value propositions, merging socio, cultural, cognitive and environment value dimensions together with an economic one (Neely *et al.*, 2002). In this perspective, dimensions such as business ethics, corporate social responsibility, sustainable economic development, corporate citizenship and stakeholder value-oriented perspectives have to be incorporated into management systems and traditional management principles must be expanded and adjusted to embed new interpretative dimensions of the nature and role of companies. By embracing the sustainability concept companies have to recognise the human-based nature of the organisation and its impact on and contribution to building the ecosystem in which it operates.

The acceleration of the pace of change

A feature of the new millennium is the pace of change. Not only has it increased, but also its nature has evolved. More and more competitive companies evolve through disruptive changes rather than by levering continuous improvements (Amis *et al.*, 2004). In this scenario, competitive advantages are less defendable and more easily eroded. This means that management has to shape organisations in which change is a 'mind status', i.e., employees continuously accept and search for new solutions in order to reactively and proactively face emergent business problems. For this reason, organisations have to nurture their employees' ability to be imaginative and motivated to give the best of themselves, as well as to embrace and promote transformation.

Competitive anarchy

In today's economy the barriers of entry across a wide range of industries are radically reducing, resulting in a fracturing of oligopolies and the rise of a 'competitive anarchy' (Hamel, 2007). This increases the chaotic nature of the competitive environment and challenges managers to navigate their organisations into a turbulent business landscape, accepting and facing unpredictable competitive events. Increasingly forecasts lose their power to predict and indicate future development paths. An example of the unpredictability of today's business landscape is the financial crisis that has shocked the global economy in recent years. Despite the surveillance of institutions such as the International Monetary Fund (IMF) and other national and international agencies and research centres, the crisis arrived as a 'bolt from the blue'.

Value networking

In the new business age the competitive success of companies is increasingly tied to the quality of their networks. This challenges managers to improve the management of organisational relationships. But most importantly, it highlights the relevance of infusing a networking culture within organisations. The ability to create superior value in and through networks requires not only the technical and contractual aspects of a relationship to be taken into account, but also very importantly people's emotional and social dimensions affecting trust, closeness, bonding, cohesiveness and mutuality, which are critical factors for the quality of a relationship (Anand *et al.*, 2002; Baker, 1990; Burt, 1992; Coleman, 1990; Leana and Van Buren III, 1999; Nahapiet and Ghoshal, 1998; Rob, 2002).

Increasing growth and role of new competitive players

The global business landscape is shaken by the 'shock waves' of the competitive growth of new players (Meredith, 2007). The rapid economic growth in Asia is gradually determining a shift in the centre of gravity of the global economy. New business players are emerging in the competitive scene that can count on multiple competitive factors ranging from traditional economic factors, to the eagerness of their citizens to improve their social and economic status. In order to meet this competition, western companies in particular will have to identify new value-creation drivers. Traditional economic, technological and production factors do not guarantee success. Companies are gradually realising that the most important strategic and context-specific competitive dimension is related to human capital.

Commoditisation of technical knowledge

More and more knowledge can be acquired in the market either by inserting know-how components in the form of organisational units, through acquisitions, mergers or partnerships, or by employing skilled people that assure the absorption of key competencies. In addition, the intense knowledge codification processes aimed at making knowledge more controllable and exploitable within organisational boundaries, have made knowledge more fluid and easily transferable. As a result technical knowledge is gradually becoming a commodity. This means that a new form of knowledge will increase in importance. It is the knowledge related to people's emotional traits. This kind of knowledge cannot be codified due to its idiosyncratic and personal nature and most importantly represents a key element distinguishing and affecting people and organisational behaviours.

Exponential technology evolution

Technologies continue to develop at exponential rates, making competitive advantages grounded on tangible infrastructure increasingly temporary. As technologies are evolving and becoming more and more pervasive, what matters for competitiveness is how companies can make the best use of them to create value. This means that organisations not only have to strengthen their technology-based know-how, but very importantly they also have to make technologies more user-friendly and intuitive.[1]

Development of an experienced-based economy

Organisations are increasingly challenged to create intangible value on the basis of an understanding of customers' perception of products. Nowadays consumers are not only becoming more diversified in terms of their needs and wants, but also more importantly they are increasingly searching for experienced-based value dimensions. Today's products are fully able to deliver material and functional value. So, successful products are those that are capable of impacting on people's emotions by levering on aesthetic properties (Austin, 2008).

The global trends outlined above are transforming companies' competitiveness and are shaping the characteristics of the twenty-first century business landscape in a way that can be summarised as: complexity, turbulence, fluidity, dynamism and unpredictability. Due to the characteristics of the new business environment it is unlikely that companies can count on lasting and sustainable competitive advantage positions. Organisations need to continuously change and renew themselves both by absorbing the external changes, in accordance with an adaptive approach, and by nourishing transformational processes in order to proactively project and induce changes in the external environment. This challenges the way organisations are managed. As the business landscape is evolving, the traditional focus on efficiency and consistency is losing its centrality and needs to be integrated with a new imperative. In a disruptive business world performance is increasingly related to the development of adaptable and resilient organisations that accept and encourage continuous evolution.

The need for new management principles

As the overall business environment becomes more complex and unpredictable, organisations are discovering that their future wealth creation is based on the development of new capabilities. To face the current global trends organisations must be dynamic, innovative, intuitive, imaginative, adaptable, resilient and tough (Hamel, 2007; Kim and Mauborgne, 2005). These capabilities can only be developed by recognising the fundamental human-based nature of organisations (Hamel, 2000). In fact, an organisation's ability to be intuitive and imaginative is related to its employees' will and power to exercise their creativity and imagination in daily work activities. This requires management systems that promote a strong engagement and deployment of human capital. Organisations willing to promote intuition and imagination need to adopt management models and approaches that create and foster a favourable organisational atmosphere in which creativity sparks and people are inspired and energised to fully use their mental faculties to explore new realities and identify hidden solutions to business challenges. Consider Google for example; in order to engage employees so that they can better identify new solutions to emergent business problems, the company has introduced practices that give time and space to employees to cultivate and express their creativity. Combining the shaping of the aesthetic properties of the workplace and the creation of aesthetic experiences Google is paying great attention to how to inspire and energise employees.

Also, organisational flexibility, resilience and toughness are linked to employees' capacity to tackle stress, anxiety, difficulties, failures and more generally negative feelings. Organisations involved in change management programmes are discovering the critical role of employees' emotions and energy to ensure they accomplish successful transformation.

Therefore, organisations aspiring to prosper have to make sure that flexibility, change and innovation are deeply embedded into employees' behaviours and skills. To support organisational value-creation organisations need to mobilise, convey and manage people's willingness to give the best of themselves to contribute to company success. Employees have to be fully engaged to put their energy into business problems and challenges.[2] According to Dick (1995: 31) 'engagement occurs when [people] experience a deep sense of caring about the work, a sense that what [they] are doing is worthwhile in and for itself'. In order to create what Dick refers to as a 'sense of caring', managers need to address people's emotions and energy (Richards, 1995). Indeed, human emotive traits such as passion, hope, morality, imagination and aspirations are gradually becoming critical strategic organisational competitive factors (Boyatzis *et al.*, 2002; Bruch and Ghoshal, 2003; Cross *et al.*, 2003; Gratton, 2007; Steers *et al.*, 2004). These dimensions affect the organisational capacity to exploit resources and to translate knowledge into action. They influence the quality of existing businesses, their growth and most importantly the development of new business solutions. In this regard, Tim Cook, chief of operations at Apple, explaining the ingredients of Apple's success, states that: 'The place is loaded with engineers, but it's not just the skills that are important, it is the ability to emote. "Emotive" is a big word here. The passion is what provides the push to overcome design and engineering obstacles, to bring projects in on time' (Morris, 2008: 42).

The above implications set the challenge for managers to infuse the ability to blend linear, analytical and rational thinking with intuitive and emotive thinking within their organisations. They need to engage employees' emotions and energy both at the individual and group levels, so that they are willing to accept and promote transformation as well as give their best for organisational success.

In today's global and complex economy, the mere interpretation of an organisation as a system made up of parts to be defined and managed in order to be efficient, controllable, reliable, stable and optimal in terms of the use of resources, is not sufficient to build successful and excellent organisations. As organisations are challenged to develop new capabilities the importance of adopting new management principles is emerging.

From a modern to a postmodern management paradigm

Management has evolved as a paradigm focusing attention on how to model and govern organisational working mechanisms in order to make sure that they are able not only to produce outputs that meet market demand, but also to guarantee the optimisation of the ratio between the produced outputs and the resources used as inputs.[3] The minimisation of the waste of resources and efforts maximising outputs through control of inputs lies at the heart of management (Mol and Birkinshaw, 2008). This fundamental principle has affected how we think about, look at and interpret organisations, their life and business models and their working mechanisms. However, the evolution of the economic and competitive scenario is gradually challenging this view, highlighting the necessity to enrich the modern management perspective with a postmodern one. By adopting the notion of 'postmodern', the aim is to denote another way in which managers need to approach the challenges and problems characterising twenty-first century organisations. The concept of postmodernism is used here not as an opposition to modernism, i.e., anti-modern, nor is it intended to denote an overcoming of the modern management paradigm, i.e., ultramodern, but rather, the concept of postmodernism is proposed to point out the importance of radically enriching the traditional understanding of organisations with a new interpretative perspective. The postmodern management paradigm is not to be considered as a 'fracture' within modern management's set of ideas, models and techniques; but rather as a significant enlargement.

The fundamental assumption is that the complexity of today's business realities makes the established linear and reductionist management thinking inappropriate. The traditional inquiring systemic approach, based on the assumption that through dividing up and analysing a system's parts it is possible to predict their behaviours and to exercise control over their activities, fails to notice that systems have self-organising principles. They are characterised by a dense web of dependent and interdependent mutual relationships that transcend the characteristics of their parts (Barrett, 2000). The reductionism that has strongly influenced the twentieth century has been challenged by complexity theory. It has shown that complex problems cannot be solved merely by understanding how sub-components work. The implications of complexity theory when applied to management highlight the shortcomings of rational thinking, advocating efficiency, consistency, predictability, determinism, simplification, control and hierarchy as conceptual categories to model and govern organisational systems (Axelrod and Cohen, 2000).

The modern management paradigm

The modern management paradigm gathers all managerial models, approaches and tools that have been developed over the twentieth century from management theory and practice, in order to plan, organise, command, coordinate, assess and control the activities of organisational systems.[4] The origin of the modern management paradigm can be dated alongside the development of the industrial age. Its fundamental question has been the technical efficiency of organisational systems. The main goal has been the definition of stable, controllable, productive and as predictable as possible organisational systems to be governed through rational thinking approaches. The solution to the problem of technical efficiency has been faced through the definition of causal explanations of business and organisational problems. Frederick Winslow Taylor is unanimously recognised as the 'father' of modern management. In his book, *The Principles of Scientific Management* (1911), Taylor delineates the reasons and the functions characterising management. His attention was addressed to the fundamental problem of defining approaches and tools to make employees' work transparent. Focusing on this problem, Taylor addressed the inefficiency of organisational components and processes. The scientific-based approach, to analyse organisational components and activities, together with the adoption of an engineering perspective, represented the interpretative platform adopted by Taylor to define the methods and tools to improve productivity. The efficiency of workers and operations was tied to the control, measurement, standardisation and coordination of organisational activities (Clegg *et al.*, 2005). In this perspective, the adoption of rationality was considered paramount by Taylor, and by all other scholars after him who have developed the managerial models that fundamentally populate today's organisational management systems. Indeed, the management frameworks and techniques adopted by modern organisations, such as total quality management, lean production, reengineering, mass customisation, supply chain management, six sigma, performance measurement and management, to name just a few, can be considered as applications and developments of the scientific management principles (Austin and Devin, 2003; Hamel, 2007; Mol and Birkinshaw, 2008).

Starting from Taylor, the rational thinking approach has been adopted to define the rules, procedures, technological solutions and best working practices to assure efficiency and that a company's productive capacity is aligned with the market demand. Consequently organisations have developed and applied scientific and engineering principles. They have rigorously implemented rational models capable of guaranteeing control, measurement and standardisation of organisational processes. The underlying assumption of the modern management paradigm is that business performance improvements and organisational value-creation depend on a rational understanding of the structure, processes and actions characterising an organisation. Therefore the management goal is to define and manage organisational systems that are governable in order to be steered along prearranged development directions, or to be reengineered in order to make them more suitable for identified environmental changes. As a result of this, the development of today's modern organisations has basically reflected the adoption of the following core principles: control, standardisation, measurability, specialisation, precision, predictability, stability, discipline, reliability, hierarchy, simplification and optimisation. Accordingly organisations have been developed as controllable, structured, bureaucratic and consistent systems.

The application of the modern management paradigm has contributed to defining and developing efficient organisational and business models, capable of generating economic prosperity and wealth. However, the characteristics and properties of the emergent business landscape highlight the shortcomings of the modern management paradigm. In the new business age, new and different managerial needs are emerging, and organisations must govern value creation, developing adaptability to rapid external change, as well as a resilient capability to proactively generate transformation. The traditional management concern for the technical efficiency of organisational systems needs to be enriched with new factors affecting the productivity and adaptability of organisations. As stated by Hamel, 'management, like a combustion engine, is a mature technology that must be reinvented for a new age' (Hamel, 2009: 91). New management principles need to be adopted in order to create organisations that truly fit the emergent business landscape.

The challenges of the modern management paradigm

In the twenty-first century, managers have to pay great attention to how to engage people. Although the importance of employees' commitment to organisational activities is not new, its nature is deeply changed in the new business landscape. Tracking the origins of modern management, the attention on employee commitment focused on how to get semi-skilled employees to perform working activities efficiently and in a controllable way. Taylor observed that workers, instead of working as productively as possible, were deliberately slowing down their activities, acting in ways he coined 'soldiering' (Mol and Birkinshaw, 2008). Taylor solved the problem of workers' commitment by examining in detail how work should be done and defined standard methods, procedures, tools and times. Over the twentieth century, the attention has moved from making employees' work transparent and controllable, to making sure that people within hierarchical and bureaucratic organisations are responsible for making the right decisions at the right time and having enough information for their tasks. In the last decades, there has been a shift of focus. The attention has moved to how to manage employees' know-how efficiently, and making sure that people share, transfer, codify and make their technical knowledge accessible. In the twenty-first century, the employee commitment problem to be faced is how to engage, energise and inspire people so that they can exercise their feelings in everyday working activities and operate as innovation and transformational agents.

Today's organisations need to expand their attention from outputs to outcomes. They have to rethink both the mechanisms and the features of their value-creation processes. Increasingly the attention has to move from a focus on efficient value-creation mechanisms to adaptable value-creation dynamics that are not only focused on efficient outputs, but also on valuable and sustainable outcomes and impacts. The goal is to encourage an organisation's adaptability and transformation. In this perspective, the traditional management principles show their limitations in mobilising and igniting human emotion and energy.

Towards a postmodern management paradigm

As previously established, the development of organisations that are able to create sustainable value, acquiring the capacity to continuously nurture and sustain innovation and transformation in their DNA, requires the embracing of new management models and tools. Hamel (2007: 19) analyses this issue, stating that to compete and create value in the twenty-first century, organisations will need to introduce 'management innovations', i.e., 'anything that substantially alters the way in which the work of management is carried out, or significantly modifies customary organisational forms, and, by so doing, advances organisational goals'. Furthermore, Hamel (2009), outlining the future of management, addresses the main great management challenges that will absorb the efforts of management innovators in the new millennium. The analysis of these challenges provides a twofold contribution. On the one hand, their identification represents an effective diagnosis of the limitations of the modern management paradigm and highlights the reasons grounding the shift from a modern to a postmodern management perspective. On the other hand, they stress and reevaluate the centrality of people, both as a key resource and source of competitiveness, and as the final recipient of organisational value creation.

From the analysis of management's challenges it is possible to distil some fundamental managerial issues that characterise the postmodern management view (Hamel, 2009). Box 1.1 proposes the main managerial challenges that characterise the postmodern management agenda. They also can be considered as the main drivers of the shift from the modern to the postmodern management paradigm. They corroborate

---

Box 1.1 The managerial challenges characterising the postmodern management agenda

- *Inadequacy of the shareholder value to explain organisation's wealth creation and recognition of the interdependence of all stakeholders.*
- *Mobilisation of human energies by creating engaging and empowering organisations.*
- *Catalysing emotions within organisations.*
- *Development of an organisational culture reflecting the ethos of community and citizenship.*
- *Adoption of a managerial philosophy aligned with people's nature.*
- *Redistribution of power, overcoming hierarchical structures and fostering emergent coordination.*
- *Linking power to value performance and making authority linked to people's value contribution.*
- *Reducing anxiety and fear, and control of the negative feelings.*
- *Promoting a risk-taking culture and allowing people freedom to dissent and express themselves.*

- *Generation of variations within the organisation by embracing diversity.*
- *Facilitating conversations and information flows, promoting people's freedom and prompt decision-making.*
- *Spurring networking and the creation of fluid organisations able to reconfigure and dynamically develop their capabilities.*
- *Developing a forward-looking approach and imagination, rather than being linked to the past, making sure that management processes do not prefer continuity to change.*
- *Building identity and sense of belonging.*
- *Developing social intelligence that values a participatory process of setting organisations' directions for the future.*
- *Arousing 'hearts' by engaging employees' passions to be committed to give the best of themselves.*
- *Sparking and sustaining people's creativity, and promoting an internal market for the best ideas and projects.*

(cont.)

- *Transforming the command-and-control systems into commitment systems promoting trust.*
- *Encouraging self-discipline and self-assessment.*
- *Engaging employees to define the meaning driving organisational behaviours and visions, building a collective wisdom.*
- *Moving from a top-down supervision control to a peer review evaluation.*
- *Getting over the traditional strategy planning and promoting emergent and evolving strategies that make organisations more adaptable and resilient.*
- *Creating an organisation which is genuinely human.*

- *Training people in competence for improving their life and for better thinking.*
- *Encouraging experimentation and bottom-up initiatives, making innovation everyone's job.*
- *Making the business closer to people's wants and needs.*
- *Infusing in the business feelings such as honour, truth, love, justice and beauty.*
- *Implementation of incentive systems encouraging long-term value creation.*

the argument that in the new business arena organisational success cannot be considered as the mere ability to define and manage technical efficient systems. New organisational capabilities are necessary to survive and prosper. In an increasingly complex and turbulent business world that requires adaptability and resilience, the excellence of an organisation depends on the integration and revision of the rationalistic vision of the organisation with an interpretation that distinguishes the deep and unique human nature of organisational life and components (Adler, 2010). This recognises that organisations are human systems whose final goal is to generate wealth for human beings.

A fundamental facet characterising postmodern management is the acknowledgement of the centrality of people in organisational value creation. People are not machine-like components, but actors shaping and affecting organisational activities with their behaviour. Employees contribute to organisational value-creation by deploying their capabilities rooted in personal and tacit knowledge, i.e., knowledge that is embodied in people's actions and behaviours (Nonaka, 1991, 1994; Nonaka and Takeuchi, 1995; Polanyi, 1962, 1966). This knowledge cannot be merely reduced to rational and technical knowledge, but includes emotive dimensions that can be conceptually represented by the notion of 'emotive knowledge'. Emotive knowledge is related to people's emotional traits and can be considered the result of aesthetic knowledge-creating processes based on human senses (Strati, 1992, 2000a, 2000b). The acknowledgement of emotive knowledge highlights the relevance of taking into account people's emotions and energy as an integral component of the organisational knowledge domains affecting business performance. Employees bring their rational faculties into organisations together with their emotive capabilities. High productivity and innovation can be more easily achieved when employees perform work activities in a passionate way (Hamel, 2000). Therefore for organisations to prosper they need to understand how to catalyse and employ not only people's rational faculties but also their emotive capabilities (Adler, 2006, 2010). Consequently organisational management systems have to be expanded with innovative models and enriched with new approaches and tools so that they can engage people to give the best of themselves and be happy in their everyday work. On the basis of these reflections, it is possible to address the fundamental managerial problem that characterises the postmodern management paradigm.

The fundamental managerial problem of postmodern management

The postmodern management paradigm places renewed emphasis on the contribution of employees to the efficiency and excellence of organisational systems. Its main concern is how to make organisations truly living organisms, capable of fully incorporating and reflecting human nature.

Organisations need to be intelligent and able to deal with any emergent business problem by identifying and interpreting business issues as they evolve. This requires the development of organisational capabilities that combines and synergistically integrates the rational organisational dimensions with the emotive ones. Therefore, the fundamental managerial problem under the postmodern management paradigm is the setting up of organisational systems that recognise the relevance of human nature and utilise people's emotions and energies as key factors affecting the capacity of organisational value creation. Accordingly, organisations have to develop human characteristics and be able to engage people's feelings both internally and externally. Internally, managers not only need to make the roles of employees more clearly defined, measurable and manageable, but also to take into account their emotions and energies. Externally, organisations and their products need to make a positive impact on all organisational stakeholders. As a result, it is of fundamental importance for organisations to manage their aesthetic dimensions, both by generating aesthetic experiences through their internal and external actions, and by manipulating the aesthetic properties of organisational infrastructure and products. The assumption at the basis of this book is that through the management of aesthetic dimensions managers can harness emotional and energetic dynamics within and around the organisation.

The techno-human nature of organisations: the role of emotions and aesthetics

The adoption of the postmodern management perspective, shifting the focus from efficiency to adaptability and transformation, takes into account the relevance and influence of people's feelings upon organisational and business activities.[5] The organisational quest for adaptability, resilience and the capability to cope with emergent business challenges through transformation, gives a renewed relevance to human capital. What changes is not the role of employees, but rather the nature of the contribution that they have to make to improve organisational performance.

A rational-based view of organisational systems

The modern management paradigm is well suited to a stable or quasi-stable environment in which it is possible to define the causal relationships and actions governing organisational systems. In this kind of predictable environment, discipline and control ensure technical efficiency through the reduction or elimination of deviation from actions that are considered desirable because they fit environmental constraints and conditions, and optimise the use of resources. By codifying and standardising organisational processes through rules, procedures and hierarchical structures, it is possible to ensure viability and consistency. It is important to stress that the very definition of bureaucratic organisational systems discourages emotional manifestations by employees. In particular, the codification of bureaucratic processes allows negative feelings, such as anxiety, anger and fear of failure, to be contained, and enables organisations to control and somehow anaesthetise employees' emotions (Menzies-Lythe, 1988). In the modern management perspective, employees essentially play the role of systems' components that significantly contribute to the efficiency of an organisation, and accordingly human traits are largely considered as variables to be controlled. In accordance with this efficiency-based view of human capital, even if employees are recognised as a strategic resource of organisational value creation, attention is focused on their rational knowledge traits rather than on the positive role and relevance of their emotions. Even the most recent knowledge management-based perspective tends to adopt a rational and efficiency-based standpoint, implicitly assuming that through rational knowledge management processes, including knowledge codification, mapping, sharing, transferring, storing and creation, it is possible to positively influence and improve knowledge workers' activities in order to drive superior business performance.

The position of emotions in the modern management view

Although Mayo's studies of the 1930s (Mayo, 1930) recognised the role of work-related emotions to explain work performance (Roethlisberger and Dickson, 1939), in the modern management view emotions in organisational life have been characterised and monopolised by a rationalistic-based management perspective. Indeed, management attention throughout the twentieth century has been mainly focused on emotions as a variable to be controlled for instrumental ends, rather than as a value-added dimension to be managed (Flam, 1993). People's feelings have been disregarded and marginalised, because they have not been regarded as a significant variable to explain organisational life according to an instrumental goal orientation. Most of the attention to the management of emotions within organisations has been focused on emotional control. The importance of controlling emotions has been in place since the design of industrial organisations.

By the 1940s, training was used to support managers to control and smooth the angers and anxieties of workers (Stearns, 1989). The fundamental idea was that organisational control of emotions would suppress disagreements, control information flows and reduce employee complaints (Waldron and Krone, 1991). The application of modern management principles through managerial actions, such as the design of space and time, the control of information flows, the definition of formal and informal disciplinary rules and the establishment of organisational culture and values by senior staff, was aimed at controlling emotions within organisations. More recently, starting from the 1980s, the control of emotional expression has been the subject of extensive attention, both in organisational and management studies. Under the concept of 'emotive labour', the control of emotive displays has been explored to determine how emotions can bend and become a commodity for achieving instrumental organisational goals (Hochschild, 1983).

With the goal of defining efficient systems, the modern management paradigm has examined feelings mainly as a variable that interferes with the regularity, stability and reliability of organisational system components due to their subjective and unpredictable nature, and because of their objective difficulty in being treated as measurable variables. So, the attention has been paid to transforming emotions into controlled variables so that they might be removed from the personal sphere of influence and transformed into commodities for instrumental ends. The definitions of norms and display rules have operated as mechanisms for affecting the expression of emotions to define what the appropriate emotive displays are and how to induce compliance (Rafaeli and Sutton, 1987, 1988, 1990, 1991).

However, in today's new emergent business landscape, organisations need to develop emotive and energetic abilities more and more. This is necessary both to improve the quality of organisational life and activities, and to face negative feelings and 'depression' that can lock in an organisation during turnaround processes. In this perspective the rational management thinking has to be enriched with an acknowledgement of the strategic relevance of the aesthetic dimensions of organising and managing. For example France Telecom has struggled to deal with a series of staff suicides during a period of transformation, showing the importance of tackling workplace stress and of recognising emotions as a critical dimension of organisational life.

The role of emotions in the postmodern management view

The relevance of emotive dimensions as components of organisational structure and working mechanisms has already been introduced in management studies. Sullivan (1986), investigating organisational working mechanisms, proposed a description of an organisation structure, distinguishing three organisational dimensions and revealing the role of organisational emotions or non-rational components. The first dimension of an organisation constitutes the 'surface reality' and is made up of components such as goals, objectives, technology, structure, power and relationships. The second dimension can be identified as the 'cognitive or rational reality' that involves the overall know-how capabilities of an organisation, such as human skills, organisation practices, procedures and routines, and more generally organisational competencies. Finally, Sullivan notes that the third dimension includes the unexamined feelings, beliefs and values upon which the other two surfaces rest. This dimension constitutes the 'irrational or emotional reality' that Sullivan (1986: 535) defines as 'the set of motives, mental and emotional capacities, and psychic mechanisms common to humans [. . .], it is a set of pan-human needs, drives, predispositions, tendencies, properties and actual behaviours'. These conceptual categories appear useful to schematically analyse the working dimensions of an organisation. In particular, the distinction between the rational reality and the emotional one allows the demarcation of two fields of influence on the quantity and quality of organisational activities. The rational approach, in the form of scientific approaches, methods, tools and practices, defines the characteristics of the quantity of organisational activities, i.e., the components, the relationships and the properties of the activities grounding the organisational working processes. On the other hand, the emotive dimension, in the form of feelings, behaviours and expressions, affects the quality of organisational activities, defining the nature and the intensity of the personal and social energy, linking the performance of organisational processes to employees' life experience. The function of any organisation is characterised and based on vital phenomena. These include, at the same time, the rational dimensions of the working processes and the emotive and inner dimensions of human experience. These two dimensions cannot be separated unless an organisation is made into a 'machine-like system' removing the human presence. They are two joined, intertwined, complementary and continuously balanced dimensions, though with different roles and importance according to the diverse situations and scope of human activities.

The techno-human interpretation of organisations

To denote the pivotal role of human beings in business activities, organisations can be seen as techno-human systems. This notion addresses the dual, inseparable, rational and emotive nature of organisational and business realities. This view is grounded in the tradition of organisation theory (Argyris, 1964; Likert, 1961; Pfeffer, 1981) and conceives organisations as living organisms (Burns and Stolker, 1961; Wheatley, 1999). However, it is mainly inspired and supported by recent organisational study streams focusing on the relevance of aesthetics and emotions in organisations (Fineman, 1993; Frost *et al.*, 1985; Linstead and Höpfl, 2000; Mintzberg, 1985; Strati, 1992, 2000a; Turner, 1990).

The adoption of a techno-human interpretation recognises that in the new business age, organisations need not only to manage the technological and the rational-based dimensions, but increasingly they have also to take into account, when organising and managing businesses, the aesthetic and emotive dimensions as explaining factors in the success and excellence of organisations (Taylor and Hansen, 2005).

Aesthetics and emotions are two dimensions which are strictly intertwined. Aesthetics generate feelings and feelings affect aesthetics. Aesthetics can be used to mobilise and manage emotions within and around organisations, and emotions can be put in place to better tune organisational aesthetic capabilities.

The recognition of the relevance of organisations' aesthetic dimensions demonstrates that human senses are factors affecting organisational life and activities (Strati, 1992, 2000a). Sensory and perceptive faculties frame people's experiences of the world (Berkeley, 1710). They affect how people perceive and interact with their inner and outer reality, how they communicate their experiences, develop mutual understanding in interpersonal dynamics, build their communities and shape the environment around them, constructing meaning. Through the sensory system people develop personal knowledge (Polanyi, 1962, 1966), which can be considered as the integration of technical or rational knowledge and intuitive or emotive knowledge.

From a philosophical point of view, aesthetics denote a specific mode of knowing that emphasises the importance of the human sensory system in creating knowledge (Baumgarten, 1750; Vico, 1968). By managing aesthetic dimensions, organisations can harness people's emotions and energy both externally and internally with a positive impact on organisational value creation. Externally, for example, the management of aesthetic dimensions allows an organisation to elicit positive responses from all the people with whom business relationships take place (Carter and Jackson, 2000). The aesthetic dimensions influence how an organisation communicates with, and is perceived by, external stakeholders, which in turn, determines how organisations' value propositions are received and valued. For example, many companies such as Coca-Cola use the management of aesthetic experiences in a very strategic way as a key competitive lever to build and support customer relationships and as an instrument to create intangible value. On the other hand, internally, aesthetic experiences affect the wellbeing of people and how they are engaged to give the best of themselves to support an organisation to achieve success and business excellence. Pixar, for example, through an artistic design of workplaces and the development of recreational activities, has traditionally paid great attention to the creation of an organisational atmosphere in which employees can be happy and inspired.

The relevance of emotions in organisations

The existence and influence of emotions in human life is proved by our heuristic experience. It is common sense that emotions deeply affect the quality and meaning of people's existence. The human capacity to perceive and interpret events taking place in the environment, as well as the ability and modality to act upon the environment, are strictly related to emotions.[6] In particular, the research on multiple intelligences has pointed out the relevance of emotions for the quality of human abilities. Emotive intelligence has been identified as a master aptitude and as a capacity profoundly affecting all other abilities, either facilitating or interfering with them (Goleman, 1995). Accordingly emotive state affects mental clarity and the efficiency of human thinking capacities. Consequently, emotions cannot be disregarded in the analysis of organisational activities; they have to represent an essential focus of the management attention.

It is far beyond the intention of this book to attempt to provide a definition of emotions or to attempt their classification. Many different theories with different ontologies of emotions have been developed with the goal of defining emotions and how they influence the way people conduct their existence (de Sousa, 2009). For understanding the importance of the arts in management it is important to recognise the position of emotions as a fundamental aspect affecting people's behaviours and abilities. This means from a managerial point of view that emotions characterise both individual and organisational actions. So they have to be considered as a fundamental dimension affecting organisational success and excellence.

According to cognitive theories emotions can be seen as an aspect of people's cognitive activities and include desires, beliefs and judgements (Neu, 2000; Nussbaum, 2001; Oakley, 1992; Solomon, 1990). However, although emotional and cognitive processes are strictly intertwined and affected by each other, for the scope of clarifying the relevance of the arts in management, emotions are considered as a dimension of the human mind that is activated by people's aesthetic experiences. Accordingly aesthetic experiential processes impact on people's emotions affecting their capacity for action. This assumption considers a schematic interpretation of the functioning mechanisms of the human mind (the hypothesis grounding this interpretation is presented in the Appendix). It assumes that people's actions and behaviours are the result of two minds: the rational and the emotive one (Ekman, 1992; Ekman and Davidson, 1994; Epstein, 1994). In virtue of this distinction and of the relevance of the emotive mind in driving people's decisions and actions, emotions can be considered as a critical element in shaping organisational life and in affecting the capacity of organisational value creation.

Emotions in organisations

Fineman (1985: 1) states that 'Emotions are within the texture of organising. They are intrinsic to social order and disorder [. . .] They are products of socialisation and manipulation. They work mistily within human psyche, as well as obviously in the daily ephemera of organisational life'. Therefore emotions are integrated in organisational activities and affect people and organisational behaviour and knowledge-creating processes. Emotions contribute to, and reflect, the tangible and intangible organisational infrastructure and the organisational capability to survive, prosper and evolve, through adaptation and transformation in the business ecosystem. The role and relevance of emotions in organisations can be understood from different perspectives. Emotions can make or break organisational structure as forces that mobilise conflict or determine a sense of belonging (Collins, 1993). Dimensions such as respect, diffidence, fear, awe or love, are components which strongly affect social transactions (Fineman, 1985). Stress, as one of the widely recognised emotions in organisations, is identified as a negative feeling to be present in work activities and needs to be controlled in order to avoid it invalidating employees' efforts and performance (Newton *et al.*, 1993). The skilful display of emotions is recognised as a key performance factor in interpersonal relationships and personal impression that needs to be managed to support organisational performance improvements (Giacalone and Rosenfeld, 1991). Work activities are steeped in emotions, as the individual and social experiences of working can be seen as a sense of attachment, tedium, gloom, enthusiasm, excitement and flow (Sandelands, 1988). Emotions play a fundamental role as personal inner forces, checking our moral conduct and making sure we comply with ethical behaviours (Callahan, 1988). Emotions influence an individual's self-control on the basis of how people think others see and judge them (Scheff, 1988). The work of professionals, such as consultants, doctors, teachers, managers, and so on, carries features that build up, and reflect, their professional identity. These features, such as being serious, analytical, understanding, cool, and so on, have to be internalised and displayed through appropriate emotion management (Fineman, 1985). Emotions provide channels to reinforce organisational values, culture and bonds, and allow the orchestration of desired moods within organisations.

The postmodern management paradigm is grounded in the recognition that in today's disruptive and chaotic competitive scenario, emotions cannot be reduced to marginalised organisational aspects to be controlled as commodities for instrumental goals. Instead, emotions are critical competitive factors that need to be appropriately catalysed and deployed to enhance organisational value-creation capacity.

Emotions for organisational excellence

The role of emotions for organisational excellence can be schematically interpreted according to an inward perspective and an outward perspective. From an inward standpoint, emotions have a fundamental role in explaining and contributing to the quality of the organisational value-creation mechanisms. Emotions, in their negative and positive twofold nature, can act as enablers or as hampers of organisational value creation. They contribute to explaining individual and organisational behaviours. They have the capacity to both moralise and demoralise, mobilise and immobilise organisational energies (Frank, 1988). Indeed, emotions affect the commitment and engagement of people and act as catalysts of important explanatory factors of business performance, such as satisfaction, enthusiasm, flexibility, loyalty, creativity, change and innovation propensity, identity, diversity, culture, risk-taking, and so on. The proliferation of negative emotions within an organisation such as fear, anxiety, panic, awe, stress, burden, anger, embarrassment, shame and guilt, have the power to immobilise an organisation and make it incapable of tackling challenges and problems (Flam, 1993). The acknowledgement of the inward role of emotions highlights the importance of putting management actions in place aimed at valuing people's emotions so that working activities have a meaningful, fulfilling, engaging and passionate result. This points out the importance of defining and managing organisational processes so that they are grounded in human knowledge that combines and integrates rational knowledge with emotive knowledge.

From an outward perspective, emotions contribute to understanding the organisational value-creation outputs and outcomes. Increasingly the value incorporated by companies' outputs involves intangible value dimensions related to the feelings that accompany a product and/or a service. The ability of an organisation to manage the aesthetic dimensions of its outputs and then to harness emotions within and around products/services represents a critical factor of value-creation (Austin, 2008). On the other hand, emotions influence the outcomes of organisational business activities. They help to explain both the failure and the success of an organisational ability to adapt to external environmental changes or to proactively create changes. The organisational capacity of being adaptable, resilient and innovative has strong ties to the development of capabilities that are rooted in organisational emotive traits and characteristics.

Organisations as techno-human systems, whose actions and reactions are expressions of vital phenomena, have their behaviours significantly affected by organisational emotions. Emotions influence how an organisation interacts and communicates with the external environment and play a critical role in framing how an organisation sees and perceives itself in the economic environment and acts on it (Brunch and Ghoshal, 2003). This is related to the capacity of building identity and self-identity, but also to the understanding of the impact on the social, cultural and physical environment of organisational actions. From an outward perspective, emotions prompt organisations to shift their attention from a mere focus on outputs to the understanding of their actions' outcomes and impacts on the wellbeing of present and future society.

The arts in management

The recognition of the techno-human nature of organisations and of the role of emotions attributes great relevance to the identification of innovative management practices and models to govern organisational value creation. In this perspective, the arts offer a new territory to inspire management (Adler, 2006, 2010; Austin and Lee, 2010; Nissley, 2010). Arts can support the definition of new organisational models and processes to drive organisational development, as well as the adoption of new managerial techniques to manage organisational aesthetic dimensions. Their working mechanisms are based on the deployment of people's emotional and energetic dynamics to support the enhancement of organisational value-creation capacity. The arts occupy a privileged position as a resource and source of human aesthetic experiences (Green, 2001; Klamer, 1996; Strati, 2000a, 2000b). They have the power to activate and develop aesthetic experiences by stimulating human senses that arouse and catalyse people's emotions and energy that can be employed and channelled for organisational and business development purposes. Therefore, the arts can play a central role in management as an instrument to generate and manage organisational aesthetic dimensions. This allows an organisation to handle emotional and energetic dynamics within organisational boundaries to improve organisational performance, as well as at the intersection between the organisation and its external environment to better build and deliver value propositions that truly meet the wants and needs of stakeholders.

Understanding the arts in business

The definition of arts goes beyond the scope of this work. The conceptualisation and nature of the arts has traditionally represented one of the greatest issues of the philosophy of arts and particularly of the branch known as aesthetics. Philosophers have discussed the meaning of the arts, highlighting the difficulty and elusiveness of the task, and even debating about the possibility and usefulness of the definition (Adajian, 2009; Kivy, 1997; Wollheim, 1980). Sceptics argue that the arts might be an open concept and as such indefinable in terms of necessary and sufficient conditions (Weitz, 1956). Instead of attempting to provide a definition of the arts they prefer to denote the arts through the definition of a cluster of properties (Dissanayake, 1990; Gaut, 2000; Wittgenstein, 1968). Adajian (2009), reviewing the definition of the arts, points out that it is possible to distinguish two main sorts of contemporary definitions: the conventionalist versus the functional perspective. These perspectives attempt to provide necessary and sufficient conditions for discriminating artworks from non-artworks (Schellekens, 2009). Conventionalist definitions focus on institutional and historical features of the arts. They consider the modern arts and start with the denial that art has an essential connection to aesthetic properties. The conventionalist perspective suggests that artworks are generated within a social and artistic context, so an artwork acquires its status in virtue of its relation to the historical and social setting. The conventionalist perspective, recognising the role and relevance of institutions, considers a work of art as something created by an artist to be presented to an 'artworld' public (Dickie, 1984). The conventionalist perspective that takes into account the position of works of art in the historical evolution of the arts considers artworks as something standing in an art-history in relation to other earlier works of art (Levinson, 1990). Instead, the functional perspective defines the work of art on the basis of the concept of aesthetic properties and connects arts to aesthetic traits (Beardsley, 1982). Adajian (2009) points out that the aesthetic definitions better account for universal features of the arts, while the conventionalist definitions consider the revolutionary modern arts well.

To understand the role of the arts in management the attention is not focused on the definition of arts in order to provide an answer to the question 'What is art?' and particularly given a specific item, either an artefact or a performance, to solve the issue 'Is it an artwork?'. Traditionally, this has been the main concern of the discussion in aesthetics in order to distinguish arts from non-arts. Notwithstanding, it is possible to acknowledge that this might be the concern of the cultural industry interested in assessing the economic value of an artwork. In addressing managerial goals the focus is on the instrumental and functional use of the arts as a means to deal with issues related to the development of organisational value-drivers affecting business performance improvements. The aim is to understand how artistic products and processes can be intentionally used to change management mindset, to evolve management systems and to develop organisational components and value capacity. On the basis of this presupposition a working interpretation of the arts is proposed. The adopted standpoint is the functionalist perspective that considers the connection of the arts to aesthetic properties and experiences. However, the conventionalist perspective is also recognised, particularly when analysing socio-cultural issues and meanings that can be associated with works of art by an organisation and/or a community.

A working interpretation of arts in business

The working conceptualisation at the basis of the understanding of the value of the arts in business considers the arts as an arena and a body of knowledge gathering all possible human expression and creative processes dealing with human aesthetics and emotions. This interpretation differs from the traditional use of the concept of 'art' in the managerial lexicon. The management literature has mainly focused the attention on its etymology. From the Latin 'aris', the concept of art has been adopted to denote any 'skill' or 'craft' aimed at designing or building something by using creativity, intelligence and mastery (Strati, 2000a). In this sense, art translates a creative process for the arrangement of elements, and indicates a creative skill, a creative process or a creative product. It is acknowledged that the arts also denote and can be used as a metaphor for indicating creative activities or a creative accomplishment (Austin and Devin, 2003), but the attention goes to the roots of their nature and properties. For managerial purposes any art form can be considered to be grounded in aesthetic properties and experiences. So the use of the arts in management is related to the employment and exploitation of the aesthetic properties and experiences associated with an artistic product and/or to an artistic process.

Regarding the concept of 'aesthetic', it is considered in accordance with the position of Maxine Green (2001: 5) who states that aesthetic is 'concerned about perception, sensation and imagination, and how they relate to knowing, understanding and feeling about the world'. Therefore, in this context, the attention is focused on the relevance that the arts can play as a means to affect the aesthetic properties and expressions of an organisation. The adoption of such understanding places the arts at the core of the management's attention in searching for models, approaches and tools to manage organisational aesthetics dimensions that can influence the emotive and energetic characteristics and components of an organisation.

The arts and organisational development

The challenge of developing organisational capabilities that promote organisational adaptability and continuous innovation requires organisations to evolve as amplifiers of human nature and abilities (Hamel, 2000, 2007). The virtues of the modern management paradigm such as stability, discipline, reliability, precision, modularisation and measurability must be synergistically integrated with new virtues such as malleability, resilience, toughness, agility, imagination, creativity, happiness and intuition (Hamel, 2009). The development of modern management's virtues had been inspired by and rooted in the principles of rational thinking. While, in order to develop the new virtues of the postmodern management paradigm, the attention has to be shifted to the emotive dimensions of human knowledge and wisdom. The arts can offer the conceptual and operational instrument to manage the aesthetic characteristics and dimensions of an organisation.

Placing the arts in an organisational context as well as inserting arts-based managerial actions into management systems can significantly affect and change the nature and manifestations of organisations. The adoption of the arts can support the transformation of organisations. Two important features of the transformation are related to the employees' engagement and to the creation of external organisational relationships. Within an organisation the arts can be deployed to make employees feel attached to the organisation and able to express themselves and of giving space to their own creative potential. While from an external point of view the adoption of the arts helps to develop new interpretative perspectives of the relationships between organisations and stakeholders. This supports organisations to better understand and evaluate the impact of their activities on the economic, social, cultural and environmental ecosystems.

The adoption of the arts in management integrates the rational and analytical thinking of modern management with the emotive and intuitive assessment that must characterise the postmodern management paradigm.

The arts in business: a utilitarian approach

The arts can serve many different purposes. In particular, as highlighted by the anthropologist Claude Levi Strauss (1962), the arts can serve diverse functions grouped according to those that are motivated and those that are non-motivated. The non-motivated purposes of the arts are related to the nature and instinct of human beings. This category identifies those functions of the use of the arts that have intrinsic value, i.e., not aimed at fulfilling external purposes. In this sense the arts denote those creative activities, outputs and experiences that humans must do, by their very nature, independently of their specific external utility. Included in the category of non-motivated purposes, the arts can be used as: a response to the human nature of searching for the appreciation of beauty; a way to experience the spiritual life and appreciate the mysterious; a way to communicate with the world and with other human beings; a way to express human imagination by using forms, symbols, ideas and feelings; a ritualistic and symbolic role for expressing a community's cultural values. The motivated purposes of the arts refers to the intentional and conscious use of works of art to achieve utilitarian goals, for example, to communicate meanings; to convey specific moods; to comment on and bring change to political, social and cultural aspects; to address personal psychology; to develop values and culture; and to market and sell products. Although, the use of the arts in management may respond and play a pure non-motivational purpose, the attention here is focused on the utilitarian adoption of the arts to support and drive organisational development and value creation. Thus, even if the use of the arts in business may have a ritualistic and symbolic value, simply aimed at making people better human beings, the investigation focus is not concerned with the intrinsic aesthetic value of a work of art, but rather on its instrumental, utilitarian and functional value. The use of the arts is interpreted as a management means to address the fundamental problem of the postmodern management paradigm. It allows the definition of management systems that integrate models and techniques recognising the human nature of organisations and harnessing people's emotions and energy.

The relevance of arts in management

The managerial role and relevance of the arts in management is based on the recognition that people's experiences, both when they act within an organisation and when they behave as economic and social agents in the market, are strongly affected and shaped by the aesthetic nature of human life. Any human activity is influenced by the senses and from the quality impact that sensations have in the human mind. People's consciousness as well as the interactions among and between people and things can be considered as the result of an aesthetic experience.

The arts shape and express human feelings, and communicate and transfer sensations in inter-personal and social relationships. The arts are aesthetic in nature and are based on the deployment of human senses. The arts provide people with a powerful means to express and to experience human feelings. In this regard, any work of art, from the most complex to the most simple, expresses the vitality of human life. So the arts convey the quality and the complexity of emotions that impregnate and surround human and social activities.

The adoption of the arts responds to an understanding of organisations as techno-human systems acknowledging the central position held by people and their feelings to enhance the capacity of organisational value creation. Through the managerial use of the arts it is possible to generate and manage organisational aesthetic dimensions. This influences the emotive and energetic traits that characterise the tangible and intangible components of an organisation as well as affect the ability to handle people's emotions and energy. The arts can support the creation of organisations that are more human – in other words, organisations that express the human nature of organisational activities, contribute to shaping the quality of human actions and develop capabilities that reflect human traits.

As it will be explored in more detail in the following chapters, the influential power of the managerial use of the arts on the development of organisational value-creation capacity is tied to the creation and transformation of organisational knowledge assets. They constitute the building blocks of organisational capabilities that in turn influence the quality and performance of business processes. In particular, through the use of the arts to generate organisational aesthetic experiences and manipulate aesthetic properties, it is possible to influence organisational knowledge that is related to the intuitive and emotive human mind faculties. The deployment of the arts allows both the activation of learning mechanisms that develop people's emotive knowledge and the incorporation of emotive knowledge into tangible and intangible organisational infrastructure so that they echo emotions and energy.

Two interpretative perspectives of the importance of arts in business

The importance of arts in management can be summarised in two main perspectives: the arts can play the role of a learning platform or they can represent a device or vector to influence organisational aesthetic dimensions. The perspective that recognises the arts as a learning platform considers the arts as a body of knowledge from which management can draw inspiration to define new organisational and business models that value the aesthetic, emotive and energetic dynamics of organisational life and activities (Boyle and Ottensmeyer, 2005; Gallos, 2009; Nissley, 2002, 2008, 2010; Seifter and Buswick, 2005). Using and interacting with artistic products and processes, management can identify the organisational ingredients, properties and relationships grounded in aesthetic experiences that can be exploited as analogical models to be imitated and/or from which to learn and spur creative thinking. In this case, the use of the arts in business aims to define analogies and metaphors as well as a context activating and supporting organisational learning. In her book *Artful Creation – Learning Tales of Arts in Business*, Lotte Darsø (2004: 31) explores what business can learn from the arts. Darsø points out how artistic products and processes can be used by managers as a powerful means for artful creation, i.e., 'art experiences that initiate an inner transformation, which opens up for special kind of consciousness [...] that involves feelings and that touches the person profoundly'. This involves the use of artistic metaphors to spark the generation of new ideas, to start conversations and dialogue for exploring and addressing important organisational questions, to prompt reflection for fostering transformation and to test new and different hypothesis for organisational problem-solving. The use of the arts as a metaphor can activate and sustain learning mechanisms both at an individual and organisational level (Argyris and Schön, 1996; Senge, 1990). In addition, the arts and particularly the artistic process can be used as powerful analogical models for benchmarking learning, i.e., for exploring and understanding how to combine and integrate rationality with intuition and emotions. Indeed, the peculiarity of the artistic process that makes it very interesting for postmodern organisations to be analysed and absorbed, is the co-presence of deep technical and emotive knowledge. An artistic process blends rationality with intuition. It requires discipline, a structured approach, hard work and techniques, but at the same time it encompasses aesthetic, emotive and energetic dimensions. Understanding how to create and manage this process is of great value for businesses. By investigating artistic processes, organisations can identify new ways of designing and managing organisational activities and models.

On the other hand, the role of the arts in management is related to the use of artistic products and processes as management devices or vectors to create aesthetic experiences within organisations, as well as to embed aesthetic properties into tangible and intangible organisational infrastructure and products so that they are able to stimulate people's aesthetic sensibilities affecting emotional and energetic dynamics. In this case works of art can be employed as instruments to develop the emotive features both of human capital and of the tangible and intangible organisational infrastructure. The arts can be also exploited as vectors to incorporate aesthetic value into organisations' products and/or to create organisational symbols aimed at building and representing the organisational identity and image.

The arts and organisational value creation

When analysing the value-creation capacity of an organisation, it is possible to adopt a dynamic or a static standpoint. The adoption of a dynamic-based view assumes that the attention is focused on the characteristics of organisational value-generation processes, i.e., on the components and properties of the mechanisms affecting the value creation. This view is concerned with the factors that define and enable the working mechanisms of a value-creation process. In other words, the dynamic perspective considers the dimensions influencing the organisational value flow. The focus is on the issue: *How do we create value?*

Instead, the static-based view is mainly concerned with the assessment of the value incorporated by an organisation and its components at a specific time. The static perspective takes into account the factors defining the organisational value stock. Its focus is on the results of a value-creation process. The fundamental question related to the static viewpoint is: *What is the generated value?* These two different, but complementary and intertwined, interpretative views of the organisational value-creation capacity suggest that the arts can play a managerial role both in improving organisational value-creation mechanisms and in increasing the value embedded in organisational components. Both perspectives are based on the assumption, as will be discussed in Chapter 4, that the arts have the power to create and transform organisational knowledge assets. In particular, the dynamic perspective considers the development of organisational knowledge assets as a way to enhance the organisational value-creation mechanism, i.e., how an organisation performs its business activities to deliver the targeted value propositions. Accordingly the adoption of the arts either as a learning platform or as a device, allows the creation and/or incorporation of emotive knowledge into organisational assets building the knowledge domains upon which organisational capabilities are grounded. This, in turn, influences the quality and performance of organisational and business processes.

By using the arts in management as a learning platform it is possible to leverage the arts as a model or as an approach that through metaphors and analogies, spark and sustain learning dynamics that involve a transformation of human and organisational capital (Darsø, 2004). The transformation of human capital is mainly based on the learning processes taking place at both the individual and group levels that nurture the development of employees and may also have a positive impact on the internal and external organisational relationships dynamics. On the other hand, the development of organisational capital can be considered the result of the use of metaphors and analogies to generate learning insights and inspiration aimed at exploring and understanding new and different organisational processes and management practices that exploit the full human potential. This promotes the definition of organisational and business models valuing emergent coordination, distributed wisdom, full engagement of people and distributed authority. Similarly, the use of the arts in management as a device allows aesthetic characteristics into organisational knowledge assets to be embedded. This affects the development of organisational knowledge domains so that they can incorporate and express aesthetic traits.

The static point of view considers the impact of the arts as a way to increase the value of an organisation and of its components in the market. In this case, the arts represent a value vector to be embedded in the organisational components and products in order to increase their value.

The two value-based views are integrated and interdependent. Figure 1.1 depicts the relevance of arts for the development of organisational value-creation capacity.

Conclusion

The arts as the arena and expression of human life provide knowledge and approaches for interpreting and shaping individual and social constructions that can be used to manage aesthetic characteristics of organisational and business activities. The domain of the arts can be employed and exploited for managerial purposes, providing managers with a learning platform and instruments to explore and rethink organisational models, to better manage the human-based nature of business processes and to enhance the value incorporated by an organisation and its assets.

To deal with the managerial challenges of the new millennium, the arts can provide a new and privileged territory to manage organisational aesthetic dimensions and to handle people's emotions and energy for managerial purposes. Thus the arts matter in management; to engage people by handling their emotional and energetic dynamics, and to create and develop the tangible and intangible organisational infrastructure assets in order to build aesthetic experiences that have a positive impact both within the organisation and at the intersection between the organisation and its environment.

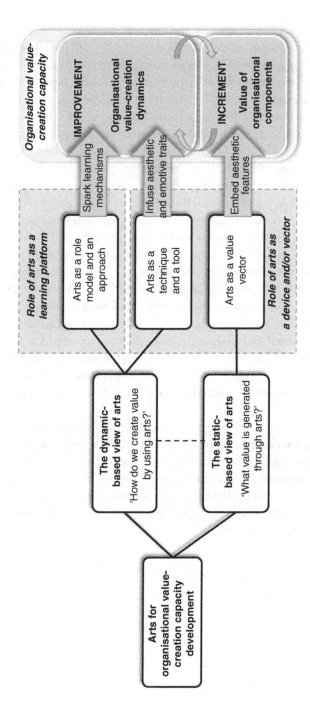

1.1 The relevance of arts for the development of organisational value-creation capacity

Using the arts in management can support the development of management innovations and the shift from the modern to the postmodern management paradigm. The arts in management can be seen as a cornerstone for the evolution of management mindsets and systems in order to integrate the rational principles of scientific management with the emotional traits of human nature. The use of art forms is at the core of managing the aesthetic dimensions of an organisation.

The arts are founded on human nature. They are the expression of human beings and contribute to shaping mankind. Therefore, the adoption of the arts as a management means recognises the centrality of people both in organisational life and in business activities. Through the arts it is possible to humanise organisations and businesses. This contributes to making organisations truly living organisms, better able to cope with evolution dynamics, through adaptation and transformation, and to create stakeholder value in a more sustainable way. The arts work by managing aesthetic experiences. They act on the human sensory system and speak directly to a person's emotive mind. This means that the integration of the arts in management systems enables emotional and energetic dynamics in organisations to be handled. Internally to an organisation, the use of the arts can drive people's development and engagement. Externally, the arts can build intangible value dimensions that satisfy the experiential-based wants and needs of stakeholders.

The arts in management can play the twofold function of a learning platform to spark and support organisational learning dynamics, and of a device to manage the aesthetic dimensions of an organisation. The management use of the arts can be recognised as a crucial way to enrich today's management toolbox and to develop new management models and systems more suited to facing the challenges of the twenty-first century business landscape.

2 | The arts into action: Arts-based Initiatives

Introduction

All organisations have the arts within their business or at least the aesthetic manifestations of art forms. The brand or the identity of a company, for example, is ultimately represented by a logo or images that are built on art symbols that present and communicate the organisation through aesthetic expressions. The use of art forms is also spread throughout an organisation. Office spaces are defined, shaped and decorated by arts-based manifestations. An explicit example of this can be found in the lobbies, recreation and meeting areas of office buildings. They look more and more like art galleries, aimed at welcoming company stakeholders by generating aesthetic experiences that affect people's perceptions and touch their feelings. But more generally, art forms can inhabit many corners of the workplace. Paintings, photographs or simply posters can be hung on the walls. Sculptures or art installations can shape and decorate internal and external office spaces. Music can be broadcasted into offices. The arts pervade organisations. However, not all organisations use artistic products and processes to address management challenges and solve business problems. Most organisations simply use the arts more or less implicitly because they are an integral part of human life and people tend to surround themselves with art forms.

Understanding the value of the arts in business is not concerned with whether or how organisational life and activities are contaminated with the arts but rather with the utilitarian and instrumental adoption of the arts to enhance organisational wealth generation. Therefore the focus is on the intentional use of the arts as a management means to face competitive organisational challenges, support business performance improvements and develop organisational value-drivers. This requires understanding of how the arts can be put into practice by management and raises the essential questions: *How can managers translate the arts into action?* And, from an operational point of view: *What does it mean to adopt the arts to address management challenges and business problems?*

The use of the arts as an intentional managerial instrument to enhance organisational value-creation capacity is tied to the implementation of management initiatives that adopt art forms as a learning platform and/or as a device to develop organisational dimensions that affect business performance. From a practical point of view, this involves specific art forms being purposely deployed in order to improve organisational value-creation mechanisms, as well as to increase the value incorporated into organisational infrastructure. The use of any art form as a management action is represented by the concept of Arts-based Initiatives (ABIs). Through the definition and implementation of ABIs, organisations can translate the arts into action using the aesthetic power of art forms to advance value creation.

In order to provide the conceptual background to clarify how the arts can be adopted by management, first and foremost in this chapter the notion of ABIs will be discussed. Understanding the characteristics of ABIs is at the basis of the managerial exploitation of the arts for improving business performance. For this reason, the nature of ABIs and the possible ways in which the arts can be deployed in business are addressed by defining a practical classification for interpreting the application of the arts as a management means. Afterwards, starting from the acknowledgement that at the core of ABIs there is the deployment of art forms, an interpretative framework for investigating the possible contents of ABIs will be presented. The distinction between artistic products and artistic processes is at the basis of the use of ABIs as a management means to generate aesthetic experiences and to manipulate aesthetic properties in organisations. Indeed, the impact of ABIs on organisational components is strictly related to the power of the arts to engage people in aesthetic experiential processes and/or to shape the aesthetic features of organisational infrastructure. This allows organisations to handle emotional and energetic dynamics.

Arts-based Initiatives (ABIs)

The instrumental and utilitarian adoption of the arts to deal with management challenges and business problems is based on the implementation of management initiatives that employ and exploit art forms. In order to denote any management initiative based on the adoption of an art form the concept of ABIs is proposed. An ABI can be interpreted as any management action using one or more art forms to enable people to undergo an aesthetic experience within an organisation or at the intersection between the organisation and its external environment, as well as to embed the arts as a business asset.

The fundamental management goal of the adoption of an ABI is to directly or indirectly contribute to the improvement of business performance. This is achieved by enhancing organisational value-creation mechanisms and/or by increasing the value incorporated into organisational infrastructure and products. Managers can use ABIs, on the one hand, as a learning platform made up of analogies and metaphors that allow people to discover new understanding, prompting organisational development and management mindset transformation. On the other hand, ABIs can be deployed as a device to enhance value dynamics and value stocks of an organisation.

ABIs can take different forms in organisations. They can range from providing an art-rich environment, by infusing the arts into different areas such as hanging paintings, photographs and posters on the walls, positioning sculptures and art installations both within office workspaces or outside office buildings, and incorporating the arts into organisational activities, to involving or instructing people directly in arts-based activities in order to exploit artistic products and processes as a learning tool or as a catalyser of aesthetic experiential processes.

An ABI can involve a wide range of art forms, such as painting, poetry, literature, film, dance, theatre, photography, sculpture, storytelling, drawing, graffiti, comics, writing, cartoons, circus and pottery (Darsø, 2004). Potentially the range of art forms and art activities grounding an ABI is limitless. Not only can different forms of arts be adopted, but they can be combined and integrated in various ways so that the modalities of their application are potentially unlimited. To understand how ABIs can be put into practice to solve business problems, it is important to start from the identification of the possible managerial forms that ABIs can assume in organisations. In the next section, the distinction between interventions, projects and programmes is discussed, offering a first practical classification aimed at clarifying how organisations can approach the use of the arts in management.

The managerial forms of ABIs

The use of the term 'initiative' generally denotes any management action based on the deployment of art forms with the aim of achieving a targeted business goal in a specific time frame. On the basis of the time frame and of the features characterising the targeted goal, it is possible to identify three main managerial forms of ABIs. These are interventions, projects and programmes. The relevance of this distinction is not only conceptual, but it also has important practical implications as the different forms of ABIs tend to have a diverse scope and beneficial impact for an organisation.

Arts-based interventions – An 'intervention' is a short-term arts-based management action, characterised by a limited time frame usually ranging from a few hours to three days, and it is aimed at accomplishing a specific managerial function. It is mainly practical in scope and tends to be focused on a specific organisational or business issue. So an arts-based intervention tends to be very narrow in scope and the underlying assumption is that its implementation allows one to perform a specific well-defined task. Most organisations' experiences with the use of the arts to address business issues fall in this conceptual category. This is the reason why the term 'intervention' is common and generally used by arts-based organisations and facilitators offering arts-based services for personal and organisational development purposes.

Traditional forms of arts-based interventions are represented by training courses and workshops that take different formats, such as storytelling, cooking, forum theatre, playing drums, chorus singing, and so on (Gallos, 2009; Seifter and Buswick, 2005). They are usually implemented with the aim of developing people's skills and attitudes, for team-building purposes, and more generally to support individual and organisational learning. Other forms of arts-based interventions are: performances that support an event and/or deliver an impactful message; meetings and group sessions using the arts to support brainstorming, codification and representation of insights as well as the creation of a context in which a meeting can take place, to come up with new and breakthrough ideas; and generally events such as official parties and openings, celebrations, private performances for employees and/or clients, festivals, product launches, brand and image activation, and so on.

Arts-based projects – An ABI can be defined as a 'project' when the duration of the initiative is longer than a few days and is characterised by a set of integrated and coordinated interventions, planned and implemented over a period of time, usually ranging from one to six months. The goal is to accomplish a people and/or an organisational development with an impact on the organisational value-drivers. The focus of a project is wider in scope than an intervention. It plays a management function and is aimed at supporting managers to accomplish their organisational and business development objectives. Arts-based projects generally tend to involve the production of a tangible or intangible output that requires professional artist facilitators or arts-based organisations to work with a company for a period of time. The targeted output might be the development, acquisition and absorption of a concrete or abstract work of art, such as an art installation, a photo gallery, or a theatrical performance. Alternatively, the output can be the creation of knowledge flows between artistic processes, carried out within the organisation, and organisational processes, so that for instance employees can improve their abilities by understanding and appreciating the traits and factors characterising the artistic activities (Austin and Devin, 2003; Boyle and Ottensmeyer, 2005).

Projects generally address challenging organisational business problems. They tend to ensure a significant impact on organisational performance through longer exposure of the organisation to the arts. Some examples of arts-based projects include long-term, modular-based courses; coaching and mentoring based on one-to-one relationships between artists and business people in order to support the development of artistic-based skills and professional capabilities; creative investigations, i.e., commissioned pieces of arts-led action research shedding light on key themes or emerging trends; and residential programmes in which artists work within an organisation's premises.

Arts-based programmes – When an ABI involves a plurality of business objectives aligned with a company's strategy and considers a set of different projects, it can be defined as a 'programme'. The result of a programme is the aggregate and possibly synergetic combination of different projects carried out over a period of time (usually longer than six months). The implementation of an arts-based programme can respond to different strategic business issues. The goal of a programme is to have a significant impact on organisational value-creation capacity by delivering different project outputs. Although arts-based programmes can be adopted for multiple strategic reasons, most of the organisations' experiences are related to change management processes.

The managerial form of ABIs clarifies how management can approach the use of the arts in organisations to run arts-based management actions aimed at developing organisational components and improving business performance. It is worth pointing out that different managerial forms of ABIs tend to have diverse impacts on organisational development.

ABIs and the development of knowledge 'osmotic dynamics'

The impact of the use of the arts on an organisation is affected by the managerial form of the ABI. When ABIs are aimed at developing people and transforming organisations, significant and long-lasting benefits can be achieved through a sustained involvement of an organisation in the arts (McCarthy *et al.*, 2004). This suggests that 'one-off' arts-based interventions can be beneficial, but their impact is usually temporary. The adoption of projects and programmes guarantee that organisations better absorb the intrinsic features of art forms. A longer exposure to the arts better facilitates the absorption of the aesthetic dimensions in an organisation's DNA. Thus, it is assumed that greater value is captured when organisations develop a sustained partnership with the arts. Isolated ABIs are useful, but unlikely to generate significant organisational development achievements. A stable partnership between an organisation and the arts very likely supports the creation of beneficial knowledge flows. From a conceptual point of view, in order to denote the influence exercised by the arts on the transformation of organisational components, the metaphoric notion of 'osmotic dynamics' can be used, assuming that the contact between the arts with the organisational context is characterised by knowledge flows. These knowledge flows are related to the emotive and energetic dimensions that are attached to the aesthetic experiences and properties characterising the arts. The fundamental idea is that by working with and through the arts an organisation can gradually and unconsciously absorb and/or generate knowledge that involves the capacity to handle emotional and energetic dynamics. This issue will be further explored in the next sections.

The formats of ABIs

ABIs can present different formats on the basis of the ways the partnership between the arts and business is created. An exploratory investigation of the use of the arts in business shows that many different approaches can be adopted. In gathering different experiences of partnerships between arts and business, it is possible to distinguish some fundamental categories.

In practice ABIs can be characterised by different ways in which the art forms are implemented by organisations. It is very difficult to outline the spectrum of the formats of ABIs due to the potentially unlimited ways of involving art forms in business. However, analysing the relationships between arts-based organisations and business organisations, it seems possible to identify some clusters of formats. It is not intended to be thorough, but to provide a preliminary and practical understanding of how organisations might approach ABIs to deal with business issues. Furthermore, it is important to point out that not only can the formats be different, but also that the same format can present a variety of characteristics. It can be influenced by the scale of the initiative; working on a one-to-one basis to enhance an individual's performance or involving a group, or even communities at large. The format of an ABI can work with diverse art forms. It can be focused on a specific form of art or span and integrate different art forms. The format is also influenced by the place where ABIs occur. They can be delivered in an organisation's offices, the arts-based organisation's space, such as theatres and concert halls, or other chosen venues. Below, a classification of the formats of ABIs is proposed.

- *Training*. This format characterises ABIs that are based on courses and workshops, and are aimed at offering aesthetic experiential learning opportunities to develop or exploit artistic-based skills and attitudes for both professional and personal development purposes.
- *Coaching*. When ABIs are implemented as a way to support mentoring they take the format of coaching projects or programmes. They involve one-to-one relationships between artists and business people.
- *Residency activity*. ABIs can take the form of artist-in-residency activities, tailored to the organisation's needs and wants. This

format aims to create more effective exposure and interaction between the arts and business, so that positive 'osmotic dynamics' can take place between artists and art forms, with business people and organisational contexts.

- *Team-building.* This format includes all ABIs working in group sessions that aim to develop networking relationships. Although the objectives of ABIs included in this format can be different, their fundamental focus is on the growth of a sense of mutual trust among the people involved in aesthetic experiential processes.
- *Creative investigation.* ABIs that take the format of creative investigations essentially correspond to action research activities that adopt artistic creative approaches to carry out investigations about business issues.
- *Event.* The use of ABIs for running events can include: conferences, organisation meetings, official openings, celebrations, awards ceremonies, hospitality, private performance for employees or clients, festivals, product launches, brand promotion, art exhibitions and installations in and around the office spaces.
- *Art collection.* The format of this ABI corresponds with the purchase and installation of an art collection, eventually also by establishing museums or permanent exhibition centres.
- *Sponsorship.* Included in this format could be all ABIs that take the form of both business donations to arts organisations and underwriting art performances, exhibitions and installations.
- *Arts and architecture.* This format of ABI combines the arts and architecture to introduce art into public spaces with the aim to improve the quality of urban or rural areas.
- *Art and design.* This format includes all the possible ABIs that support, particularly, the design of an organisation's products and the interior design of organisational workspaces.
- *Corporate social responsibility.* This format embraces all ABIs implemented as a way to forge organisational relationships with the local community and the society at large.
- *Embedding the arts into organisational life.* This format denotes a large typology of ABIs covering all the possible managerial uses of the arts that are not included in the previous categories, and are aimed at shaping, executing and communicating organisational dimensions and activities.

The above categories identify the main ways that ABIs can be adopted by business organisations. The different formats are not mutually exclusive and they can overlap. The specific characteristics of ABIs in each category are defined and tailored on the basis of the specific organisational needs and wants. Their identification provides the first interpretative basis to understand how business organisations can approach ABIs.

The definition of the managerial forms and of the possible formats of ABIs provides a practical understanding of how the arts can be deployed in business. But how ABIs can be designed and implemented to deal with business issues is a concern related to the definition of the art forms defining the content of ABIs. Therefore it is important to shed light on the content characterising ABIs. For this reason, from an operational point of view, a distinction has to be made between artistic products and the adoption of artistic processes. This distinction identifies the building blocks of ABIs. Accordingly, the adoption of an ABI can be based on the use of artistic products or on the adoption of artistic processes, as well as a combination of the two.

The building blocks of ABIs: artistic products and processes

The definition of an ABI can be based on the use of both artistic products and artistic processes (Darsø, 2004; Taylor and Ladkin, 2009). Although, in practice, most ABIs tend to integrate the deployment of both artistic dimensions, their distinction is of fundamental importance to understand how ABIs can influence the creation of people's aesthetic experiences as well as the manipulation of aesthetic properties of organisational infrastructure. Different contents have different impacts on organisational aesthetic dimensions, with the generation of different effects on the development of organisational components.

In Figure 2.1, a classification of the contents of ABIs is proposed. The identified categories represent the building blocks of ABIs. The proposed framework is drawn from the distinction between artistic products, i.e., works of art, and artistic processes, i.e., activities of artistic creation, which can be labelled as 'artistry activities'. Therefore the underlying assumption is that an ABI can be constructed deploying works of art and/or employing artistry activities.

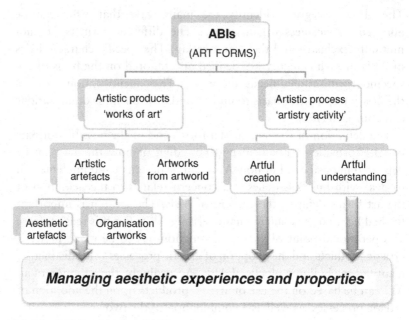

2.1 The building blocks of ABIs

The use of artistic products and artistic processes can be further split into two sub-categories. The ABIs that use works of art can include two main typologies of artistic products. Taking into account the properties of the works of art, it is possible to distinguish between 'artworks from the artworld' and 'artistic artefacts'. The former typology represents those artistic products that are recognised as works of art by the public artworld.[1] The latter typology of works of art intends to denote those artistic products that are made by an organisation for the organisation. This category, in particular, can be further divided in two sub-categories of works of art: the 'aesthetic artefacts', i.e., those artefacts made by people working for the organisation with the support of artists acting as facilitators and instructors, and 'organisation artworks', i.e., works of art commissioned by the organisation from artists and arts organisations. On the other hand, ABIs that adopt artistry activities can be distinguished on the basis of how they exploit artistic processes. Thus, artistry activities, on the basis of the kind of aesthetic experiences they generate, can be distinguished as: artful creation and artful understanding.

The analysis of the contents of ABIs represents the conceptual foundations to understand, for descriptive and normative purposes, how ABIs work in affecting organisational aesthetic experiences and properties.

ABIs based on artistic products

All ABIs that are based on works of art fall into the category of 'artistic products'. In order to understand the traits that characterise this typology of ABI, first the meaning of a work of art has to be addressed. It is possible to take for granted that works of art are artefacts (Davies, 1991). Coherently with the position adopted in aesthetics, the concept of an artefact is considered in a wide sense and it can be supposed that a work of art is essentially an artistic artefact, i.e., an object – which is contrasted with a natural entity – that has been intentionally made through human actions in order to respond to a specific author(s)'s intention (Hilpinen, 2004). This interpretation identifies three main characteristics of a work of art. First, a work of art corresponds to a product that is opposed to the concept of activity that denotes how the product has been made. Second, ontologically, a work of art can be a concrete or an abstract object that has been made by an individual or a collective activity (Petroski, 1992). Third, due to its intrinsic human nature, any work of art is characterised by an intended character, that essentially defines the properties reflecting the author(s)'s intention of making the artefact. In particular, the properties characterising a work of art can be distinguished between those that are defined by author(s) in order to make the artefact suitable to play a specific function and to achieve targeted purposes, and those that are independent of the specific intended character (Simon, 1996). This clarification means that an ABI can be based on two different types of works of art. An ABI can use works of art the intended character of which is not at all related to business issues, but the artistic properties of which can be deployed for addressing business problems. For example, Shakespeare's *Henry V* is an abstract artwork that can be used to address leadership development issues in a business context (Whitney and Packer, 2000), even if Shakespeare's intention was certainly not the improvement of corporations' executives' competencies. Similarly any other artwork, even if created with a specifically intended artistic character, can potentially be deployed through appropriate facilitation to activate aesthetic experiential processes intended to face business issues. Alternatively, an ABI can be based on the adoption of works of art that are purposefully made to deal with business issues. In this case, artistic artefacts can be created at the outset with a specific business intent. For example, at The Banff Centre, ABIs are implemented for leadership development and involve executives making 'leadership masks' with the aim of expressing and representing their leadership practice (Nissley, 2010; Taylor and Ladkin, 2009). The leadership masks are aesthetic artefacts made by the organisation for the organisation. Other examples may include the creation of art installations or group paintings and drawings visualising the features of intangible organisational assets such as culture, values, identity and image, or representing managerial aspects such as a management philosophy and strategic planning. Consider, for instance, the approach of adopting visual arts to represent the traits of a strategy plan. In this regard, companies are experimenting with the adoption of works of art as an innovative way of formulating and communicating their strategy (Burgi et al., 2005; Roos et al., 2004). They invite visual artists to attend board meetings during which different aspects and characteristics of the strategy plan are discussed. The task for the artists is to capture and interpret, together with strategy consultants, the key messages emerging in the conversations at the meetings and to artistically represent them through drawings and images. The created works of art define an analogical model helping executives to further analyse and comprehend the hypothesis at the basis of their strategy. The artistic artefacts can be further revised on the basis of executives' feedback, making sure that they represent and communicate the key messages and strategic objectives linked to the organisational vision.

On the other hand, an organisation can also commission artists to create a work of art with the purpose of addressing and communicating specific business issues. In this case art symbols are deployed to communicate messages that are able to engage people in aesthetic experiential processes.

Thus ABIs using artistic products can be based on two categories of works of art: the artworks from the artworld, that is works of art that are made by artists to respond to their own personal intended purposes, but that are subsequently adopted to address business issues; and the artistic artefacts that are created or commissioned by an organisation with the specific intent of dealing with business issues. Both typologies of works of art can be used as a management means to address business problems and support organisational value-creation. Their essential working capacity is related to the power of generating and manipulating aesthetic experiences and properties that can have a positive impact on organisational assets.

ABIs using artworks from the artworld

The category of the artworks from the artworld gathers all the works of art related to an art theory and recognised as arts in the public domain (Danto, 1981; Dickie, 1984). They are 'borrowed' by an organisation in order to purposefully enable people to undergo an aesthetic experience and/or to appreciate aesthetic properties. In this case a company can bring an artwork into the organisational context or take people to experience a work of art in a theatre, museum, art gallery or concert hall, and with the support of facilitators use the artwork to spark reflection and conversations that aim to deal with business challenges faced by the organisation.

ABIs employing artistic artefacts

All works of art, such as paintings, photographs, drawings, sculptures, stories, theatrical performances and so on, that are made by an organisation for the organisation, fall into the category of artistic artefacts. It includes all works of art that are made either by people working for the organisation, with the support of artists who act as instructors and facilitators, or by artists who are commissioned to produce a work of art for business purposes. In the case of artistic artefacts, people within an organisation are involved in the creation of artefacts, i.e., concrete products, such as a collective painting, or abstract objects, such as a theatrical performance, that can be considered works of art due to their aesthetic nature. The intended character of these works of art is both to engage people's emotive and rational mind, and to create experiential processes. This allows people to create and express emotive knowledge; be involved in a reflective process; develop their own competencies; build relationships; and more simply, just have fun and be happy in the workplace or with work-related activities. The works of art made by artists or arts organisations for a company can be defined as organisation artworks. In this case artists are appointed

to create a work of art which responds to specific organisational business needs ranging from the design of products, workplaces, logos and
images to the creation of emotional and energetic catalysers for people working within the organisation as well as for people outside the
organisational boundaries.

ABIs *based on artistic processes*

This category includes ABIs that use artistic processes for managerial
purposes. The main focus is not on the product, but on the activities related to the production of a work of art, and specifically on
the features of the artistic creation. In order to denote the properties characterising an artistic process the concept of 'artistry' can be
adopted. Artistry is an inherent quality of any artistic process and can,
generally speaking, be interpreted as the practice of artistic performance (Davies, 1991). Eisner (2002: 81) states that 'artistry consists
in having an idea worth expressing, the imaginative ability needed to
conceive of how, the technical skill needed to work effectively with
some material, and the sensibilities needed to make the delicate adjust-
ments that will give the forms the moving qualities that the best of them
possess'.

The notion of artistry can be adopted in a wide sense to indicate any
activity that aims to create or infuse artistic qualities into an artefact,
which shapes and affects the aesthetic properties of tangible and intangible objects. However, the concept of artistry not only indicates that
an artistic activity creates aesthetic properties, but also highlights that
in performing any artistic activity people are engaged with their senses
and they undergo an aesthetic experience touching their emotions and
energy. The notion of artistry has to be considered as being associated
with an author who is engaged in the creation of an artistic process.
The author can be an individual or a group of people. In this perspective artistry is a conceptual category that can be adopted to denote
any activity carried out by people within the organisation. This recognises that organisational activities can be executed so that they involve
aesthetic experiences and generate outputs characterised by aesthetic
features. Accordingly, the quality and productivity of working activities in organisations are not only tied to technical knowledge, which
pertains to rational thinking, but also to emotive knowledge which
entails human emotive faculties.

On the basis of the above reflections, an artistic process can be interpreted as a set of artistry activities performed intentionally by authors who employ and exploit their sensory systems to define objects that incorporate and evoke aesthetic properties. In accordance with this interpretation ABIs using artistic processes tend to fundamentally exploit the artistry in order to involve people in aesthetic experiential processes. This helps people to understand both how to create objects that are characterised by aesthetic features, and how to be engaged in what they do so that they can deploy their senses and be in touch with their inner reality. In other words, ABIs based on artistic processes allow people to discover and be aware of their senses in performing activities so that they can undergo aesthetic experiences and can appreciate the process of infusing aesthetic properties into the creation of both tangible and intangible artefacts.

ABIs employing artistic processes engage people both rationally and emotionally (Darsø, 2004). This can support employees in organisations in understanding how to reconcile what they do in the domain of technical knowledge with the realm of emotive knowledge.

On the basis of the purposes related to ABIs it is possible to distinguish two types of exploitation mechanisms of the artistic processes: artful creation and artful understanding. This distinction considers that ABIs can exploit artistic processes either as a means of fostering people to use their senses in carrying out activities and letting them explore how they can generate emotive knowledge, or as a role model to identify and investigate the dimensions of the artistry affecting the creation of artefacts.

ABIs activating artful creation

The adoption of artistic processes to shape ABIs creates people's aesthetic experiences that can be fundamentally analysed in accordance with Darsø's (2004: 31) interpretation of artful creation, i.e., an 'art experience that initiates an inner transformation, which opens up for a special kind of consciousness "that" [. . .] can be developed only through direct experience, that involves feelings and touches the person profoundly'. For ABIs levering artful creation, independently from the characteristics of the artistic process output, what matters is the involvement of people in the art-making. This has two functions. On the one hand, it helps people to discover the relevance of performing activities in an artful way. People can understand both the importance of being in touch with their emotions in whatever they do, and how to link the execution of everyday working activities with their inner life. Consequently, ABIs grounded in artful creation can allow people to detect the artfulness of their working activities and to appreciate the ingredients that characterise an artful work; performing work activities with passion and commitment (Richards, 1995). On the other hand, the art-making allows personal contemplative dynamics that drive learning to be activated (Dissanayake, 2000; Kolb, 1984). People involved in artistic processes are quick to reflect on issues using the metaphors and analogical models provided by the aesthetic experience in which they are involved (Scharmer, 2009; Scharmer and Kaeufer, 2010). Consider the case of some arts organisations, such as the Welsh National Opera, that carry out people learning and development programmes in which, for example, managers are trained how to conduct a chorus. People, in conducting their peers, appreciate, reflect and understand both the pleasure of being engaged with their emotions and explore the key challenges of leading a group and making it collaborative and synergetic. The art-making – in this case 'conducting' – allows people to be aware of the feelings and passion of guiding a group with full involvement and commitment towards the achievement of a common objective, as well as support learning about the challenges that managers face in their everyday activities in steering people towards the achievement of shared targeted objectives.

ABIs activating artful understanding

ABIs that use artistic processes as role models play a different function as they are not necessarily aimed at involving people in aesthetic experiential processes, but rather at building an aesthetic reality that can be observed, investigated and interpreted. This reality is aimed at letting people mirror themselves and what they do, in order to discover how to benchmark and imitate the mechanisms and organisation of artistic processes. In order to denote ABIs that are aimed at understanding and imitating artistic processes the notion of artful understanding is proposed. Artful understanding can be considered as the approach of revealing and knowing the artful dimensions that characterise an art-making process. It is about knowing the artistry by identifying and analysing the dimensions at the basis of an artful work. Through artful understanding it is possible to disclose the factors that characterise an artistic activity. This is crucial when managers, for example, are interested in understanding either how they can shape and run organisational processes so that they are soaked with aesthetic features, or how to organise and structure activities so that they are able to create outputs that incorporate and evoke aesthetic properties. Austin and Devin (2003) address the relevance of understanding how artists work in order to drive business performance improvement in knowledge-intensive business sectors. They focus their attention, in particular, on software development, in which exploration, adjustment and improvisation play a fundamental role, and stress that mangers can look at the collaborative arts to understand how to develop new capabilities to deal with uncertainty and ambiguity. To denote the process of creating something entirely new which involves exploration, adjustment and production, Austin and Devin (2003) adopt the metaphor of artful making and address how theatre rehearsal and collaborative arts processes represent key models for knowledge work. The scholars stress how the agile software build process parallels theatre rehearsal and they can be considered as specific cases of artful making. So, the understanding of artful making can offer learning insights that help employees to learn and practise how to create forms out of disorganised materials. In addition it helps to maintain focus on a knowledge creative process and develop self-confidence about the final result, as well as the capacity of managing emergent situations and taking advantage of them.

The function of ABIs: managing aesthetic experiences and properties

ABIs are defined by adopting one or a combination of arts-based contents as described above. In addition, the choice of adopting one specific art form or an integration of different art forms depends on the managerial intentions motivating the implementation of ABIs. It is important to point out that independently from the managerial reasons driving the implementation of an ABI, whatever art form grounds its definition, the fundamental working mechanism at the basis of the impact of arts-based management actions is related to their capacity to affect aesthetic experiences and properties of organisational components. By deploying artistic products and/or artistic processes in the form of ABIs, the management team is able to influence the organisational aesthetic dimensions. The managerial use of art forms as a management means can be aimed either at directly enabling people to undergo an aesthetic experience, or can address the infusion and insertion of aesthetic properties into tangible and intangible business assets. Therefore, the fundamental focus of an ABI is neither a work of art in itself, which can be a painting, poem, story, film, photograph, dance, musical or theatrical performance, nor an artistic process in itself, which can be any set of artistic activities aimed at generating a work of art, but the aesthetic-based nature of the use of the arts instead. The focus is the use of art forms to engage people in aesthetic experiential processes and/or shape the aesthetic properties of organisational products and infrastructure that in turn can affect people's perception.

The impact of ABIs on organisational components

The impact of ABIs on organisational value-creation capacity is related to their influence on two fundamental organisational components: the people related to the organisation, or stakeholders; and the organisational infrastructure, or structural resources. This distinction reflects the two key constituent parts of an organisation: its actors and its structural parts. The former essentially involves the people working for an organisation as well as the people who are external to the organisational boundaries, but interact directly or indirectly with the organisation as economic agents, such as the customers, the investors and the policy-makers, but also families and society at large. The latter entails both the tangible and intangible organisational structural resources grounding the working mechanisms of an organisation. The tangible infrastructural resources correspond to the overall tangible organisational components ranging from working equipment, machines, information and communication technology infrastructure, to buildings, workplaces and the portfolio of products. While the intangible infrastructural resources represent all those organisational components that are intangible in nature, but grounding and affecting the working functions of an organisation. Some important components of an organisation's intangible infrastructure are: brand, culture, routines and procedures, leadership and management philosophy, identity and image, organisational climate and, more generally, the 'spirit' of the organisation, i.e., the specific atmosphere, energy and feelings that characterise an organisation (Schiuma *et al.*, 2008b).

The impact of ABIs on people and infrastructure is considered related to their capacity to create and manipulate aesthetic experiences and properties. Through ABIs, organisations can manage aesthetic experiences and properties in order to influence the emotional and energetic dynamics characterising people, and tangible and intangible infrastructural components. In particular, distinguishing the impact on people from the impact on organisational infrastructure it is possible to recognise two fundamental aesthetic actions of ABIs. On the one hand, ABIs can be deployed with the goal of letting people undergo aesthetic experiences that have the power to touch their emotions and energy levels. This can be used by an organisation internally in order to engage employees to exercise their passion in daily working activities, and externally to the organisational boundaries to generate experiences that create intangible value for all the organisation's stakeholders. On the other hand, ABIs can be employed in order to embed aesthetic properties into the tangible and intangible organisational infrastructure and products. This allows an organisation to develop its structural resources so that they are capable of expressing aesthetic qualities that in turn have the power to generate aesthetic experiences with an impact on people's emotional and energetic levels both within and outside organisational boundaries.

Therefore an ABI has to be fundamentally considered as an instrument for managing aesthetic, experience-based dynamics that directly or indirectly have an impact on people, both internally and externally to an organisation. By using artistic products and processes an ABI can directly engage people both rationally and emotionally through either active or passive participation. While indirectly, ABIs impact on people by infusing and incorporating aesthetic properties into organisational assets that in turn evoke aesthetic experiences influencing people's perceptions within and outside the organisation.

Particularly, internally to an organisation, ABIs are able to define aesthetic experiential processes that provide different perspectives on and analysis of the business challenges and problems (Boyle and Ottensmeyer, 2005). They have the power to put people directly or indirectly into a different context, forcing them to get out of their comfort zone and to explore new perspectives and ways of seeing the reality around and within them (Darsø, 2004). They are thought-provoking and capable of engaging people in reflection, self-assessment and in developing a new and different understanding of the competitive, managerial and organisational issues (Taylor and Ladkin, 2009). This encourages and supports organisational development (Senge *et al.*, 1999).

In order to understand how ABIs contribute to organisational development, it is relevant to point out that their impact starts and ends at the individual level. The adoption of an ABI is grounded on the fundamental assumption that organisations are made of people and work for people. This means that ABIs are essentially aimed at developing the human-based traits of organisational life and components. They are managerial instruments to humanise an organisation and to engage employees in their daily work activities. The adoption of an ABI can explicitly address people, or its focus can be a tangible or an intangible organisational infrastructural component, but always with the inherent aim of affecting people.

Analysing the impact of ABIs on organisational components it is possible to presuppose that the individual's experience is the building block upon which social experiences and any other effect of the aesthetic experiential processes are built. This means that no social experience can exist without an individual experience. In other words, the construction of a social experience is always subordinated to the individual one.

ABIs have the power to touch an individual's emotive mind as well as to define the conditions that move people towards the creation of a social experience. At the individual level an ABI engages a person emotionally and intellectually. When it is implemented as a social experience it involves a group of people that are engaged in building and sharing emotions and energy states. In this case an ABI is capable of stirring social intelligence with an influence on collective and social processes.

Understanding the organisational aesthetic dimensions affected by ABIs

To analyse the impact of ABIs on organisational components an abstract representation is proposed. In Figure 2.2 the impact of an ABI is conceptually represented by means of a segment where two opposite

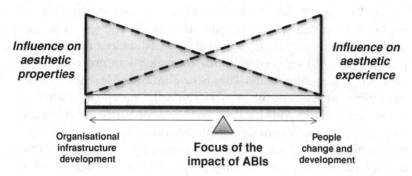

2.2 A conceptual representation of the organisational aesthetic dimensions affected by ABIs

extremes are located: people change/development and organisational infrastructure development. Each position of the segment conceptually denotes the potential impact of an ABI on the two fundamental organisational components: people and infrastructure. In accordance with this visualisation, the focus of an ABI can either be people change and development, which corresponds with the right end of the segment, or the organisational infrastructure development, represented by the left end of the segment. ABIs that focus both on people and infrastructure development are positioned between the two extremes of the segment on the basis that they mainly affect people or infrastructure. As we move from one extreme to the other, the focus of the impact of ABIs changes. In particular, when an ABI is focused exclusively on people change the focus of the impact is essentially on the creation of an aesthetic experience engaging people emotionally. ABIs act by directly stimulating people's sensory system in order to enable them to undergo an aesthetic experiential process that sparks and develops emotions and energy. While, if the ABI is focused fundamentally on the development of organisational infrastructure, the impact is on the aesthetic properties of the organisational assets. In this case the attention is paid to embedding art forms as business assets. ABIs infuse and insert aesthetic traits into the tangible and intangible organisational assets that in turn allow the infrastructural components to evoke and catalyse aesthetic experiences impacting on people.

For interpretative purposes, as shown in Figure 2.2, it is assumed for simplicity's sake that the impact on aesthetic experiences or on the aesthetic properties of an ABI decreases or increases linearly, as we move from one extreme to the other of the segment. The goal of this conceptualisation is to provide a visual understanding of the impact of an ABI on organisational components in order to clarify how ABIs affect organisational aesthetic dimensions. It is not a framework aimed at assessing the impact of an ABI. Conceptually, when an organisation adopts ABIs focusing exclusively on people development, its impact corresponds primarily with the generation of aesthetic experiences directly involving people. This is the case, for example, in the use of art forms for people training purposes. While, if the attention is paid entirely on the development of organisational infrastructure, the primary focus of the impact of an ABI is on the manipulation of the aesthetic properties characterising the tangible and intangible organisational assets. An illustration is provided by the use of the arts to design or shape products. This distinction is useful in order to understand how ABIs can be adopted to manage aesthetic dimensions of an organisation. If ABIs are adopted to support people development, then they are mainly constructed using art forms that manage or create aesthetic experiences. If ABIs are focused on the development of organisational infrastructure, such as products and facilities, then they allow aesthetic properties to be defined and/or manipulated.

The above conceptualisation stresses that when managers adopt ABIs they have to clearly understand what kind of organisational aesthetic dimensions they are addressing and affecting. They need to identify what the managerial reasons are that justify the adoption of ABIs, and whether they are mainly focused on the creation of aesthetic experiences directly involving people, or whether their attention is on the aesthetic properties of organisational infrastructure.

The focus of the impact of ABIs on organisational components is strictly related to the value-creation goals addressed by the management. If the arts are mainly adopted as a management value vector aimed at increasing the intangible value incorporated by organisational products and assets, the managerial focus is essentially on the manipulation of aesthetic properties. While, if ABIs are adopted with the goal of enhancing organisational value-creation mechanisms, then the managerial focus is on blending the creation of aesthetic experiences with the manipulation of aesthetic properties. In this case, even if the primary focus of an ABI might be the development of organisational tangible and intangible infrastructural components there is great attention on the indirect aesthetic experiential effects generated by the initiative on people.

In summary, it is possible to state that ABIs are a management means to affect the organisational aesthetic dimensions. The managerial goal can either be to increase the organisational value stock or the enhancement of the organisational value-creation mechanisms by directly or indirectly affecting and/or shaping people's aesthetic experiences. In both cases, ABIs can be seen as instruments to support the development and transformation of organisations into adaptable techno-human systems that recognise the central and focal position of people in value-creation dynamics and purposes.

How ABIs work by creating people's aesthetic experiences

The relevance of ABIs is essentially related to their power to directly or indirectly activate people's aesthetic experiences that enable management to handle individual and collective emotive dynamics (Klamer, 1996). In order to understand how ABIs act by creating aesthetic experiential processes, the nature of the people involvement in the art forms needs to be clarified.

The participative role played by people in ABIs can be of a twofold nature. People can be involved in an aesthetic experience either through a 'hands-on' or a 'hands-off' participation. Both approaches activate experiential learning mechanisms engaging people aesthetically. ABIs stimulate people's sensory system so that they can be in touch with their feelings and energy. Although both the hands-on and the hands-off participation fully involve people in aesthetic experiences, the dynamics of the experiential processes activated by the two approaches are fundamentally different. In the case of the hands-on approach, people are directly physically engaged in an arts-based experience. They play the role of actors or protagonists in the creation of an artistic product or in the construction of an artistic process. The experiential learning mechanisms taking place mainly present the properties of a 'learning by doing' process, and people develop emotive knowledge by directly acting and going through trial and error activities. Alternatively, the hands-off approach involves people as 'members of an audience'. In this case people are not physically engaged. They are spectators of an artistic product or process and fundamentally have a passive role. Nevertheless, they are actively involved in an aesthetic experience, but this takes place through vicarious experiential process dynamics. This means that even if people are not directly physically involved in the creation of a work of art and/or do not act in an artistic process, they feel attached and engaged as if they have created the contemplated artwork or have performed in the observed artistic process. In this case, the experiential learning dynamics taking place tend to be 'learning by observing' mechanisms and people can learn by observing and reflecting on the reality under investigation.

To clarify how ABIs provide management with approaches and tools to generate people's aesthetic experiences, a framework that distinguishes four main working mechanisms of ABIs is presented. Understanding the working mechanisms of ABIs is at the basis of the managerial use of the arts to affect people development and organisational behaviour.

The working mechanisms of ABIs

The working mechanisms of ABIs are based on the activation of people's experiential mechanisms that allow them to be in touch with their feelings, and to externalise and express their inner reality (Kolb, 1984). The creation of aesthetic experiences touches and sparks people's emotions and energy. They are an important source of feelings, and influence personal cognitive life by driving the exploration, understanding and imagination of the external world. This has an impact on people's awareness and self-consciousness.

The experiential process activated by ABIs allows people to grasp as well as to distinguish and bridge their inner reality made of personal psychological and emotional traits, with the external reality which is represented by the world that surrounds individuals. People continuously interact with and shape the external reality through their actions that involve work activities, decision-making processes, communication and social interactions and constructions. How people interact with the external reality is influenced by their inner reality, which in turn is continuously affected by their experiences of the world.

The use of art forms as a way to bridge the inner and external reality of people can drive a joyful experience that creates a kind of pleasurable break in everyday life; or can be deployed as a medium to convey messages, ideas and feelings, and then act as an instrument to shape expressive forms; or can even represent a means to spark and

	Hands-on	Hands-off
Artistic process	Artfulness creation	Absorbing artistry
Artistic product	Making aesthetic artefacts	Attending artworks

Contents of ABIs

Hands-on   **Hands-off**

People's participation roles in ABIs

2.3 The working mechanisms of ABIs

support reflection and learning that reframes people's mindsets and generates self-assessment of behaviours and attitudes (Nissley, 2010).

The use of artistic products and artistic processes works differently in connecting people's inner reality with their external world. An artistic product is essentially about projecting the inner reality so that it becomes part of the external reality (Taylor and Ladkin, 2009), while an artistic process is mainly about creating a connection between the inner reality and the external one (Darsø, 2004). In performing an artistic activity people exercise their sensory system in such a way that they can not only interact with the external world, but also savour the emotional and energetic states attached to the aesthetic experiences.

In order to shed light on the working mechanisms characterising ABIs, a framework to understand how people can be involved in the aesthetic experiential processes is presented. The framework is based on the combination of the participative role of people, distinguishing a hands-on versus hands-off approach, with the two fundamental categories of contents that an ABI may present, classified as artistic product versus artistic process. The framework is depicted in Figure 2.3. It classifies the typology of the working mechanisms by indicating, along the horizontal axis, people's participation roles and, along the vertical axis, the contents of ABIs. Four main working mechanisms of ABIs can be so identified. They represent the modalities through which ABIs are able to create people's aesthetic experiential processes. They represent the 'engine' of the arts-based managerial actions and denote how ABIs act by creating people's aesthetic experiences.

Making aesthetic artefacts

Making aesthetic artefacts involves a hands-on participation of people in the creation of a work of art that can be tangible, such as an art installation, a group painting, making masks and creating an art exhibition; or intangible, such as creating a live performance, singing in a chorus or making music, e.g., a drum performance. In this case, the focus and the relevance of people's aesthetic experience are fundamentally related to the characteristics of the created aesthetic artefact. The aesthetic experiential processes revolve around the creation of an aesthetic artefact that acts as a means to externalise people's embodied emotive and tacit knowledge (Taylor and Ladkin, 2009). In the creation of the aesthetic artefact, people deploy their sensory system, expressing their feelings and exploring their deep understanding of the activities to be carried out and/or of the objectives to be achieved.

When ABIs are based on the working mechanism 'making aesthetic artefacts' the production of a work of art is carried out on the basis of a specific theme. For example, people can be asked to represent their leadership or management style, or the organisational culture, values and atmosphere. For example, tradesecrets, an arts-based organisation, uses group paintings to engage leaders in expressing and representing their understanding of the fundamental hypothesis at the basis of their vision and strategic objectives. In this way the painting becomes a visual codification of the organisational strategy and can be exploited either as a platform to animate conversations among the top management or even as an alternative communication medium that sparks inspiration and imagination. This illustration shows that an aesthetic artefact can operate as a projective technique objectifying personal experience so that it can be handled and understood (Langer, 1942). The aesthetic artefact becomes a metaphor to explore the inner reality as well as an analogical model to present and communicate meanings and feelings. Thus 'making aesthetic artefacts' allows the projection of the inner reality of individuals and groups by creating objects that condense and reflect people's points of view, feelings, values, beliefs and perceptions, so that they become part of the external reality and can be shared, discussed and reflected upon.

Attending artworks

Attending artworks involves a hands-off participation of people in an aesthetic experience of a work of art. In this case, people play the role of spectators. For example, they can experience an art collection or an art performance within or outside the organisation. An organisation can decorate and beautify workplaces with art forms, can create an art collection and scatter works of art in the workspaces or display them in a private museum or exhibition. Artists can be brought into the organisation to perform, or simply, an organisation can take people to experience artworks in galleries, museums or theatres and concert halls. In all these cases, people are engaged in aesthetic experiences that use the aesthetic properties of the experienced artworks.

ABIs based on the working mechanism 'attending artworks' use artworks that are part of the public artworld or that are commissioned by the organisation to artists and arts organisations, with the goal of inviting people to appreciate and understand a work of art. This has the power of catalysing, attuning and developing people's sensibilities. Indeed, by experiencing an artwork people can awaken their passion and get in touch with their deep emotions and energy. This aesthetic experiential process can be deployed for managerial purposes in order to help people to discover and express their inner reality, and develop a better understanding of themselves and of organisational life and components (Adler, 2006, 2010). The works of art are used as a vicarious means to recall personal experiences and to analogically project personal knowledge into the artistic product so that it raises awareness and makes self-assessment possible. Therefore, 'attending artworks' works by creating an association between people's inner reality with an artwork that has the power to evoke emotions and generate personal energy.

Artfulness creation

Artfulness creation is characterised by a hands-on participation of people in an art-making process which usually, but not necessarily, produces a work of art as an output. Through art-making people discover the properties of being involved in artistry activities that engage their feelings, full attention, presence and appreciation for what they do. ABIs based on the working mechanism 'artfulness creation' allow people to understand the artfulness of an artistic process, i.e., the passion and commitment involved in art working (Richards, 1995). This can be inspiring for people to realise how they should feel at work and how they can approach working activities so that they can perceive them differently. Unfortunately, most of today's working activities are characterised by being anaesthetic. They tend to suppress or control feelings. People are fundamentally requested to put in place their rational faculties to perform tasks and activities. This is a major shortfall because it prevents a full engagement of employees in their activities (Hamel, 2000). Indeed, as addressed in Chapter 1, traditionally companies aspire to define their business models as technical efficient systems. The definition of rules, procedures and standards responds to the need to control the efficiency of organisational processes making sure the organisation achieves, without surprise or eventfulness, the targeted business goals. The technical efficiency characterises business operational contexts in which the level of ambiguity and uncertainty is low. The definition of standardised rules and procedures guarantees that work activities are performed in accordance with the known best practices. However, productivity is affected not only by technical efficiency but, very importantly and increasingly, in today's complex and dynamic business landscape, by an organisation's ability to engage people with their emotions and energy.

The goal of artfulness creation is to let people appreciate the emotional and energetic dynamics characterising an artistic process. This can help them to understand how to be in touch with their feelings at work and be positively in touch with their inner reality (Richards, 1995). In fact people at work can operate experiencing their activities and the space around them without an emotional attachment. In this case the activities tend to be rational, practical and routinely executed and people are fundamentally detached from what they do. The rational mind is driving behaviours and attitudes. In extreme cases, this can also generate alienation and depression. On the other hand, people can experience their work activities by engaging their positive feelings so that the activities and the space become a source of personal satisfaction. In this case not only the rational mind is engaged in the experience, but also the emotive mind leading the generation of feelings which enriches personal life.

The engagement of feelings in the execution of work activities can drive self-consciousness and can support people to discover flow, i.e., to feel a sense of transcendence as the boundaries of self are expanded and the awareness of time disappears and people feel pervaded by a subtle pleasure (Csikszentmihalyi, 1990; Csikszentmihalyi and Robinson, 1991). Artfulness creation allows the key factors for fully engaging people in what they do to be identified and the discovery that work can be executed in such a way that pursues joy and does not separate feelings from organisational working activities.

Two fundamental approaches exploited by ABIs based on 'artfulness creation' are: 'rehearsal' and 'artists in residence'. They are particularly important in the definition of ABIs aimed at developing employees.

Artfulness creation and the practice of rehearsal. The practice of rehearsal to face management problems is fundamentally a concept coming from the performing arts. Rehearsal is something that is commonplace in the world of the performing arts, but not in the business world. Usually businesses do not rehearse. Rehearsal offers the possibility of experimenting with different situations and simulating behaviours and approaches to problem-solving. People can create prototype situations, reproducing the possible business realities, and test hypotheses by understanding what would happen 'if', or simply by stretching themselves to learn how to face difficult circumstances in a safe environment. Rehearsal is a key process in live performances during which experiments about the different aspects and characteristics of the performance take place, and behaviours are explored, tested, repeated and refined to improve performance. A rehearsal, in the artistic world, is a time when the public is not watching the performance and actors can comfortably try different forms of expression and test their abilities, strengths and weaknesses. During a rehearsal process the pressure of performance is suspended and risks for experimenting with new things and/or exercising specific activities can be taken without any consequence. The principles at the basis of rehearsal are particularly important in the management arena and particularly for executives who are continuously under pressure for performance results (Corsun *et al.*, 2006). In business, very rarely do people have the opportunity to experiment, being under pressure to deliver. Very rarely in the business world do people have the opportunity to ask anything, and to practise stretch and fail, which is critical for improving performance and also for creativity. However, this is the kind of thing that during theatre-based initiatives business people can do in the rehearsal room, i.e., to reflect, to explore, to experiment, to try and to

risk failure. What ABIs based on rehearsals do is create an opportunity
to immerse people in artful creation and to develop self-consciousness
and awareness as well as to discover the ingredients of artfulness. For
example, in particular, theatre-based initiatives leverage artfulness creation to spur different emotions in people through their involvement
in a drama, a comedy, a tragedy or a farce.[2]

Through the theatrical experience employees are forced to explore
issues such as identity, passion, conflict at work, work–life balance,
personal performance, and so on. Moreover, theatre-based initiatives,
as well as any other live performance, allow employees to focus on
how to provide and get feedback, and most importantly how to act
upon it. Today's business people often receive huge amounts of feedback, but most of the time they do not know what to do with that feedback. In the rehearsal room they can receive feedback and immediately
try and try again based upon it. People usually struggle because they
are not used to systematically learning through trial-and-error mechanisms. Rehearsal offers this opportunity, giving people the opportunity to experiment, reflect, test and learn from failure. The experiential
learning processes grounding the rehearsal mainly involve learning by
doing, learning by experimenting and learning by trial-and-error, but
also learning by observing and learning by reflecting. All these different
learning mechanisms benefit from the ever-present cycle of feedback
which characterises a rehearsal process.

Artfulness creation and the relationships with artists. The relationship between artists and an organisation can be configured in accordance with two main approaches: artist-ex-residence and artist-in-
residence. The difference lies in how artists are integrated into organisational life. In the case of artist-ex-residence, artists are brought in
the organisation as temporary 'injections'. Artists are invited to visit
the organisation only for the time required to perform the ABI. In the
case of artist-in-residence, however, artists are integrated into organisational life. They are invited to stay and work in the organisation
so that socialisation dynamics between artists and business people can
take place. Through socialisation people can exchange tacit knowledge (Nonaka, 1991; Nonaka and Takeuchi, 1995). Thus employees
can be exposed to artful creation and by observing artistic work and
interacting with artists they can intuitively and empathetically capture
the artfulness of artists' jobs. People can learn the passion and commitment that artists put into what they do. They can discover that artful

creation involves a collection of joy and disciplined work. Artists love what they do, enjoy making art, and know how to motivate themselves. Artists are not fundamentally driven by extrinsic motivation, they care about what they do. This can inspire and enlighten business people about the intrinsic rewards they can get by discovering how to reduce the distance between their work and their positive emotions. Caring for and enjoying work activities is a key path for self-motivation and self-actualisation which ultimately is the top dimension of Maslow's (1954) hierarchy classification of human needs.

Absorbing artistry

Absorbing artistry involves a hands-off participation of people in an art-making process. This working mechanism of ABIs is based on the exploitation of artful understanding. In this case, people take an external perspective and observe an artistic process. The fundamental difference between absorbing artistry and artfulness creation can be interpreted on the basis of the conceptual category of the participation consciousness (Berman, 1984). In artfulness creation, people are in the position of a participative consciousness, i.e., they are in a recipro-cal relationship with the artistic process and they are at one with the process. As outlined above, artfulness creation is mainly about sensing and connecting the inner reality with the external world. This process is fundamentally subjective and strictly related to the personal expe-riential process. In absorbing artistry, people are fundamentally in a position of non-participation consciousness. They are separated from the process and are focused on the identification and understanding of the key dimensions that characterise the artistic process. People's aesthetic experience is mainly aimed at objectifying the artistic activ-ities. This may also involve an externalisation and codification of the phases, inputs, transformation, outputs and organisation of the com-ponents characterising the artistry grounding the artistic process. ABIs based on the working mechanism 'absorbing artistry' can fundamen-tally be deployed for managerial purposes aimed at using the artistic process as a metaphor or role model for understanding the stages, components and properties characterising a specific artistic process in order to imitate and replicate it into organisational processes (Austin and Devin, 2003). This involves absorbing the artistry in order to improve business processes.

The reinforcing cycle of ABIs

The fundamental underlying assumption of the working mechanisms of ABIs is that they are capable of engaging people in aesthetic experiential processes. This is a personal process that is strongly affected by the levels of individual's familiarity and propensity to experience the arts. This means that the potential impact of ABIs is influenced by people's attention, propensity and openness to undergo an arts-based experience. So, ABIs can produce different impacts on the basis of the different levels of people's willingness to participate in the arts.

To understand the relevance of the levels of participation in the arts and the benefits that an individual can get from experiencing art forms, McCarthy *et al.* (2004) propose the 'model of participation process'. This model identifies the factors explaining the different patterns of people's participation in the arts and how this participation can change over time. Although this model is not specifically addressed to investigate the impact of ABIs in organisations, it is useful because it highlights that the effects of arts-based experiences are related to their capacity of engaging people. It helps to clarify what the factors affecting people's involvement in the arts are. In addition, it provides relevant implications for the definition and implementation of ABIs within an organisation, identifying the causes affecting people's capacity to properly accept and absorb arts-based experiences. The model of participation process helps to clarify the conditions that guarantee a successful implementation of ABIs as well as providing indications about the most appropriate managerial forms of ABIs to implement on the basis of the targeted impact on organisational components.

The model of participation process identifies three main factors explaining the level of participation of people in the arts. The first factor is the 'gateway experience'. This denotes people's initial experience with the arts. It can occur at any age. The gateway experience tends to have a strong influence on people's arts involvement. Positive gateway experiences increase the likelihood of developing a constructive attitude towards involvement in the arts. This attitude is also influenced by personal beliefs about the arts and the perception of social norms (McCarthy and Kimberly, 2001). The importance of the first experience to explain the participation in the arts has important implications for the definition and implementation of ABIs in organisations. First, it stresses that people's willingness to be involved in arts-based experiences is higher if people had constructive gateway experiences and/or are currently involved in the arts. Previous experience with the arts creates people's propensity to actively participate in ABIs. This means that if employees have not been consistently exposed to the arts in their life, it is quite important for an organisation to take this into account when introducing ABIs. Second, it is crucial, particularly when an organisation is experiencing an ABI for the first time, to make sure that it is structured in order to positively touch and involve people creating a positive gateway experience that further spurs people participation in arts-based actions.

The second factor is the 'quality of the experience'. This is the aspect which transforms an art participant from an occasional to a frequent one. It presupposes that a positive experience drives an increase of the personal attitude towards arts participation. People who develop an appreciation for the arts are essentially better able to capture the benefits of arts-based experiences. In other words, the level of familiarity with and knowledge of the arts allows people to better savour and absorb the value of an ABI. This suggests that ABIs in order to better engage people have to be properly introduced in organisations so that people can find them enjoyable and develop familiarity and knowledge around them.

The third factor is the 'intrinsic worth of arts experience' to an individual. Once people discover the deep gratification that the arts produce for them, they tend to be engaged in a life-long participation in the arts. The quality of the arts-based experience drives people's propensity to seek further, continuous and deep involvement in the arts.[3] This means that once employees discover the benefits of being involved in arts-based experiences they are keen to take part in ABIs and are also more capable of capturing the related benefits. Therefore within an organisation, employees who find ABIs worthwhile are inclined to further use the arts for addressing business issues.

The above reflections define the arts-based reinforcing cycle of ABIs. As shown in Figure 2.4, the framework proposes that the positive impact of ABIs is affected by people's propensity to be involved in the arts. As people are involved in arts-based experiences their familiarity with and knowledge about ABIs grows, and this in turn allows people to better appreciate and capture the benefits of the aesthetic experiences. Then, finally, this can support the production of benefits for the organisation. The identified dimensions are linked to each other in

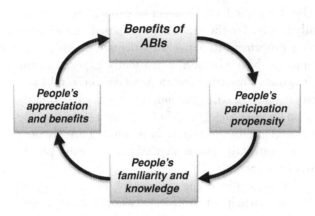

2.4 The reinforcing cycle of the arts-based experiences

accordance with a closed loop cycle, which highlights that a sustained and a greater level of people involvement in ABIs is a key aspect for gaining benefits from the management adoption of the arts.

ABIs, emotions and energy in organisations

A fundamental premise of the implementation of ABIs is their power to handle people's emotional and energetic dynamics in organisations. This is the result of the ABIs' working mechanisms of developing and managing experiential processes that are grounded in people's aesthetic experiences. The arts engage people with their sensory system in building experiences that blend emotive and rational knowledge. In particular, the use of the arts allows people to live, express, share, transfer and communicate emotions that affect thinking and behavioural capacity and attitudes. Indeed, any art form has the power to represent, communicate, transfer and induce emotions. So an ABI can be exploited to catalyse positive emotions or to calm down negative tensions and dissolve depressing feelings. They can marshal people's positive feelings, such as enthusiasm, zeal, confidence, pleasure, happiness, joy, self control, persistence and the ability to motivate oneself. This is crucial to enhancing an organisation's ability to achieve better performance. On the other hand, ABIs can break cycles of depression and anxiety that can lock-in the thinking of individuals and groups, so that they can overcome organisational emotive distress, such as anxiety, anger, fear, sadness and pressure that can cause negative feelings hampering the capacity and potential to achieve high performance. Therefore, ABIs allow managers to harness emotions in organisations.

The analysis of the typology of emotions that might characterise an organisation represents an important research area, but it goes beyond the scope of this book. As already discussed in Chapter 1, the relevance of emotions in organisations is a fundamental factor affecting employees' engagement in everyday work activities, as well as the role that emotions can play in organisational life and activities. In this section, the focus is essentially on emotions and energy as a composite element that influences organisational business performance.

The concept of energy at work is addressed by pointing out the role of ABIs to handle emotional and energetic dynamics in organisations. The fundamental assumption is that people's emotions and energy can be interpreted as two interdependent and interconnected dimensions of human life. Emotions affect energy and, vice versa, energy influences how people feel. Although it can be recognised that conceptual differences between emotions and energy can be addressed, particularly for managerial purposes, they can be considered as two facets of the same phenomenon and reality, i.e., the creation of people's emotive knowledge. This can be considered as the result of the fundamental capacity of art forms to speak directly to the human emotive mind so that people's emotions and energy are catalysed and put into action.

Understanding energy in organisations

The concept of energy is intuitively understood and it is quite pervasive in much of organisational life. It is fundamentally associated to individuals and widely recognised as a key factor affecting people's performance. Indeed, the more energy an individual has, the more effort they will be able to put into their work. In addition, energy is linked to individual and team performance, innovation and job satisfaction. Although the concept of energy is quite widespread in management literature, it is quite an elusive notion and difficult to define. It is often expressed by other conceptualisations as energetic arousal (Thayer, 1989), positive affect (Watson *et al.*, 1988), emotional energy (Collins, 1993), subjective energy (Marks, 1977), vitality (Ryan and Frederick, 1997), zest (Miller and Stiver, 1997) and affective experience/arousal (Quinn and Dutton, 2005), as well as associated with other conceptual organisational dimensions such as the atmosphere 'around a project or people' (Cross *et al.*, 2003). The analysis of the literature provides implications supporting the assumption that energy and emotions can be considered as two facets of the same reality. Thayer (1989) defines energy as the feeling that one is eager to act and capable of acting. Watson *et al.* (1988) consider energy as an umbrella concept that includes emotions, moods and dispositions. Brehm and Self (1989) define energetic arousal as a bio-psychological mechanism for translating interests into action. Quinn and Dutton (2005), on the basis of a literature investigation, argue that energy is a type of positive effective arousal, i.e., positive feeling, which people can experience as emotion. These interpretations, mainly aimed at clarifying the nature and content of energy, are further integrated by other conceptualisations that point out the goal of energy at work. Loehr and Schwart (2001) provide an operative conceptualisation as they define energy as the capacity to do work. Similarly, Lounsbury *et al.* (2004) argue that energy denotes the strength, vitality, power and capacity to perform tasks and drive towards the execution of activities.[4]

The investigation of energy in organisations clearly shows that it can be classified in three main categories: individual energy, group energy and organisational energy. Individual energy is a complex result of multiple causes, which can be traced back to the fundamental laws affecting the condition of human wellbeing: the physical state, i.e., the body's condition;[5] the cognitive state, i.e., the mind's condition;[6] and the emotional state, i.e., conscious and unconscious feelings.[7] These causes of individual energy should not be interpreted as hierarchically structured, but rather as factors that are combined and integrated to define the resultant energy condition. So, individual energy is the result of a synergetic combination of physical energy, cognitive energy and emotional energy.[8] This interpretation remarks that energy and emotions are not the same thing, but nevertheless they are strictly interwoven and integrated.

Regarding group energy, it can be interpreted as the energy of its members, but it is not simply identical to the sum of the energy of individuals. It is rather a composite result of the individual energy plus a quantity of energy associated with the systemic and synergetic combination of its members. Indeed, at a group level, energy comes from relationships or networking linkages.[9] Finally, organisational energy can be considered as the result of the integration and combination of individual energy and group energy. Like group energy, organisational energy is a social outcome and is related to both individual and group energy by mechanisms of aggregation, cross-level transfer and distribution. Organisational energy can be considered as the sum of the energies of all the employees, plus the sum of the social network energy created within and between groups, and an emergent energy that is the result of a synergetic integration and combination of all the other forms of energy.

Individual, group and organisational energy represent fundamental drivers affecting organisational performance. Internally to an organisation, the bundle of emotions and energy drives people's behaviours, powers team-working and fosters creativity and imagination. It is a key factor affecting employees' engagement in working activities and particularly driving motivation. Steers *et al.* (2004), on the basis of a review of the main definitions of motivation, highlight that all conceptualisations are mainly concerned with the factors that energise, channel and sustain human behaviour over time. Hence, emotions and energy represent fundamental drivers of the motivational force.[10] They affect both the direction a person chooses to act in and the efforts a person invests in what they do (Marks, 1977). In addition, emotions and energy determine the perception of the attractiveness of various alternatives. They support risk taking behaviour and represent a good indicator to predict the capacity to achieve results (Collins, 1981; Marks, 1977; Vroom, 1964).

Energy and organisational capacity for actions

The emotional and energetic level characterising an organisation can be qualitatively assessed on the basis of two main variables: intensity and quality (Bruch and Ghoshal, 2003; Loehr and Schwartz, 2003). Intensity refers to the strength of organisational emotions and energy. It can be arrayed on a continuum ranging from low, to moderate, to high. Instead, quality is essentially considered as the role or impact of emotions and energy on a process execution, and can be arrayed on a continuum ranging from negative, through neutral, to positive.

The emotional and energy levels determine the quality of a person's experience, the state of wellbeing and happiness, the effort a person is likely to invest in the activity and how attractive a person considers the alternatives to be (Collins, 1981; Quinn and Dutton, 2005; Rafaeli and Sutton, 1987; Ryan and Frederick, 1997; Thayer, 1989). It can be considered as an indicator of how much effort an individual or group is able to invest. It is possible to assume that people who feel high and positive levels of emotions and energy tend to view events positively, expect positive events to occur and invest efforts to achieve objectives. Positive emotions and energy make people more likely to appraise subsequent events positively (Arkes *et al.*, 1988). Summarising, emotions and energy are critical factors for engaging people and making sure that they deploy their passion in working activities.

Any organisation at any given point in time is characterised by a specific energy state. It involves aspects such as emotional excitement, alertness, the engagement of people, emotional intelligence, creativity and imagination and the shared sense of urgency for taking actions as well as enthusiasm and satisfaction. Bruch and Ghoshal (2003) propose four main energy zones characterising an organisation's energy state. They are defined on the basis of the interaction of energy intensity and quality as: 'comfort state', 'resignation state', 'aggression state' and 'passion state'. The authors assume that each state dictates how the organisation will cope with environmental pressures, and this defines their modus operandi. Those companies in the comfort state 'have low animation and a relatively high level of satisfaction. With weak but positive emotions such as calm and contentedness, they lack the vitality, alertness and emotional tension necessary for initiating bold new strategic thrusts or significant change' (Bruch and Ghoshal, 2003: 46). Companies that are in the resignation state 'demonstrate weak, negative emotions – frustration, disappointment, sorrow. People suffer from lethargy and feel emotionally distant from company goals. They lack excitement or hope' (Bruch and Ghoshal, 2003: 46). The aggressive state is associated with 'internal tension founded on strong, negative emotions'. Companies in this state have 'high levels of activity and alertness – and focused efforts to achieve company goals' (Bruch and Ghoshal, 2003: 46). According to scholars the ideal energy state is the passion state: 'In the passion zone, companies thrive on strong, positive emotions – joy and pride in the work. Employees' enthusiasm and excitement mean that attention is directed toward shared organizational priorities' (Bruch and Ghoshal, 2003: 47).

The above energy states highlight the relevance for an organisation to harness emotional and energetic dynamics. They are important dimensions affecting and driving organisational behaviour and business performance particularly in complex and fluid competitive environments. By harnessing emotions and energy, organisations can develop competencies and dynamic capabilities that allow them to be adaptable, resilient, agile and innovative.

The emotions and energy associated with an individual, a group or an organisation are specific and context-related characteristics. They represent strategic soft resources and sources of value-creation. Organisations that recognise emotions and energy as strategic sources of value-creation have to put in place actions for taking care of their development and regeneration. Indeed, individual, group and organisation emotional and energetic levels are dynamic in nature. Energy can be both created and depleted over time (Frijda, 1988), and emotional and energetic levels can be influenced in various ways by handling people's aesthetic experiences.

Emotional and energetic dynamics in organisations

Emotions and energy within an organisation are dynamic in nature. Emotions may change on the basis of people's aesthetic experiences; while energy oscillates on the basis of energy expenditure or creation, and energy renewal or recovery. Quinn and Dutton (2005), interpreting coordination as energy-in-conversation in a software company, show how energy levels change and how it is perceived as changed by people within the organisation. People are aware of their emotions and of their own energy, and this affects how they experience and approach events. Furthermore, a person continually communicates empathetically, i.e., they are able to read and ultimately affect another person's emotions and energy. An individual's or group's emotive and energetic state is shown in facial expressions, postures, tone of voice and non-verbal expression, as well as in words and actions.[11]

Organisational emotional and energetic dynamics are the result of multilevel processes that involve individuals, groups and organisational infrastructure (Schiuma *et al.*, 2007b). In order to investigate these dynamics, it is possible to distinguish two main organisational sources: people, which accounts for the emotional and energetic dynamics associated with individuals and relationships among them, and organisational infrastructure, which accounts for the emotional and energetic features related to the organisation's tangible

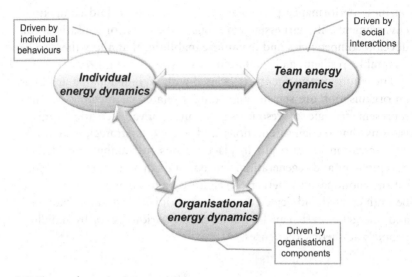

2.5 Energy dynamics in organisations

and intangible assets. The functioning and interaction of these dimensions dictates the organisational emotional and energetic conditions at any given point in time. They represent the mechanisms and levers for creating and harnessing emotions and energy in organisations. Figure 2.5 shows the sources of emotional and energetic dynamics and their relationships within an organisation. The main characteristics of individual, team and organisational energy dynamics are introduced below.

Individual energy dynamics. They depend on three main factors as follows: physical, emotional and mental capacity. The physical capacity is related to an individual's physical health and conditioning. Factors such as fatigue, sleep, stress, nutrition, intense work activities, and so on, affect the level of physical energy. The emotional and mental capacity denotes the individual psychological condition. It is related to various dimensions such as the seeking of pleasure and the tendency to avoid pain, the search for safety and security, the sense of belonging, self-esteem, self-actualisation, the search for achievement, affiliation, power and autonomy, and so on. Individual behaviours affect both physical and psychological capacity. Physical capacity goes through a continuous rhythmic cycle between energy expenditure and energy recovery that is affected by healthy rituals such as appropriate training, good sleeping and eating (Loehr and Schwartz, 2001). The psychological capacity can be developed by self-reflection processes (Boyatzis *et al.*, 2002) as well as by stimulating and nurturing individual emotions, passions, cognitive challenges and life interests.

Team energy dynamics. They are driven by social interactions. Any social interaction is characterised by a sender and a receiver who are engaged in a two-way conversation which involves an exchange of information and emotions. The overall transactions generate, over time, both social emotions and energy and social cognition. In particular, the cognitive transaction can be described as a process in which a sender codifies knowledge into information and transfers this information to a receiver, who on the basis of his/her own mental models interprets the information and recreates the knowledge. Afterwards the receiver responds with implicit or explicit feedback about the acquired knowledge. On the basis of this interaction, it is possible to identify a cycle that enables the creation of social cognition. It involves three sub-processes: explanation, understanding and reaction. At the same time, people interacting cognitively also exchange emotions. A sender conveys emotions to a receiver, who responds with implicit or explicit feedback about the continuation of the displayed emotion. The sender of the emotion reacts to such feedback by modifying his/her emotions. This conversation process can be considered as the basis of the creation of social emotion and involves three main sub-processes: display of emotion, reaction and readjustment (Rafaeli and Sutton, 1987).

Organisational energy dynamics. They are affected by the components of an organisational infrastructure defining the organisational platform for developing and harnessing emotions and energy at individual and group levels. Organisational infrastructure, including the overall tangible and intangible dimensions grounding the working mechanisms of an organisation, can be intentionally designed and managed in order to spark, develop, maintain and drive emotions and energy in organisations. The tangible infrastructure corresponds with the facilities, equipment and any other tangible organisational assets that can affect emotions and energy in people and/or in relationships among people. The traditional management literature about workplace ergonomics has largely investigated and proved the relevance of workstation design in order to reduce workers' physical and physiological fatigue. In the last few decades, many organisations have created areas in the workplace that are explicitly dedicated to meditation, relaxation, rest and fitness activities with a more or less explicit intention to affect employees' emotions and energy. Increasingly, today's organisations are also embracing interior design and generally the use of the arts not only to decorate workplaces, but also as a management means to harness emotions and energy in organisations. The intangible infrastructure accounts for all organisational assets that are intangible in nature and may influence emotional and energetic dynamics. In particular they include, among others, leadership,[12] management practices,[13] organisational culture[14] and management systems.[15]

In summary, any organisation can be interpreted and, as an emotive and energy system, characterised by different forms of emotional and energetic dynamics. They are idiosyncratic, unique and changeable over time for each specific organisational context. A fundamental challenge for management is how to generate and channel emotional and energetic dynamics in order to support the enhancement of organisational value-creation capacity. In this perspective ABIs are of fundamental relevance. As discussed in this chapter, they support the management of organisational aesthetic dimensions with the capacity to affect people's emotions and energy. Thus, through ABIs managers can ignite, generate and channel emotional and energetic dynamics both within an organisation and at the intersection between the organisation and its external environment.

Conclusion

The interpretation of organisations as techno-human systems recognises the fundamental human-based nature of organisational components and working mechanisms. In accordance with this perspective, to excel in the twenty-first century business landscape, organisations need to combine the management of people's technical know-how with the capacity to harness their emotions and energy both within and outside the organisational boundaries. This raises the challenge for managers of how to humanise organisations in order to make them real living organisms capable of adaptation and sustainable evolution in today's economic, socio-cultural and environmental ecosystem. This requires a focus on the development of the human traits of organisational components. In other words, it is necessary to manage people and organisational infrastructure taking into account their emotive features and facets. Organisations are made of people and work for people. To disregard people's emotional and energetic characteristics means to approach an organisation as a machine-like system that just produces outputs on the basis of market demand. But the new economic age calls for both an understanding of the outcomes generated by organisations, and for the development of organisational capabilities that enhance value-creation capacity. In this context ABIs represent a management means to translate the arts into action and to develop the human dimensions of an organisation. Through the adoption of art forms, it is possible to manage organisational aesthetic experiences and properties in such a way that directly or indirectly engages people's emotions and energy.

ABIs are management actions that are based on the deployment of any art form in order to enable people to directly undergo an aesthetic experience, or to manipulate aesthetic properties of organisational infrastructural components so that they can evoke aesthetic experiences in people. This means that ABIs represent a fundamental instrument to create and manage emotive knowledge within and around an organisation. By managing aesthetic experiences and properties, ABIs handle the emotional and energetic dynamics that affect the organisational capacity for actions. They are instruments that can be implemented to generate and channel people's emotions and energy so that organisations can enhance their value-creation capacity.

3 | *The value of Arts-based Initiatives in business*

Introduction

Understanding of the value of the arts in business is the central issue of the managerial use of Arts-based Initiatives (ABIs). The economic literature and particularly the so-called cultural economic research stream encompasses numerous studies investigating the value of the arts from an economic perspective (Bianchini, 1993; Brooks and Kushner, 2001; Florida, 2004; Myerscough, 1988; Radich, 1992). These studies analyse the reasons and the modalities of the partnership between business and the arts, mainly addressing the relevance of the cultural industry as a driver for wealth creation. They distinguish two main categories of benefits related to the use of the arts in business: direct and indirect economic effects. The direct economic benefits are those generated by arts-based economic activities. In this case, the arts are recognised as the resources of the cultural industry and, as such, they generate employment, income and tax revenue. The indirect economic benefits are associated with the benefits that the arts can create in terms of their capacity to generate a context supporting economic development by attracting and developing talent, creative people and firms (Florida, 2004). In this case, the role of the arts is recognised as a factor generating socio-cultural effects that can benefit economic development dynamics. The application of the economic-based perspective aims to express the value of the arts for business in monetary terms. In particular, the attention is focused on the price that people are willing to pay to acquire or enjoy a work of art. Alternatively, the focus is on the economic return associated with investment in the cultural industry.

It is undoubted that money is the best unit of measurement to communicate economic value. However, the organisational benefits related to the adoption of the arts to deal with management challenges and to solve business problems cannot be directly defined in financial terms.

The arts in management represent a knowledge domain to inspire managers and to develop organisations (Adler, 2006, 2010; Austin and Devin, 2003; Darsø, 2004). They can drive the enhancement of management mindsets and support the evolution of traditional modern management systems with the integration of new approaches and techniques that value the human-based nature of organisational models and activities. So, the use of art forms in management has an impact on bottom line results, but this has to be fundamentally considered as the result of a set of dependent and interdependent links between the development of organisational assets and the performance improvement of organisational processes.

The adoption of ABIs enables organisations to manage the creation of aesthetic experiences and/or the manipulation of aesthetic properties in order to handle people's emotional and energetic dynamics within and around the organisation. The relevance of harnessing people's emotions and energy both within an organisation and at the intersection between the organisational boundaries and the market cannot easily be stated in monetary terms. ABIs ultimately generate economic value, but as the outcome of the positive effects on organisational value-drivers. Thus, the value of the arts for business has to be found in the benefits that the adoption of ABIs can generate in terms of the development of organisational components grounding the value-creation capacity of an organisation. In particular, the arts have the power to develop organisational pillars at the basis of organisations' capabilities. They act through the creation of cause-and-effect chains that impact upon the quality and productivity of organisational and business processes and, in turn, allow the achievement of operational and strategic performance objectives.

At the basis of the understanding of the value of arts for business there is fundamentally the comprehension of how the management of organisational aesthetic experiences and properties can be translated into business performance improvements. Starting from an analysis of the characteristics of the benefits and of the beneficiaries of ABIs, in this chapter the attention will be focused on the organisational value-drivers that can be affected by ABIs. In addition, it delineates the strategic intents for implementing ABIs in order to enhance the organisational value-creation capacity. This represents the conceptual basis to further investigate how to assess the impact of ABIs on business performance improvements.

The benefits of ABIs for organisations

The identification of the organisational benefits of ABIs is based on the dominant belief in the world of the arts that the value of an art form is found in its aesthetics (Klamer, 1996). This means that the positive impact of ABIs on organisational value-creation capacity has to be searched in the aesthetic power of the managerial use of art forms to deal with business issues. Through the use of ABIs, managers can affect aesthetic experiences and manipulate aesthetic properties both internally and externally to an organisation with an impact on organisational components.

In the economic and political arena, the accounting of the benefits generated by the arts has been, particularly in the last decades, the focal concern of arts advocates promoting private and public investment in the arts. They have emphasised that the arts have a positive impact on public welfare and have addressed the need to prove the value of the arts for social and economic goals in order to design policies to support the allocation of financial resources to the arts. The analysis of the studies related to this debate provides an important starting point for understanding the nature and characteristics of the benefits related to the use of the arts in organisations for management purposes.

On the basis of a systematic multidisciplinary literature review on the role of the arts for the creation of value in the public domain, McCarthy *et al.* (2004) acknowledge that the arts can have both private and public benefits, as well as instrumental and intrinsic benefits. The private benefits are considered as those that pertain to individuals, whereas the public benefits accrue to society at large. The distinction between instrumental and intrinsic benefits aims to emphasise that the arts can support the achievement of broad social and economic goals as well as the enrichment of individuals' lives. The two classifications address important aspects of the potential value of the arts. In particular, the distinction between private and public benefits highlights that there are different beneficiaries of the arts that in the public domain are identified with individuals and society. On the other hand, the division between intrinsic and instrumental benefits stresses that the impact of the arts can be twofold in nature. The value of the arts can be analysed either in terms of the benefits produced for individuals, or interpreted on the basis of the positive impact that the arts create for society. Both classifications are greatly relevant in the public discourse, since the allocation of public funding has to address broad social and economic goals. They also represent important conceptual categories in investigating the benefits of art forms in organisations. Indeed, the distinction between private and public benefits, when applied to organisations, suggests that the benefits generated by the use of the arts can be analysed at a people and an organisational level and, in addition, it is important to distinguish the intrinsic and instrumental value of the managerial use of the arts.

Beneficiaries of ABIs

When the arts are applied in organisations as a management means to deal with business issues, it is possible to distinguish three fundamental beneficiaries of ABIs. They can be classified as follows: individuals; teams, groups or communities; and the organisation.

When approaching the use of art forms in organisations, it is important to be aware that the benefits of ABIs can be understood at different levels of analysis. A pivotal role is played by individuals. Indeed, individuals are those that finally capture the benefits of using the arts in business. An individual involved in the arts can enjoy and learn from experiencing art forms. The arts, in all their manifestations, act through and on the personal sensory system (Strati, 2000a). They create aesthetic frames and perceptions that affect the quality of individual experiential processes (Klamer, 1996). In turn, through aesthetic experiences people build their understanding of the world, and act on and transform the world around them. Through the sensory system people experience the qualities of the environment and these qualities affect their emotions. So, ABIs are able to communicate and/or create aesthetic experiential processes that can affect people's emotional and energetic states, such as joy, fun, excitement and enthusiasm.

The individual experience of the arts becomes a social experience when ABIs involve a group of individuals. This has an impact on people's networking and social dynamics and generates benefits for groups and communities within and around the organisation. For example, the arts have the power to represent and affect the culture of a community (Guss, 1989). Through the arts, the values, norms and behaviours of a community can be reflected and formed.

When ABIs are focused on organisational structural assets the generated benefits tend mainly to impact upon the organisation. This is

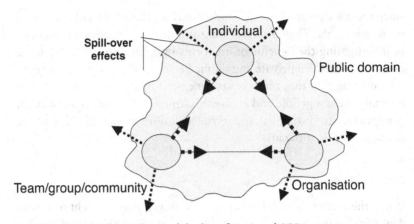

3.1 The conceptual categories of the beneficiaries of ABIs

the case, for example, when ABIs are aimed at developing organisational dimensions such as activities, identity, brand, reputation and
management practice. However, it is important to stress that the implementation of ABIs always, directly or indirectly, involves people, who
ultimately are engaged in the aesthetic experiential processes activated
by arts-based actions.

The above classification of the beneficiaries of ABIs has two main
managerial implications. The first and foremost insight corroborates
the assumption that the benefits of ABIs have to be investigated distinguishing between people and organisational structural assets. The
conceptual category of people involves both individuals and groups.
The organisational structural assets denote all tangible and intangible
resources building the infrastructure of an organisation. The second
implication is the recognition that ABIs can impact at multiple levels.
As shown in Figure 3.1, it is possible to assume that the three conceptual categories of the beneficiaries are strictly interconnected and integrated. They are linked to each other through spill-over effects. Benefits
captured at the individual level in terms, for example, of lessons learnt
through an arts-based training course and/or the positive impact on a
person's mood and feelings triggered by an arts-based experience, such
as attendance at an artistic show, may affect the organisational group
dynamics in which individuals take part, and may also have a direct or
an indirect impact on the organisational activities in which individuals
are involved. Similarly, arts-based experiences that involve and benefit

a group of people within an organisation not only have an impact on the relationships between the group members, but also influence individual behaviours and organisational dimensions such as culture, identity, activities, climate and trust. Finally, ABIs that specifically address organisational structural components, such as the embellishment and redesign of workspaces, can generate benefits both for the organisation and people. In addition, ABIs can also have an impact on the public domain in which organisations operate. In fact, the use of the arts in organisations can generate spill-over effects that impact upon the public domain. The involvement of an organisation in the arts can generate positive effects for the communities in which the organisation operates, and/or for society at large when the benefits go beyond a local dimension. Therefore, it is possible to claim that a distinctive feature of ABIs is their ability to operate at multiple levels and to generate multiple benefits.

The intrinsic and instrumental benefits of ABIs

The distinction between intrinsic and instrumental benefits within an organisation is useful to understand the nature of the impact of ABIs and to identify how arts-based experiences can generate organisational benefits. The concept of intrinsic benefits has been the object of studies in aesthetics and philosophy, art-based education, cultural industry, literacy and art criticism (Benedict, 1991; Budd, 1995; Deasy, 2002; Goldman, 1995; Jensen, 2002; Levinson, 1996; McCarthy *et al.*, 2004; Shusterman, 2002; Stecker, 1997). It draws attention to the personal effects of the involvement in the arts. Accordingly, people are fundamentally engaged in the arts because arts-based experiences have a cognitive and emotional power. Through the arts people can get unique emotional and energetic stimulation. The arts have what Eisner (2002) calls physiognomic properties. Art forms possess qualities that are able to evoke emotions. The arts have the power to embed high aesthetic qualities and to affect an individual's ability to be open and perceive the aesthetic features of the world. They are the gateway for aesthetic experiences. A work of art is able to awake and stimulate a person's sensory system, generating aesthetic experiences that open up a personal interior landscape and drive a deeper knowledge of the world (Green, 2001). This makes an art form a means of helping people to go through aesthetic experiential processes that activate and develop their emotions and energy. On the basis of this interpretation, it is possible to state that the concept of intrinsic benefits stands for the personal pleasure and inner value that an arts-based experience can generate for people. Intrinsic benefits are considered inherent in arts-based experiences. The implicit assumption is that experiential processes generated by the arts are self-relevant, i.e., they are always satisfying in themselves. Therefore, intrinsic benefits represent those value dimensions related to the emotional and cognitive sphere that are directed to fundamentally satisfy people's personal goals, creating value in their lives.

The conceptual category of the instrumental benefits denotes those pragmatic objectives that can be achieved directly and/or indirectly through the use of artistic products and/or artistic processes (Deasy, 2002; Fiske, 1999; Jackson, 1998). The concept of instrumental benefits presumes that an arts-based experience can be used as a means to achieve different benefits from those pertaining just to the satisfaction of personal goals (Griffiths, 1993; Lowe, 2000; Marwick, 2000; Myerscough, 1988; Verghese *et al.*, 2003). The traditional argument lying behind instrumental benefits is that the arts can be used to generate value in terms of achievement of broad socio-cultural and economic goals that have nothing to do with the art per se.

The distinction between intrinsic and instrumental benefits is of great relevance for the public discourse when analysing the benefits of private and public investments in the arts. This is because it is at the basis of the arguments distinguishing between those arts policies aimed at generating value in the public domain, which have to be supported, from those that should be discouraged due to their focus on private and intrinsic benefits not pertaining to society (McCarthy *et al.*, 2004).

When applied within an organisation, the distinction between intrinsic and instrumental benefits becomes fuzzy and has a different relevance. Its importance is mainly related to understanding the nature of the ABIs' outcomes, i.e., the recognition that an ABI will operate by affecting individuals' inner emotional and energetic spheres and/or by addressing organisational objects. It is possible to state that in both cases an ABI generates benefits for an organisation. Indeed, even though an ABI can grant an individual benefits that are strictly and exclusively linked to satisfy their inner goals, that could apparently not be at all related to organisational and business issues, the intrinsic benefits can be considered as a factor that operates within an organisation with an influence on the capacity of organisational value creation. According to this perspective, intrinsic benefits can be viewed in terms of their functional value, recognising that they can stimulate and support organisational growth and wealth creation. In fact, internally to an organisation, individuals who are affected by arts-based experiences tend to be in a good mood, feel better and are happier, and in turn they feel more satisfied and motivated. In other words, they tend to be more passionate and this influences their engagement in everyday work activities (Richards, 1995). However, externally, an organisation can use arts-based experiences that involve people in order to build and transfer a more appealing organisational image, which in turn can have a positive impact on reputation, brand recognition and marketing attraction. Therefore intrinsic benefits can be considered as a factor that potentially contributes to the enhancement of organisational value-creation capacity. In accordance with this view those ABIs that are thought to solely generate intrinsic benefits may also respond to an instrumental function as long as they are aligned with the organisational value propositions and strategic objectives.

ABIs that are explicitly aimed at generating instrumental benefits exploit the aesthetic nature of art forms in order to solve business problems. In this case ABIs represent an instrument of managing aesthetic experiences and/or properties, so that organisational components can be developed.

It is relevant to point out that the intrinsic benefits represent the fundamental layer on which the instrumental benefits are built. In fact, ABIs fundamentally work by acting directly or indirectly on people; and the value of the arts for people is essentially related to their capacity to generate intrinsic benefits. This recognises that the end result of an ABI is fundamentally to have a rewarding and fulfilling experiential impact on individuals. On the basis of the above reflections, it is possible to presuppose that for business purposes the intrinsic and instrumental benefits represent two integrated aspects of ABIs.

The spill-over effects of ABIs

Considering the central position held by individuals for understanding the organisational benefits of ABIs, the relationships linking the different categories of the organisational beneficiaries of ABIs can be depicted in accordance with concentric logic. Figure 3.2 shows the

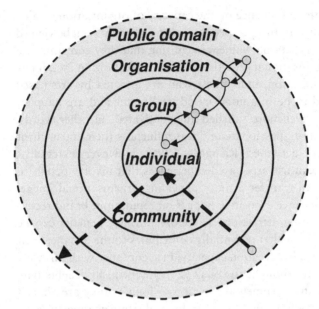

3.2 Spill-over effects linking the organisational beneficiaries of ABIs

three conceptual categories of the beneficiaries of ABIs together with the public domain. The hypothesis underneath the framework is that the value of any ABIs originates or ends with benefits generated for individuals. Within an organisation the individuals' benefits related to an ABI can be disseminated at the group level and subsequently at the organisational level, with benefits also linked to the public domain. Thus, the impact of an ABI on an organisation can move from the inside to the outside of the concentric framework or vice versa. This denotes the spill-over mechanisms characterising ABIs.

An ABI can start with an impact at the individual level and the benefits gradually spread outwards to finally reach the organisational system. Other ABIs can first have an impact on organisational structural components, or on organisational community, and subsequently involve individuals. For example, ABIs that are defined and implemented with a focus on collective effects and social processes first have an impact on networking relationships and afterwards pertain both to people at the individual level and organisational dimensions. Similarly, ABIs addressing organisational structural components, such as an arts-based interior design of the workplace, first have a direct impact on organisational infrastructure and afterwards an indirect influence on social and individuals' emotional and energetic states. ABIs can also be defined by an organisation with the explicit intent to have an impact on the public domain, through the creation of a museum or art gallery for example. In this case, the benefits start at the level of the public domain, but they spread to organisational components. Therefore, the benefits created by ABIs tend to be diffused between the four categories, namely individuals, groups, organisation and public domain. Continuous conversations take place between and among these categories allowing for the generation and exchange of benefits.

The above analysis highlights that ABIs can be adopted as a management means to spark and sustain both people and organisational infrastructure development. This represents the assumption to map the value of ABIs.

The Arts Value Matrix: mapping the value of ABIs

The implementation of an ABI can have an impact on two fundamental dimensions of an organisation: (1) the people, and potentially any other organisational stakeholder; and (2) the organisational infrastructure, i.e., the overall tangible and intangible structural assets grounding the working mechanisms of an organisation's business model. Therefore, understanding the value of an ABI has to take both dimensions into consideration.

The benefit of an ABI for an individual and/or a group comes at the people level. The organisational infrastructure level considers the benefits that an ABI can generate in terms of the development of both tangible assets, such as workplace components, equipment and working facilities, and intangible assets, such as culture, values, identity, brand and reputation, morale and organisational climate.

An ABI can play different roles in organisations and can be adopted for diverse business purposes, with direct and indirect impacts upon business performance. In order to understand the potential benefits of ABIs for organisational development purposes, the Arts Value Matrix is proposed as a framework to map the organisational value-drivers that can be affected by ABIs. It is presented as a holistic model that can be used for interpretative and normative managerial purposes in order to classify and assess the potential impact ABIs can create as a management means. It identifies value categories against which ABIs can be understood and defined.

The adoption of ABIs as a management means can produce multiple organisational benefits ranging from the development of products and workplaces, to the enhancement of competencies and organisational climate. The assessment of the impact of ABIs upon an organisation has to be carried out taking into account the potential effects of art forms on people and infrastructure. With this aim, the Arts Value Matrix is built on the dimensions of people and infrastructure development. Accordingly, the categories of the matrix identify the possible impact that an ABI can have in terms of benefits related to people change and/or of the benefits linked to organisational infrastructure development.

ABIs can have an impact on people and infrastructure with different intensities. Intensity refers to the strength, capacity and depth of advantages and functional characteristics of an impact, at both the people and organisational infrastructure development level. In general, ABIs can be used by organisations as a managerial instrument to induce transformation in people both at the individual and group levels. The nature and intensity of the ABI determines the effect on people. For the sake of simplicity, the intensity of the people change and development can be assessed by using simple 'low', 'medium' and 'high' measures.

- A low-level development occurs when the transformation is constrained by time and space, and has a 'transient impact' on people and their emotional and energetic states. During the time in which people experience an ABI they feel engaged, emotionally and energetically aroused, but the ABI's effects fundamentally disappear after the arts-based experience has finished and people generally maintain just a short memory of their temporary change.
- A medium-level development is achieved when the arts-based experience has an influence on people's attitudes. In this case, an ABI stimulates feelings and particularly, in addition, is able to touch the inner dimensions of the emotive mind in such a way that people feel mentally energised for some time after having experienced the ABI. This emotive and energetic state affects people's way of seeing and approaching the reality around them for a longer period of time. This energy results in a short-term behavioural change that can be properly channelled for action.

- Finally a high-level development involves self-reflection and self-evaluation that leads people to analyse and eventually challenge their beliefs and values, deeply affecting their attitudes that in turn can drive change with the emergence of new personal behaviours. In this case, ABIs play the role of a trigger and catalyser to the rational and emotional mind, leading people to understand themselves and the world around them differently.

The infrastructure of an organisation denotes the tangible and intangible assets that define the operative context in which organisational processes and functions take place. They are the components shaping the organisational business model and also include the portfolio of products and services that characterise the organisation. Even if people, as employees, could be considered as an integrated part of an organisational infrastructure, it is possible to distinguish the actors of an organisation from the tangible and intangible infrastructural components that are left in the organisation when employees go home at night. The continuous development of the organisational infrastructure affects the quality and productivity of business activities and more generally the capacity to create value (Carlucci *et al.*, 2004). To denote the possible levels of organisational infrastructure development, again, it is possible to identify three measures 'low', 'medium' and 'high'.

- A low-level of organisational infrastructure development guarantees that the functioning of the components of an organisational system maintains its positivity without changing the features of the operative platform. At this level ABIs have a low level of transformational impact on the organisation's infrastructural components and mainly involve people.
- A medium-level development of organisational infrastructure involves a partial change, although restricted by some components of the organisational infrastructure. In this case an ABI can be adopted as an instrument to restore, renew and modify some characteristics and traits of the infrastructural components of an organisation, such as the design and setting of the workplace or to strengthen the image of the organisation.
- Finally, a high-level of organisational infrastructure development is achieved when new components are introduced in the organisation or the existing components are deeply modified. In this case, the ABIs can operate as change devices or as a value vector of organisational

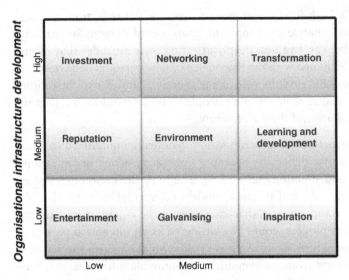

3.3 The Arts Value Matrix

infrastructure affecting, for example, the organisational culture, the property stock, or the characteristics of the products and services produced by the organisation.

Depending on what organisations seek to achieve through the implementation of ABIs, whether they are focusing on people change, on infrastructural development, or both, it is possible to represent the benefits in the Arts Value Matrix. As shown in Figure 3.3, the Arts Value Matrix identifies nine categories of organisational value-drivers that can be affected by the adoption of ABIs. Each position of the matrix identifies and classifies the potential benefits of an ABI and defines the reasons that can explain the implementation of ABIs. Combining the assessment of the effects of ABIs, in terms of people change and infrastructure development, nine fundamental categories of organisational value-drivers are proposed. They are defined as follows: Entertainment (L:L); Galvanising (M:L); Inspiration (H:L); Reputation (L:M); Environment (M:M); Learning and development (M:H); Investment (H:L); Networking (H:M); Transformation (H:H).

The nine categories of benefits represent the fundamental organisational value-drivers that managers can influence through ABIs with the aim of enhancing the value-creation capacity of organisations. The Arts Value Matrix as a holistic framework explains the benefits of adopting ABIs for organisational development. It supports the analysis of the potential impact of ABIs on the development of organisational components and provides managers with a framework to understand and assess the role of an adopted ABI in the organisation. The managerial adoption of the framework can play both a descriptive and normative role. From a descriptive point of view, the Arts Value Matrix helps to explain why managers are adopting ABIs. It supports the interpretation of the managerial role of ABIs in organisations and explains what kind of impact managers can expect by using the arts as a management means to deal with business issues. Through the Arts Value Matrix managers can make sense of the implementation of ABIs and assess what benefits the organisation can achieve. From a normative point of view, the Arts Value Matrix can support managers and arts-based organisations in managing ABIs so that they meet the organisational development needs and wants. The framework identifies the potential value-drivers that can be addressed by the implementation of an ABI. Although they are not mutually exclusive as they may overlap, their identification clarifies how management can adopt ABIs aimed at enhancing organisational value-creation capacity. In order to explain how ABIs can impact upon the organisational value-drivers identified by the Arts Value Matrix, in the following sections each value category will be investigated, explaining its role and relevance for organisations.

Entertainment: using the arts to create joyful experiences

The main goal of using ABIs focusing on entertainment as an organisational value-driver is to release adrenalin and create a pleasant arts-based experience. Any ABI exposing people to art forms has the capacity to touch people's feelings and create a joyful experience. The arts have the power to project feelings and engage the emotive mind. Through the arts people can express and make their deep emotions tangible, as well as express images and feelings that populate their interior life. The direct contact with art forms or artists can be satisfying and create happiness. However, the implementation of ABIs to entertain means that people's participation in the arts tends to be limited in time and space. As a consequence the beneficial effects of the arts-based experiences are simply related to the stimulation and an awakening of people's emotions and energy.

By recognising entertainment as a relevant organisational value-driver, managers can adopt ABIs to create aesthetic experiences that can emotionally involve people within the organisation as well as to evoke excitement around the organisation. In this perspective, a work of art or an artistic process is adopted by an organisation as a leisurely means of offering people an opportunity for fun and enjoyment. The ABIs become a management means to involve people in a happy experience. Indeed, attending cultural events such as concerts or exhibitions produces positive personal physiological effects that let people feel satisfied and in good spirits (Konlaan *et al.*, 2000). For example, creating an artistic piece or appreciating an art form can be relaxing for many people and can help them to cope with daily pressures or extreme situations.

As neuroscientists and biochemists are mapping the brain and its functions, they are discovering new clinical, experimental and anthropological evidence suggesting that personality has special areas, and in particular the emotional mind, which can best be reached through the arts. The arts stimulate emotional responses. They can infuse happiness, create a relaxed context and reduce stress that, particularly nowadays, in many organisations represents a major concern reducing effectiveness and productivity.

Implementing ABIs for entertainment
An organisation can adopt ABIs to generate entertainment benefits either by running in-house events or promoting employees' involvement in public arts events. An organisation can invite artists in-house and/or create recreational time and space within the organisation. Consider Standard Chartered Bank for example: in order to mark the official opening of their global headquarters in London, they adopted an arts-based event to entertain their employees and most prestigious clients and guests. The Welsh National Opera (WNO) was brought in to design and deliver an ABI, incorporating the bank's corporate art collection, which includes an installation of a 'Thai house' in their new reception area. This was used as a backdrop for a customised performance of Puccini's *Madame Butterfly* that reflected and symbolically connected with Standard Chartered's corporate branding. Similarly, it is quite common for organisations to integrate art forms in the

development of important events ranging from annual meetings or other social events, to the launch of a new product or the opening of a new shop.

An organisation can also offer employees the opportunity to visit, see and enjoy a work of art in-situ, for example in a museum, art gallery, theatre, concert hall, circus and so on. Many companies today give their staff cards for free entry to arts exhibitions, museums, galleries and historic houses, and many arts organisations offer entertainment packages to companies. For instance, the WNO offers hospitality packages to entertain business organisations' clients and employees. The business' guests are welcomed with a pre-performance reception, hear an engaging talk from a member of WNO's music staff to introduce the production and enhance their experience, whether it is their first opera or they are seasoned opera-goers, and they get the best seats in the house to enjoy the opera performance. As one illustration, consider the case example of Fidelity International, the UK's largest mutual fund manager, who used WNO's hospitality services to entertain existing and prospective clients. Particularly, on one occasion, after a black-tie reception and world-class gala performance of the opera *Falstaff*, Fidelity's guests were escorted onto the stage at Wales Millennium Centre, in Cardiff, and into a special dining area, in a backstage rehearsal room that had been dressed as a magical woodland glade complete with birdsong. Fidelity's guests dined by the light of Elizabethan lanterns suspended above and were joined by members of the cast, including Bryn Terfel who starred in the leading role.

Any organisation can potentially list many examples of the use of art forms as an entertainment. However, it is worth stressing that in most cases executives adopt the arts as something 'nice to have' or just because they know that art forms create an enjoyable experience. The Arts Value Matrix suggests that entertainment has to be considered as an organisational value-driver and managers can exploit art forms bearing this strategic purpose in mind. For example, consider the strategic approach of Elica Group, world leaders in the cooker hood market, with a long-standing link with the world of modern art, considered by the company as an important source of inspiration. In 2008, with the purpose of celebrating their relationship with modern art, Elica organised 'Elica Contemporary'; an arts-based event aimed at creating a mix between entertainment and industrial marketing. By mixing artworks with specially designed company products, part of

the 'Elica Collection', Elica created a unique entertainment experience
in which people could enjoy contemporary artworks and discover the
artistry of the company in the creation of products that embed the
aesthetic qualities of works of art. This is just one example of how
the arts can be deployed as a strategic entertainment means to achieve
other aims besides the creation of a joyful experience for people.

The transformational impact of entertainment

It is important to point out that the impact of ABIs implemented
with the pure goal of entertainment is transient and ephemeral. At the
people level, after having experienced an art form, a person is left with
a pleasant memory of the experience itself, without, however, involving
any behavioural mindset change. In such instances, after being involved
with the arts-based experience, people essentially go back to their
life as usual with no change in their mental energy and attitudes or
ways of seeing reality and the world around them. At infrastructural
levels, entertainment does not generate a transformation of tangible or
intangible assets. However it can be used as a value vector to create
experiences within and around organisational infrastructure.

Entertainment represents a key organisational value-driver of ABIs
and it is at the basis of any arts-based experience. It can be considered as a building block for all other value-drivers affected by ABIs.
Indeed, ABIs exploit the emotional and energetic power of art forms
that affect the pleasure and joy of people who undergo an arts-based
experience. Art forms have the power to lift people out of the mundane
and to catalyse happiness and excitement. A key factor of their working mechanisms is the involvement of people in an aesthetic experience
that is similar to the one generated by play, and as such produces psychological arousal, making people feel good and letting them be in the
moment (Brown, 2009).[1]

Galvanising: catalysing people's emotions and energy through the arts

ABIs adopted to galvanise people aim to provoke a mood change or
a tension for action by creating people's emotional state and mental
energy. An ABI generates a galvanising value when it is able to captivate
people in an intense, revealing and meaningful experience, in a way

that produces excitement, joy and a general deep feeling of passion and energy. Through arts-based experiences, people can feel passionate and energised, with high levels of involvement and concentration. So, ABIs produce both a sense of satisfaction and create a frame of mind.

The ABIs adopted with the goal of addressing galvanising as an organisational value-driver tend to create a psychological and social tension towards action and change. To translate this stimulation into action, the direct contact with art forms has to be followed up by a process of applying and channelling the emotional and energetic arousal. This releases and puts people's emotions and energy into action in order to carry out organisational activities that solve business problems.

Implementing ABIs for galvanising

Generally galvanising is rarely sought after and seen by organisations as an isolated value-driver. It exploits the same working mechanisms as entertainment, involving people in a fulfilling and joyful experience, but it extends the intensity and breadth in order to create an emotional and energetic state that can be deployed for organisational development purposes. Consider, for example, the approach taken by Nestlé to enhance creativity as well as to develop communication skills and collaboration in terms of sharing ideas and expertise. Looking for innovative approaches, Nestlé's marketing team worked on an initiative, mixing the BBC TV shows *Dragons Den* and *The Apprentice* with tradesecrets. The marketing team were taken to the venue where the original TV series was filmed and spurred on to develop ideas for generating new products with a combination of industry outsiders and brand specialists acting as facilitators. Participants were coached on their presentation style and then had to pitch to a panel of five 'dragons', made up of entrepreneurs and actors. The teams were allowed to view each other's presentation on monitors in a specially designed studio in the basement in order to learn from each other's successes and failures. This ABI generated benefits in terms of learning insights against the targeted people development objectives, but very importantly, overall it was considered to be galvanising. In this regard, stressing the energising power of the ABI, Natalie Bentley, Beverage Innovation Manager at Nestlé UK, commented: 'The team were still buzzing about the event and I had numerous visits from people keen to share their thoughts about the day and to say how much they loved it and got out of it'. This example shows that galvanising is a value dimension that is not necessarily addressed as the foremost focus of an ABI, but nevertheless it is fundamental and can be considered as a relevant side-effect of a deep involvement of people in art forms. Galvanising can be considered as the result of ABIs' power to harness emotional and energetic dynamics. In fact, the aesthetic experiences created by ABIs tend to communicate directly with people's emotive mind, stirring and arousing emotions and energy.

Galvanising appears particularly useful in cases where an organisation wants to emote and energise people in order to face specific important management challenges, such as the development or launch of a new product, the execution of a change management programme, the implementation of a successful merger, acquisition or joint venture, the definition and communication of a new strategy plan, or simply the creation of enthusiasm within the organisation to stimulate people's conversations, imagination and creativity. For example, consider the approach taken by Nicoletti, a leading international sofa production company, dealing with the challenge of engaging its staff to shift from the management platform AS/400 to SAP. They opted for an ABI in order to galvanise people and create an emotional and energetic state to face the organisational change. After twenty-five years of using the same management operative system, people were attached to AS/400 and there was a general concern about the failure to adopt new business software. This required all the technical know-how developed over decades to be given up and new competencies to be acquired to make all the business functionalities operative in the shortest possible time in order to avoid any negative influence on organisational performance. Top management recognised the need to create excitement among employees that would prompt them to accept and face the management challenge. For this reason a team of artists was brought in to define a theatre-based initiative. The artists and managers worked together, first addressing the main cultural and operative issues related to the change management programme. Then, after a set of arts-based workshops facilitated by artists, a final theatre event was performed in the company. All the company's staff was involved in a collective show in which employees were playing the role of actors. The show first represented the funeral of AS/400 and afterwards the welcome of SAP. The overall event created an emotional and energetic state that helped the organisation to successfully implement the new business platform.

The transformational impact of galvanising

Galvanising represents the way managers can ignite organisational energy and create 'hot spots' (Gratton, 2007).[2] Accordingly, ABIs can be deployed as management means to catalyse and nourish people's emotions and energy. They can ignite emotional and energetic dynamics in different ways. In particular, six fundamental functions of art forms as ignition devices can be identified as follows: questions; visions; contexts; tasks; conversations; and social activities. These functions correspond to the definition of an ignition purpose, i.e., something that excites and engages people that represents a key factor affecting the creation of organisational traits soaked in energy (Gratton, 2007). Each ignition function is introduced below.

Ignition questions – ABIs can ignite emotions and energy by framing ignition questions that propel people into the unknown, stimulating their imagination and pushing them to look for new solutions and different ways of seeing and framing reality. Specifically the ambiguity that can characterise an art form raises questions that invite people to think about past, present and future situations, driving the interpretation and construction of knowledge, which allows inward or outward assessments.

Ignition visions – ABIs can galvanise people towards a vision. In this case art forms are used to frame compelling images of what the future could be, propelling collective emotions and energy towards the same trajectory.

Ignition contexts – exploiting the galvanising effect, ABIs can address the creation of ignition organisational contexts. Through art forms it is possible to shape the organisational environment and atmosphere in order to create contexts in which people feel excited, happy, engaged, assured and feel the pleasure of attachment.

Ignition tasks – ABIs, particularly when they are based on hands-on approaches, can engage people in igniting tasks that spark and nourish people's emotional and energetic dynamics. In this case, art forms can be exploited to challenge people's abilities in order to arouse excitement and joy.

Ignition conversations – ABIs allow people to be engaged in ignition conversations. Art forms define a powerful platform to stimulate, engage and drive people towards a rich communication that involves both people's emotional and rational mind. Indeed, art forms can be utilised to express, share and communicate emotions that allow richer communication across cultural and mindset barriers.

Ignition social activities – ABIs can be adopted to create ignition social activities. Accordingly art forms can be exploited as social activities during which people relax and get to know each other a little more beyond their work life. This allows trust and reciprocity to flourish as well as providing an opportunity for people to learn about each other outside the context of work in an exciting and engaging way.

Particularly important is the role of the galvanising effect when ABIs are aimed at helping employees to reinvigorate and share their passions for their work. Energy surrounds artists and the arts. It appears as a spin-off effect of working with artists and having an artist-in-residence. Artists appear strongly energised and self-motivated; they are passionate about their work and most artists are good at finding their own passion. This can be used as an instrument to touch and inspire employees in such a way that they can feel energised or be engaged to find ways to discover their passion for what they do. This is particularly powerful in order to intrinsically motivate people within an organisation.

In summary, assuming that organisations are emotive and energetic systems, it is possible to interpret galvanising as a fundamental organisational value-driver to emote and energise organisations. This can serve different organisational development purposes such as people's motivation and engagement, knowledge creation and sharing, organisational competence development and enhancement of creativity and innovation.

Inspiration: inspiring people with the arts

ABIs can be adopted as powerful inspirational levers to prompt self-reflection and meta-understanding that can drive mindset and behavioural changes. ABIs can provoke people to question and reflect upon the way they act and make decisions. They encourage self-assessment, self-discipline, self-efficacy, self-confidence and self-esteem, which can make people reflect on life, on who they are and who they would like to be (Eisner, 2002). This in turn can drive the development of personal attitudes and behaviours towards an organisation and work activities. ABIs are therefore able to generate mechanisms of self-awareness and critical thinking, while simultaneously driving assessment and understanding of an individual's external reality and other people's behaviours and actions; in turn, this can induce change in personal mindsets and behaviours.[3] Indeed, through a profound consciousness people are able to see the world and themselves differently. Consequently, they can rethink their assumptions, concerns, values and beliefs, and change their behavioural attitudes accordingly. Inspiration leads to aspiration and, as a result, to transformation, through engagement and the desire to do something worthwhile. The studies on attitudinal and behavioural stimulations of the arts point out that the process of individual change first affects beliefs and attitudes followed by intentions and behaviours (Stone, 1997; Stone *et al.*, 1999). The possible benefits associated with an attitudinal and behavioural change can cover a wide range of aspects from motivation and critical thinking to pro-social actions. This involves inspiration being seen as a first beneficial step towards the achievement of other benefits associated with personal learning and development, and interpersonal networking and bonding. Furthermore, inspiration is at the basis of people's motivation to go through transformation, and accept and promote changes in what they do.

The relationship between ABIs and inspiration is twofold. An ABI has the power to inspire by deeply touching people's emotional dimensions and, at the same time, it sparks a learning-based process fostering reflection (Taylor and Ladkin, 2009). Through the use of ABIs, people undergo aesthetic experiences that touch their feelings encouraging the development of awareness about themselves and the reality around them. The felt-sense of emotions is a gateway for a learning-based process that allows reflection on the personal experience of the issues under investigation. ABIs offer metaphors and analogies to explore and interpret reality in order to develop a meta-understanding.

An artistic product or an artistic process is able to engage people with both their emotional and rational faculties, building a connection between the personal self-conscious and the investigated reality. This allows key insights to be projected and/or extracted. The process of projecting and extracting meanings from a work of art or an artistic process in order to develop a meta-understanding of issues is an idiosyncratic personal process that involves an individual's interpretation grounded in rational and emotional experiences. The use of an artistic product, which can be either an aesthetic artefact or an artwork, allows tacit understanding that drives self-consciousness and self-reflection, to be externalised and made explicit. Meanwhile, the artistic process and particularly the artful creation, i.e., the process of making an artistic product, activates a personal meditative and contemplative process that allows people to access remote parts of their mind (Dissanayake, 2000). In accordance with Taylor and Ladkin (2009: 60), art-making offers modern individuals 'a means by which they can re-evaluate and reflect on their own deep feelings about events in their life'.

Implementing ABIs for inspiration

A key example of the use of ABIs aimed at generating inspirational benefits for people development is offered by the large adoption of Shakespeare's work, and more generally of films, to support executive education and management development, to spark reflection about organisational and business issues in order to capture insights for managerial lessons and implications (Burnham *et al.*, 2001; Champoux, 1999; Corrigan, 1999; Shafritz, 1999; Whitney and Packer, 2000). In addition to the use of Shakespeare's works of art as inspirational sources, a widely adopted typology of ABI to drive people's self-reflection and meta-understanding is a theatre-based one. The use of improvisational theatre games is reported by Corsun *et al.* (2006) as a way to inspire managers to reflect on the possible general tendency to shortcuts.

Regarding the inspirational power of theatre-based initiatives, Terry Willie, chief executive officer (CEO) of Hall and Partners, recognises as one of the most important impacts of their theatre-based development programme, the change of employees' behaviours and approaches towards clients: 'One of the most brilliant folks in New York was struggling to understand how she could make the next step. She was young, super smart, confident, articulate – but more concerned about herself rather than the client, and talked rather than listened. The walking in other's shoes bit was a revelation for her – she came out of the Actor's Studio absolutely understanding it was smarter to make her clients successful'. A further case example is provided by Unilever UK, which has used theatre-based activities to inspire people change. In particular, the ABI named 'Unleashed' was implemented to help people develop their potential and make a difference to the business in which they worked. This arts-based project aimed at building people's confidence, self-awareness and helped them to understand the impact they could have on the business and on those around them. The project covered six areas: *belief,* to consider or reconsider personal values, vision and goals; *personal risk and courage,* how to learn from success and failure and to be open to new experiences; *presence,* how to use personal body language, awareness of how to present oneself and build self-confidence; *energy,* understanding the role of personal energy and how to call upon and renew it to create an impact; *ideas,* how to generate new ideas and work through them; and *communication,* understanding how to use and develop writing, dialogue and visual communication abilities. The overall project helped people to reflect upon their own abilities and how to develop themselves and others.

An interesting case example of how ABIs can be adopted with an inspirational value purpose is represented by the arts-based project implemented at Unilever UK named 'stimulating reflection'. This ABI aimed at raising awareness of behaviours by tracking people's moods. People were asked to choose between statements related to their daily business behaviours (such as: having fun; you have let a colleague down; this is the place to be; you have taken a risk; bureaucracy got in your way; you have passion for winning) by landing on mats that had the statements written on them. These mats incorporated sensors that made it possible to record the number of landings. This not only provided an assessment of the organisational atmosphere, but supported a self-reflection and self-awareness about people and organisational behaviours, and developed within the organisation a better climate.

The transformational impact of inspiration
The value category 'inspiration' not only accounts for the benefits related to individuals' self-reflection and meta-understanding, but also includes the potential positive impacts of the arts for personal health.[4] ABIs can contribute to improving people's health within organisations. The recognition of the therapeutic effects of the arts is not new. In the last two decades many studies have systematically investigated the role of the arts on health and, particularly, on clinical outcomes.[5] Today, the medical literature on the arts and health provides evidence that the arts can have a positive impact on health and wellbeing (Staricoff,

2004). Theoretical and empirical knowledge, addressing the therapeutic effects of the arts on health, shows the importance that arts-based experiences can play as devices to reduce anxiety, stress and depression states and to improve physical conditions (Heber, 1993; Marwick, 2000; Staricoff, 2004; Verghese *et al.*, 2003). Psychoanalysts address the use of arts as a non-verbal tool for expression. The arts can be used as a vehicle for establishing self-expression, self-esteem and communication with others.[6] So, it is important to recognise the therapeutic use of the arts as a way to generate high intensity levels of benefits for people with a positive impact on personal emotional and energetic states.

The inspirational impact is rarely obtained as an isolated benefit, unless the ABI is specifically intended to just have an effect on people transformation. Usually it is strongly tied to other value-drivers identified by the Arts Value Matrix, particularly with those that are associated with 'networking' and 'learning and development'. Since inspiration involves people's inner-dimensions, it is quite difficult to assess and detach them from other organisational benefits related to the adoption of ABIs in organisations. Fundamentally, it is manifested by a change in people's attitudes and behaviours.

Reputation: strengthening organisational image by using the arts

ABIs focused on reputation aim to raise the organisational profile and image by displaying attention and interest in the arts. The association of an organisation's image with the arts represents a powerful means to improve organisational reputation and to strengthen identity. ABIs supporting this goal can be gathered under the conceptual umbrella of sponsorship. By sponsoring artworks and/or artistic processes, an organisation assumes the role of a patron shaping a relationship with the public artworld. This allows the interaction and building of relationships with artists and arts organisations. In this perspective, it is possible to consider patronage and sponsorship as two overlapping concepts, even if slight differences between the two notions can be discussed. They can take different formats such as art events, projects, programmes and productions in the cultural institutions where the arts generally take place, or can be focused on initiatives in the workplace, such as using corporate public spaces for temporary or permanent art installations and exhibitions, which may be also related to educational programmes such as lectures, films and performances. ABIs based on patronage and sponsorship may also focus on public spaces and particularly urban spaces, from gardens, squares, buildings and courtyards, to atriums and warehouses.

Patronage and sponsorship serve the same fundamental purpose. They are both different from philanthropy, which is mainly a charitable act, and describe the support that a business organisation might provide to artists and arts organisations. Although patronage and sponsorship may denote a pure form of arts support aimed at contributing to cultural and societal enrichment, they represent a management means to achieve organisational benefits. They can even be considered as investments, when they are interpreted as a way to gain future economic benefits. This is the case when purchasing artworks or investing in cultural industry activities.

Implementing ABIs for building reputation

In the perspective of adopting ABIs as a management means to raise an organisation's reputation, it is possible to see patronage and sponsorship as a managerial action to forge a partnership between business and the arts that produces mutual outcomes, though the goals of the relationship are different and only partially aligned. By building associations with art forms, it is possible to give a specific image of the organisation to the organisation as well as to all organisational stakeholders (Darsø, 2004). It creates an opinion about the essence of the organisation. For example, an organisation supporting contemporary art may portray an image of itself as a dynamic and modern organisation that pays attention to the modern trends that contemporary arts reflect. ABIs as a communication device can express and represent meanings and messages that shape the identity of the organisation both internally and externally. In this case, the use of art forms acts as a kind of symbolic statement and message that expresses and communicates the organisational identity internally and externally. Organisations can adopt art forms as the embodiment and projection of the attitude that they want from their people. As an illustration, consider the case of Diesel, an international fashion company. Since its foundation the company has attributed a fundamental importance to the arts in workplaces as a way to prompt and represent the innovative organisational spirit. Contemporary artworks are spread throughout the office spaces as they express the kind of dynamic, collaborative and innovative mindsets that Diesel wants from its employees. Similarly, other companies use the arts as a symbol to shape the image and the identity of the organisation. Unicredit Group, one of the leading European banks, with the ABI named 'sharing passions' exhibits artworks in offices and bank branches to communicate to employees and stakeholders the relevance attributed to the cultural activities as a fundamental facet of the company's identity. A further case in point is offered by Teseco, an Italian company and national leader in the environmental engineering sector. This company has adopted the arts as a way of shaping its organisational identity. Since 1989 with the creation of a foundation 'Fondazione Teseco per l'Arte', Teseco has integrated arts-based activities into organisational life. With the development of a modern art collection, the 'Collezione Teseco per l'Arte', gathering artworks mainly from local artists, Teseco has developed a strong organisational membership consciousness forging its identity. A case example of a company that uses the arts to communicate its identity and values externally is represented by Enel Group, the second largest European listed utility producing, distributing and selling electricity and gas. Enel has promoted 'Enel Contemporanea', an ABI dedicated to the world of contemporary public art, based on art installations of different internationally acclaimed artists who worked mainly in urban areas of Rome. This initiative is contributing to raising the identity and reputation of the company showing its commitment both to cultural institutions and communities, and to research and innovation.[7]

The transformational impact of reputation

The use of art forms allows management to express and build awareness of the organisational culture and values. Through ABIs it is possible to give a social expression to the values and traditions of the organisation, developing and sustaining a cultural heritage, for both internal and external purposes (Lowe, 2000; Stern, 2000). Tim Stockil, a professional artist at Ci: Creative intelligence, points out: 'Most of the time organisational values are conceptual and people cannot get a handle on them. So talking about words like respect, leadership, transparency, mutuality, trust and so on, they do not practically mean anything to people. A forum theatre workshop [for example] aims to let people really understand what values mean when they are lived, or particularly not lived in the company.'

The communication activated through patronage and sponsorship can be aligned with the characteristics of the organisational business. For example, consider the strategic approach adopted by some companies that have created a strong link between their image and reputation with the arts as a symbol of the highest human expression and traits. A key example is represented by Vitra International, a leading German manufacturer of modern and innovative furniture. This innovative company founded the Vitra Design Museum in 1989 with the mission of gathering artworks and exposing products that are aligned with the organisation's area of expertise and documenting the history of the Vitra company. The museum has played a fundamental role in promoting an identity and developing a reputation for the organisation as a supporter of the most innovative designers in office furniture.[8]

A further case example of how it is possible to form a strong link between business image and the arts is provided by those companies that use corporate art collections to shape organisational reputation and strengthening identity. Consider the approach taken by the Hess Family Estates, which has created The Hess Collection gathering contemporary paintings, sculptures and mixed media on display in Napa, California and now in two other museums at Glen Carlou Winery in South Africa and at Bodega Colomé in Argentina. Donald Hess is using art in a strategic manner by creating a strong connection between his business, and particularly his idea of doing business, with the contemporary art world. He has housed the winery and a contemporary art collection in the same facility in order to strategically intertwine art and business. His collection, rather than gathering isolated and varied artworks, focuses on around twenty living artists from whom artworks are purchased at regular intervals. This allows, as he stresses, 'for a fascinating exploration into their development both as artists and human beings. And since what resonates in their work highlights aspects of one's own path, a parallel discovery of oneself and another is facilitated through the art' (Hess, 2009). So, the high-standing collected artworks are capable of reflecting the fundamental principles of the company and communicating the link between wine and art as a symbol of the passion for life.

Still with a focus on raising the reputation of the organisation, ABIs can be implemented with the aim of increasing brand awareness and strengthening ties with the local community. This is the case with

Atradius, a global credit insurance and risk management company, which not only sponsored the WNO's main scale productions, but arranged a free programme of events and activities in order to add value to their partnership with the WNO. The company, whose UK headquarters are in Cardiff, added value to their sponsorship by supporting the WNO's Open House, which provided local residents and visitors with the opportunity to go behind the scenes and experience workshops, tours, demonstrations, masterclasses and performances. This enabled Atradius to build brand awareness while making an impact in their local community. Atradius also benefited from logo presence on all promotional print, branding on t-shirts and balloons, press and PR opportunities.

Other benefits related to the increase of brand awareness by associating the organisation to high-profile art forms can be the specific marketing advantages. Usually organisations sponsoring arts productions and events get marketing benefits, such as credit on television and press publicity as well as print advertising in the form of credit on all arts events related materials, including banners, posters and performance programmes. In particular, these marketing benefits can be considered as an organisational investment and can be translated into economic figures when assessing the arts-related promotional activities in terms of purchasing equivalent advertising space.

Through patronage and sponsorship, business organisations can get the attention of institutions and society. In this regard, those ABIs that aim to transform urban and rural areas might be particularly effective. Business organisations, autonomously or in joint ventures as well as in collaboration and cooperation with public institutions, can renew and transform urban spaces through outdoor initiatives that create an interplay of arts and architecture. As an example, consider the ABI labelled 'Diesel Wall' promoted by Diesel. This arts-based project offered young artists and designers the opportunity to showcase their works of art on giant urban canvases in city centres around the world. The goal was to bring intriguing, inspiring, insightful and inciting contemporary ideas into urban areas and to salvage prominent precious public space.

Other reasons for sponsoring art forms include ethical, social and cultural motivations in order to build public relations and contribute to the wealth generation of society at large. In this regard ABIs are increasingly integrated into corporate social responsibility strategies. Today, most corporations can list in their corporate social responsibility activities a number of projects aimed at supporting cultural and arts institutions.

Environment: creating an arts-based organisational atmosphere

ABIs addressing the environment as an organisational value-driver mainly aim to create an engaging organisational atmosphere by infusing art forms into the organisational infrastructure. In particular, art forms, through their symbols and expressions, can be adopted in an organisation as a management instrument to shape physical spaces and the environment within and around the organisation. Art forms have the power to decorate and beautify workplaces. By shaping the physical space ABIs create an organisational atmosphere capable of affecting people's attitudes and behaviours. By adopting art forms it is possible to form an organisational context in which people feel comfortable and are spurred to express themselves and communicate with others. This affects people's emotional and energetic dynamics with a significant impact on people's motivation and satisfaction.

The influence of the characteristics of the workplace on employees' performance is widely recognised. In particular, the workplace design is identified as one of the major factors affecting the performance of knowledge workers and knowledge-based organisations (Davemport *et al.*, 2002). The physical setting and workplace environment have significant effects on building a relational capital, social life and organisational context, which in turn influences knowledge work (Davemport and Beers, 1996). Knowledge workers are therefore more productive when working within a positive, stimulating and enjoyable environment.

Implementing ABIs for shaping environment
Commissioning artworks to be displayed in the reception areas, organisation public spaces, board rooms and conference rooms as well as in atriums and outdoor spaces is not new. Starting from the eighties many corporations, such as IBM, First Bank System, La Caisse des Dépôts et Consignations, Cartier and Chase Manhattan Bank, set the art commissioning practice by purchasing artworks, developing in-house galleries and founding museums (Jacobson, 1993). Focusing on the adoption of art forms, and particularly of art collections, to be displayed in workplaces, the attention in this book is not about the

assembling of portfolios of artworks that have an economic value for the corporate art market. Although this is a relevant economic value dimension, the functional value of art collections is considered as a way to build a passionate organisational background that fosters the development of emotional and energetic dynamics in organisations. Thus, the premise underlying the adoption of ABIs targeted at levering the organisational value-driver 'environment' is that through the employment of art forms it is possible to aesthetically beautify organisational workplaces generating multiple benefits for organisational constituent parts and particularly for people.[9] The fundamental idea is that artistic artefacts, through their aesthetic properties, become an element of the passion, spirit, culture and life of an organisation. They are able to spark and catalyse reflections and conversations about personal and organisational issues. So, ABIs implemented with the goal of creating an engaging organisational atmosphere act as enlightening and delighting instruments that aesthetically enrich the spaces of the organisational office buildings, the buildings themselves, the facilities and the outdoor public spaces. Hanging art on walls, positioning sculptures in the reception areas, performing plays in organisational public spaces, arranging temporary exhibitions and art installations and shaping the office spaces combining arts and architecture, allow staff to read, talk, hear and feel art forms. This triggers and nourishes emotions and energy both at the individual and group level. So the incorporation of art forms into tangible and intangible organisational infrastructure facilitates the creation of an emotive and energetic organisation. In addition, the implementation of ABIs aimed at transforming the organisational atmosphere can be strategically integrated by people learning and development activities. For example, using an art exhibition explicitly produced for a location in the workplace, people can be asked to write wall labels to express their feelings and impressions about artworks in order to elicit personal judgements and raise consciousness within the office community. Artworks can play the role of metaphors to address business issues that involve intuition and require analogical methods to capture insights. For example, consider the case of Unilever UK, which has used art forms to shape the organisational environment. This was based on the recognition of the role of visual imagery, such as paintings, drawings and photographs, as a powerful management means to shape an organisational atmosphere capable of creating and communicating the organisational culture. Among many other ABIs adopted by Unilever, they created an art collection purchasing artworks from British artists with the scope to decorate the workplaces and stimulate conversation among staff. People were involved in the process of choosing the artworks and were invited to write captions about their favourite artworks and display their thoughts together with the works. Furthermore, in order to prevent the office's art collection turning into wallpaper, in addition to the permanent collection, Unilever established two temporary photographic galleries showcasing regularly changing exhibitions. This contributed to creating a visual culture to communicate not only internally to Unilever staff, but also to customers and consumers. Similarly, Darsø (2004) reports that Novo Nordisk used visual arts as clear signals of the managerial intents to employees. By bringing in young artists and displaying their works of art, the organisation aimed at creating an environment that allowed people to think differently, to take risks, to accept mistakes, to ask questions and reflect and learn how to learn.

The transformational impact of shaping environment
The ABIs that are implemented as art for the workplace represent management actions that aim at infusing the aesthetic properties of art forms into organisational workplaces so that they can stir emotions and energy. This fundamentally corresponds with generating and shaping an organisational atmosphere that pervades and surrounds workplaces and idiosyncratically characterises the organisation.

Infusing art forms into the organisational environment exercises an influence, primarily on the internal organisational components; but also contributes to improving the external perception of the organisation. Everyone that comes across the organisation can appreciate the uniqueness of the atmosphere that characterises and surrounds the organisation. However the benefits of creating arts-based workspaces have significant outcomes in terms of the influence on people's attitudes and behaviours as well as on their level of satisfaction and motivation. By adopting works of art, the organisational environment can engage people. Through the arts people are more likely to feel creative and comfortable, and capable of expressing themselves and communicating with others. Art forms in the office environment can stimulate people's emotive mind, challenging the perception and interpretation of the reality. This helps people to become more intuitive, imaginative, tolerant and flexible. In other words they become more adaptable. This contributes to shaping the adaptability of the organisation. Moreover, considering that people spend a great portion of their waking hours in the office, it is important that the organisational environment is pleasant and comfortable. This guarantees that people are more likely to feel happy to spend time in their workplace. In this regard, Elica Group has strategically used art forms to shape workplaces so that they promote innovativeness, imagination and creativity, but also offer a source of inspiration, wellbeing and serenity to employees. For Elica, workplaces have to be a dimension of emotions; spaces where people can investigate, discover, and exhibit ideas and projects resulting from their creativity and innovation. Workplaces need to be able to lead people towards the essence of their human nature. This also entails that workplaces have to be conceived as social places where minds can be inspired and refreshed. Among other factors, this way of conceiving the working environment has contributed to Elica receiving the 'Best great place to work Italia' award in 2009 and also to getting the 'Etica d'impresa' (ethical enterprise) award.

Thus artists and designers, and generally art forms, can be brought into organisations to decorate and affect workplaces. The direct objective is to shape the organisational environment, but essentially with the final goal of influencing people's perception about the workplace. By shaping the office space it is possible to challenge people to reflect on the way they see and act within the organisation.

Learning and development: arts-based experiences to build people's soft skills

Learning and development is the organisational value-driver that recognises the fundamental importance of developing the soft skills of employees. Most of the ABIs traditionally implemented by organisations address this benefit area. In the last decade both corporate and public organisations have experimented with the use of the arts to support their staff learning and development programmes by bringing in artists to deliver arts-based experiences (Nissley, 2010). Most of the attention has been paid to the use of arts-based methods as an alternative approach to the conventional organisational development approaches mainly focused on technical knowledge and conceptual frameworks. Artistic skills have been deployed to build different learning contexts based on experiential development pathways (Darsø, 2004).

Learning and development through arts-based methods is not meant to make people artists. ABIs are neither intended to transform people into artists nor make them 'art literate'. Endowing people with knowledge and understanding of the technical, aesthetic or historical contents related to art forms are the main goals of arts education.

The fundamental idea at the basis of using ABIs as a management means for people development is that arts-based experiences offer a learning platform to spark and sustain experiential learning mechanisms (Beckwith, 2003; Gibb, 2004; Monks *et al.*, 2001; Taylor and Ladkin, 2009; Vaill, 1989). The underlying assumption is that the arts represent knowledge domains spurring reflection and learning, and from which artistic skills and competencies can be acquired with the intent of improving people's abilities, particularly for management and leadership development (Adler, 2006, 2010). ABIs can address the improvement of specific management competencies that can benefit from the acquisition of artistic skills, such as the use of body language, the ability to intonate the voice and the use of eye contact during communication and presentations, as well as the enhancement of meta-competencies such as self-management and the understanding of complex organisational issues. As one illustration, consider the arts-based project labelled 'Take your best shot!' undertaken at an international company with the aim of supporting learning and development. This ABI used photography as a learning platform to encourage staff to improve their visual awareness and critical skills. Other arts-based learning initiatives included a series of writing workshops focused on raising the standard of people's written communication in order to effectively express personal and business information and to deliver brilliant marketing messages.

Implementing ABIs for learning and development
One of the essential premises of the adoption of ABIs for learning and development purposes is that artists can transfer their artistic skills, such as creative writing, advertising, journalism, reading, storytelling, listening, seeing, presenting, coordinating and improvising, and that by exposing people to artistic products and processes, their soft skills can grow. It is possible to identify some fundamental soft skills that can be developed through engaging people in art forms, as

follows: creativity, imagination, risk-taking, improvisation, observation, criticism, awareness, flexibility and energising themselves and others. Box 3.1 presents the main characteristics of the soft skills that can potentially be influenced by art forms.

Box 3.1 Key soft skills influenced by arts-based learning

Creativity – the arts can help people to be more creative by improving how individuals see, interpret and represent their reality and problems. They provide insights and methodologies to understand how to pay attention to detail as well as to the whole, stimulating metaphorical and analogical thinking, and letting people recognise the importance of representing the world so that they engage their feelings and deep motives.

Imagination – the arts represent a fertile soil to grow imagination as a source of possible solutions and content. The arts can change the way people perceive the world, providing new interpretative frames to see their reality differently and to envision a possible new reality. The arts are similar to the act of play. Indeed, through the arts people can play and be engaged in an exploration process, exercising imagination, which helps to create and see the reality differently from what it is and to think about new possibilities. The use of imagination allows us to see things other than the way they are. It helps us to see how things might be and can foster efforts and the employment of technical knowledge to pursue what has been imagined. In addition, imagination provides a safety net for experiment and rehearsal.

Risk-taking – as outlined by Eisner (2002), working in the arts involves microdiscoveries providing surprise, and surprise is one of the rewards of working in and with the arts. To pursue surprise requires the willingness to take risks. Appreciating the discovery process and the satisfaction that this process involves is a source of learning how and why to take risks.

Improvisation – improvisation is a key ability in those organisational and business contexts that are characterised by high uncertainty and ambiguity in which it is necessary to develop flexibility. This ability pertains to the capacity to shift direction, even to redefine aims when the environment changes and new options

(cont.)

---

emerge in the course of the activities. Improvisation is a managerial ability that is acknowledged as an important factor, grounding the capacity to respond spontaneously and under pressure to problems and opportunities as they arise (Crossan, 1997). People can learn how to improvise by learning some key skills from improvisation in theatre (Corsun *et al.*, 2006), or can draw learning insights from reflecting on how jazz players improvise, taking advantages of errors (Barrett, 1998).

Observation – observation is about tuning the sensory system so that it is fully aware of the reality under investigation. The arts can help people to learn how to better use their sensory system. People explore and understand the world through their senses. Every artefact or activity is experienced through the sensory system that provides the data and information to be elaborated by the personal mind to create knowledge. The world around people is made of aesthetic qualities. So people's aesthetic experiences are shaped not only by the qualities of the artefacts and activities, but also by how individuals approach the world. The ability to perceive aesthetic qualities depends on how individuals tune their senses, and art forms provide ways for this purpose.

Criticism – the arts provide a platform to understand how people can see things in a variety of ways. This helps different points of view to emerge as well as to converge towards a common frame of reference. The arts can help people to see and interpret things aesthetically. This brings people's different sensibilities into place and explores how they can use their senses to better understand the world and problems.

Awareness – the arts support the development of people's awareness of their emotional response to situations. This helps individuals to become more aware of themselves and to gain control of their actions. This also concerns the refinement of people's perception. Through art forms people can be made aware of the reality around them and of the transformations taking place in reality. This helps to improve the capacity of enquiry about possible futures.

Flexibility – the arts can teach people how to be flexible, accepting and handling diversity, variability, uncertainty and ambiguity. In

(*cont.*)

the arts there is always more than one interpretation of an art work. Furthermore, the arts highlight the importance of being flexible in the course of actions, particularly in fast-changing contexts. This entails that the definition of goals and objectives has to be followed by people's ability to keep their eyes on the context in order to shift the goals and objectives when needed.

Energising themselves and others – the arts invite individuals to pay close attention to their emotional and energetic states. They help people to both savour the aesthetic qualities of an experience, and create aesthetic properties to generate experiences soaked in emotions.

Through the arts, people can learn techniques to better perform specific activities that require particular artistic skills. In this perspective, an ABI works essentially as an instruction guideline. For example, ABIs can be valuable to: develop people's breathing in a way that enhances their presentation style; structure and articulate messages in a way that brings them to life; identify people's unique tone of voice and how to vary their intonation to get the best communication effect; inject more energy into people's performance; improve the choice of words to gain a better impact in people's work; manage and organise people's thoughts for mutual benefit; understand how to look at people to capture their attention and better communicate with them; and develop people's ability to sense themselves and others in order to communicate empathetically.

ABIs can have a particularly powerful impact on communication skills. Understanding how to use voice and body to connect with an audience can help employees to give a better performance on the telephone, in a face-to-face relationship with customers, in a meeting, in the board room and at public occasions. In today's businesses this is increasingly a critical competency for everyone within an organisation, but it is particularly important for chief executives and managers who continuously stand in the spotlight and have to be able to communicate effectively. Being a good communicator is the result of a variety of factors, which are related to both technical communication skills, such as the use of voice and body language, and to personal attitudes, such as confidence, self-consciousness, passion and personal energy. These factors can be developed by involving people in arts-based experiences.

The case study of 'creative pitching' at Hall and Partners
A case study highlighting the relevance of using ABIs to support people learning and development in organisations is provided by 'creative pitching' at Hall and Partners. Creative pitching is a theatre-based programme designed and implemented at Hall and Partners, a successful advertising research agency, to encourage and support people learning and development. Hall and Partners were expanding rapidly in America, and needed their key personnel to develop the strength and confidence to win and keep clients and businesses such as Microsoft. Hall and Partners' approach to advertising research was innovative for the industry and part of this strategy was to recruit young and very smart people. As an extremely successful and rapidly growing company, the people at Hall and Partners simply had too much work from the senior partners and they needed to learn to rely on their instincts in all the critical negotiations, and to solve problems in meetings where the projects were relevant and the clients were very senior. Also, because of the fast growth of the company, people were being promoted quickly and their responsibility became significant, working with important clients. In this context, people were asked to learn fast and particularly to understand how to deal with client relationships. Terry Willie, CEO, recognised that their people needed to develop and maintain the skills and experience to handle the strenuous situations that arise when dealing with important clients. Looking for innovative approaches for training and developing people, in terms of their self-confidence, self-expression and communication skills, Hall and Partners identified ABIs as a way to speed up the process through which their people could become adept at handling difficult situations, difficult clients and negotiations. To address these issues, Dramatic Resources was brought in to design a theatre-based programme, aimed at enabling employees to handle unexpected situations. The premise underneath the ABI was that handling an encounter, a presentation and/or a relationship with a client is like a creative pitch. Just as in the theatre, where a performer must engage the audience both emotionally and intellectually to have an impact, relationship managers have to be able to engage clients' hearts and minds. The ABI implemented in the organisation sought to develop this sort of capacity through the use of theatre-based skills and the practical application of theatre techniques in order to increase people's confidence and resourcefulness in

the handling of client relationships. The main identified learning and development goals of the ABIs can be summarised as follows: learn and develop the confidence of how not to be intimidated by senior figures; be able to get the best out of situations; and develop a self-management orientation and the ability to improvise.

A theatre-based approach using improvisation skills was used. Different scenarios were created and diverse roles were played in order to improve people's improvisational skills and equip them with the expertise to handle demanding situations. Working with artist facilitators, people focused on the ability to listen, respond, empathise and negotiate. The model of rehearsal was used to give people a forum to practise challenging encounters in a low-risk environment. Through the rehearsal people could experience working with clients and examine their own style. Theatre was used to rehearse meetings with senior clients, played both by actors and trainers. Many different live situations were tried, with diverse things happening, involving improvisation, experimental approaches, tools and behaviours to improve people's competencies. Geoff Church, director of Dramatic Resources, recalls that 'initially, there was some fear among participants of being revealed in front of each other and there was also a degree of scepticism among a few about the usefulness of a theatre-based process to address their own practical situations. But, once they had been immersed in the process, they found it a very different experience from anything they had done before, especially the improvisation, and showed interest, pleasure and enthusiasm for the entire rehearsal process.' According to Terry Willie, 'there were some fantastic skills we could draw from theatre – especially the ability to walk in other people's shoes and be able to read and understand roles, characters and plots. We also loved the idea that it was learning by doing, not just telling – and using the acting/theatre approach got people to relax and try new things. It is proved to be just a lovely fresh perspective.'

The ABI changed participants' whole thinking about their relationships with clients. Through the initiative they heightened skills in communication and improvisation, and learnt how to cope with difficult situations requiring self-confidence, self-expression, empathy and how to properly use body language and other communication means. The initiative also provided personal benefits to participants, helping them to see themselves and others differently, stimulating self-assessment and self-reflection. The senior managers from Hall and Partners said that the ABI provided benefits in terms of people development 'as if they had grown up ten years'. Moreover, they highlighted that the rehearsal and coaching developed through the theatre-based initiative, challenging and stretching people, made a real difference to their day-to-day performance, particularly in terms of changing people's attitudes and behaviours.

Hall and Partners was voted as one of the top small businesses to work for by the *Sunday Times*. This can be considered as a consequence, among other factors, of the adoption of innovative training approaches for people development, such as the theatre-based programme. Terry Willie stressed that 'we passionately believe the reason why the business has been successful is because we care so much about not just attracting the best and most creative talent, but keeping and developing them. And to that end we have developed an extensive "curriculum" for training people at every level in the place... [this] work is by far the most influential work we do – people universally came out of it raving about how much they got out of it; you could immediately see the change in their day to day work'.

The learning and development mechanisms activated by ABIs

The learning and development mechanisms activated by ABIs can exploit works of art both as metaphors and analogies to explore reality and/or as aesthetic experiences and properties that spark learning reflections and conversations (Taylor and Ladkin, 2009). Works of art such as photographs, theatre representations, videos and films, paintings, drawings and music, can provide metaphors that offer time and space to acquire and/or generate new knowledge and insights. Metaphors can spur new ideas as well as stimulate a conversation between people. By exploiting the power of a metaphor it is possible to frame and analyse an issue by using a different model which keeps some similar properties and/or characteristics of the investigated reality. This allows questions to be raised and implications to be explored that help people to face problems by applying taken-for-granted knowledge and/or by generating new knowledge.

People involved in ABIs can go through experiences that touch their inner feelings and energies. This allows for the creation of connections between personally felt experiences and organisational issues. For example, the vicarious experiences created by reading and seeing Shakespeare's *Henry V* allow managers to feel emotions and personal connection with the concept of leadership, that helps to better understand and discuss its essence and key dimensions. Selected plays by Shakespeare can be exploited to teach lessons to business people.

The works of art can be used to generate aesthetic experiences that encourage people to reflect on their own management and leadership style, and think about alternative approaches. Art forms help people to develop an aesthetic perspective of the issues, situations and problems that they have to deal with, and in which they are immersed. This endorses and develops emotional sensitivities, allowing people to make informed decisions based on logical and linear thinking and grounded in emotions and intuition. This activates a learning-based process which is based on 'knowing in your gut' together with 'knowing in your head' (Taylor, 2003). For example, at Unilever UK, different arts-based experiences based on cooking, theatrical performances and boxing were used in the arts-based project named 'top dogs'. This project, delivered by The MAP Consortium, aimed at enabling people to explore their understanding and relationships with the concept of 'competitiveness'. This contributed to strengthening people's attitude and mindsets for competing, but living more consistently and with greater belief.

The learning mechanisms activated by ABIs are related to the capacity of art forms to operate as an analogical device to mediate, externalise and discuss tacit knowledge and personal understanding (Barry, 1994). Thus, for example, the use of photographs can be exploited as an arts-based method to express and present personal points of view fostering conversations and learning among people in complex organisational issues. In this case, ABIs act as a projective technique that helps managers 'to understand and work with the multiplicity of meaning making that surrounds complex organisational issues' (Taylor and Ladkin, 2009: 65).

Through ABIs it is possible to explore management challenges and business problems from different perspectives that enable executives to develop learning insights that spark creativity, imagination and enhance personal competences. Adler (2006: 494) states that executives can learn different competencies from artists and the arts, like for example 'the courage to see the reality as it actually is; the courage to envision previously unimagined and unimaginable possibilities; and the courage to inspire others to bring possibility back to reality'. In addition, executives can learn how to better lead and manage their organisations by paying attention to dimensions such as time, energy, space and human interactions (Denhardt and Denhardt, 2006), as well as by discovering how to approach work activities with emotional energy so that people's spirit can be nurtured and they can be engaged in a sense of ownership and self-awareness (Richards, 1995).

An example of the application of ABIs for leadership development at PricewaterhouseCoopers

One illustration of the relevance of the adoption of arts forms for developing executives is represented by the arts-based programme 'PwC Young Leadership Programme', implemented by PricewaterhouseCoopers, and designed and delivered by The MAP Consortium. The aim of the ABI was to create an innovative development pathway for the leaders of tomorrow. Using different art forms the young managers were involved in an experiential context capable of letting people explore leadership capacity and think about their own vision and choices of leading. The arts-based practices created a learning platform based on metaphors and analogies that stimulated reflection on the differences between management and leadership. For instance, a warm-up exercise using objects where participants had to use an object to talk about themselves and what they felt about leadership. These objects became metaphors to project their personal understanding of leadership allowing for descriptive discussion and conversations that fostered both individual and group learning. Another exercise was based on setting a leadership challenge. Each individual was tasked with presenting a vision to their team on how they would lead the group in the creation of an abstract work of art. The tasks contained both a challenge in terms of communication and leadership themes/values, such as: 'compose a soundscape that investigates communication', or 'create a movement sequence that explores progress'. Participants were given a short lesson in arts practice, supplied with materials, and were given an hour's preparation time to reflect on what they wanted to bring to the exercise in terms of leadership style, approach and vision. This also included their style of presentation and the quality of the message they wanted to convey to an audience. Then, individuals had to introduce their ideas, and lead the discussion and rehearse in their working group. This experience moved people out of their comfort zone and forced them to think about what vision is and concerns. People had the opportunity to explore the emotional aspects of leading and co-creating, forcing them to be authentic. The challenge to set out an idea was stimulating in terms of reflection around creativity and the creative process. The explanation of the idea to their peers challenged individuals to discover what they wanted and needed to communicate their vision to others. Finally, they had the challenge of leading their group, giving them the experience of learning how to forge a group to become co-creator.

The overall process was accompanied by feedback given by facilitators around key issues such as leadership style and presentation. Participants were invited to reflect and discuss the different patterns and processes of leading. Questions such as: 'What did it feel like to lead?' or 'Did your presentation say what you wanted to say?' or 'Where were you true to your chosen leadership style and where did you revert to a manager?' allowed participants to develop awareness about leadership and assess their leadership style and its impact on others. Feedback was given on how to powerfully communicate ideas rather than just articulate them. The feedback represented the basis for identifying areas of improvement and individuals were given further rehearsal time with their groups in order to refine their presentational aspects. A final presentation allowed the participants to show their learning insights about the capacity of leading a group as well as to demonstrate their imaginative use of resources.

The qualitative assessment of the ABI, on the basis of a structured set of questions, revealed that the participants considered the arts-based development initiative highly positive in terms of: capacity of giving a practical framework in which to lead; enabling participants to reflect on their vision and choices in how to lead; and providing an experiential context in which to explore leadership capacity. Further identified learning insights involved: level of confidence in responding to leadership challenges; assessment of risk-taking in leadership; and assessment of the ability to give feedback.

The transformational impact of learning and development

An ABI adopted by an organisation with the aim of supporting people learning and development is intended to generate benefits in terms of people's abilities to address business issues that require intuitive thinking, emotive arousal, aesthetic understanding, social intelligence and more generally adaptability. ABIs adopted for learning and development may share several approaches and tools with arts education and therapy, although their goals are fundamentally different. ABIs revolve around business goals, however they may also have some educational and therapeutic effects once implemented, albeit unintentionally.

Evidence on the positive impact of arts-based training is reported by a number of studies conducted with regard to the links between arts-based learning and health practitioner development. Some of the main topics emerging from these studies are reported by Staricoff (2004) who has effectively addressed that arts-based learning experiences produce beneficial outcomes in terms of mental task performances in surgeons, such as observational skills and ability in drawing, stereo vision and three-dimensional thinking. Dolev *et al.* (2001) reported that the use of art history seminars, to be integrated into clinical tutorial sessions, together with the use of photographs for describing dermatological lesions, improves medical students' diagnostic skills. This is because medical students become better equipped to see the details of paintings and photographs, which seem to drive them to better analyse the constellation of symptoms manifested by patients they examine. The use of works of art also has a role in encouraging medical practitioners to be more humane, understanding and sympathetic. The exposure of medical and nursing students to visual arts, music, dance, theatrical performances and literature has proved to be beneficial for improving professional decision-making, communication skills and understanding of the relationships between doctor and patient through, for example, clinical empathy (Dow *et al.*, 2007; Jeffrey *et al.*, 2001; Kottow and Kottow, 2002; Skelton *et al.*, 2000). The evidence gathered from the studies in healthcare organisations can potentially be generalised and extended to other public and private sectors.

Investigating the cognitive benefits and the relevance of the arts to develop learning skills and academic performance, arts education literature has shown that arts-based experiences produce positive learning and social effects. More specifically, a review of the literature of arts-based education shows that it is possible to identify three main cognitive benefits related to arts-based development processes: improvement of academic performance, improvement of basic skills and improvement of attitudes promoting the learning process itself (Deasy, 2002, 2004; Eisner, 2002; Fiske, 1999; McCarthy *et al.*, 2004). Arts play a fundamental role in the development of cognitive capacities, including perception, elaboration, problem-solving and creative thinking. Literacy, interpreted as the process used to acquire and express meaning in symbolic form, can be benefitted by arts-based education (Deasy, 2002, 2004; Eisner, 2002).

Finally, arts-based learning experiences stimulate and develop group and collaborative learning. This is the case, particularly, of arts-based experiences based upon ensemble arts that prompt people to feel a sense of responsibility to a group and/or to a project (Fiske, 1999). Indeed, theatre productions, music ensembles, dance presentations, collaborative creative writing and group paintings are all examples of group activities involving group members' learning processes. Learning in the arts encourages the development of cognitive capacity and the ability to learn in other domains (Deasy, 2002; Fiske, 1999). In this light, even if there are some empirical difficulties in proving the existence of knowledge transfer from the arts to other fields, from a quantitative perspective, qualitative and theoretical implications show that skills learnt through arts education can benefit other capabilities and professional skills (Perkins, 1994). The relevance of ABIs in creating value in terms of learning and development is further highlighted by the ever-increasing adoption of arts-based courses in the curricula of many business schools.

The use of ABIs in business schools

The competitive challenges of the new business landscape and the business problems related to the relevance of ethical issues have pointed out the importance of adopting innovative means to train and develop managers and leaders (Adler, 2010). The integration of arts-based learning processes in business schools' curricula is gradually spreading. For example, business schools such as MIT Sloan, INSEAD Business School, Warwick Business School, University of Glasgow Business School, the IMD Business School Lausanne, Cranfield School of Management, Aston Business School and F.W. Olin Graduate School of Business at Babson College, to name a few, have adopted ABIs either as added learning courses or as an integrated approach in the delivering of the traditional learning modules. These business schools have adopted ABIs in their master of business administration (MBA) courses, master of the arts (MA) courses and other executive courses. For example, at Babson College, in order for MBA students to learn the principles of a creative process, they are exposed to arts-based experiences under the guidance of an artist facilitator who acts as a creative consultant. Students learn how to use their senses in order to better grasp things that are happening around them, as well as to react to them by being immersed in artistic creative processes. This results in the development of MBA graduates' creative skills, and show: confidence in their ability to express themselves creatively; willingness to accept and deal with ambiguity and uncertainty; openness to reframe problems, solutions and scenarios; and develop trust in themselves and in their potential creativity (Pinard and Allio, 2005). In other business schools art forms are used to lead students to understand how to become more receptive by relaxation in order to let their imagination run free. By exposing students to artistic products and processes, through a hands-on approach, they can learn to be more in touch with their senses, emotions and thoughts. Students take classes of puppetry, dance and movement, music, fiction, writing, theatrical improvisation, painting and poetry in order to learn how to handle ambiguity, be more adept in discovering new things and seeing things from different perspectives, take risks, communicate more efficiently and improve problem-solving capabilities. Art forms are therefore increasingly recognised as a powerful means to develop students' imagination and creativity. Furthermore, the technical skills attained through the exposure to the arts are transferable and can be applied in the workplace and within a business context.

Investment: using the arts as a value vector

ABIs can be adopted as a management means to increase the value of organisational assets. They can play the role of value vectors aimed either at creating and incorporating intangible value into products and other organisation's infrastructural components, or as a management action to achieve economic financial benefits. The use of art forms as a management means to address business issues can trigger a variety of direct and indirect economic benefits. The direct benefits are those related to the use of the arts as an economic activity in which case the arts represent financial assets or they are sources of income. In today's economy, art can represent relevant economic assets. The art market puts an economic value on artworks. Thus, organisations can approach the creation of art collections with the specific intent of making an economic investment and entering their artworks on the balance sheet as an economic asset. Furthermore, art collections or underwriting arts activities and organisations can be considered, in some countries, as part of a tax strategy. On the other hand, the arts can be exploited for commercial purposes. In this case, works of art can be seen as commodities that have their value determined by the interplay between demand and supply in the marketplace. In particular, the attention is focused on the role of the arts as an industry. This is the so-called business arena of the creative industry, such as film and music businesses, design, architecture and more generally the arts businesses, in which case the arts are converted into products and/or services to be sold in the market.

The above economic roles of the arts represent an important perspective to interpret the value of the arts for business. They have been largely recognised and investigated in the economic literature. In this book the use of the arts as a financial investment is not addressed – although it is acknowledged that the arts can generate economic benefits – as the focus is on the deployment of the arts as a value-added vector to increase the value incorporated into products as well as in organisational infrastructure. The fundamental idea is that art forms can be deployed to create intangible value to be embedded into organisational products and infrastructure. The interest is focused on the use of artistic products and processes to shape the aesthetic properties of products and infrastructure in order to increase their embedded value. From a purely economic perspective, this corresponds with recognising that the price of a product incorporating arts-based traits and features is affected by its aesthetic value. This is becoming increasingly important in today's economy, because for many products the margins to improve the functional and material value are narrow, and customers search for experience-based consumption. The employment of art forms to shape the aesthetic properties of products is crucial. They allow the creation of products that are capable of engaging people in aesthetic experiences that evoke emotions. These are the essential aspects of the intangible value that increasingly characterises the products of twenty-first century business organisations.

Implementing ABIs as a value vector

By acknowledging the importance of incorporating intangible value dimensions into products, many companies are starting to position themselves at the intersection of commerce and the arts (Bangle, 2001). The idea is not that a company's competitiveness is based on the creation of artworks; but that the incorporation of the quality and features characterising works of art into products is increasingly crucial.

The use of art forms to infuse arts-based qualities into products and create intangible value can take different forms. A traditional approach is the convergence of art and design. In this regard, a number of examples can be provided from diverse industries. For instance, car manufacturers such as Ferrari, Lamborghini, Maserati and Aston Martin, pay great attention to artistic components of their products from design to colour and materials and to any other components, which as a work of art can affect clients' experiences. Chris Bangle (2001: 48), global chief of design for BMW, considers his company's products as 'moving works of art that express the driver's love of quality', and considers his job as director overseeing 220 artists, mediating the corporate pragmatism and the artistic passion and mindsets within the company. On a similar note, Robert Lutz from General Motors pointed out: 'I see us being in the art business; art, entertainment and mobile sculpture, which, coincidentally, also happens to provide transportation' (Hakim, 2004). The arts can also be considered as a fundamental component of the success of Italian home-furnishings companies, such as Alessi, Artemide, Cassina, Flos, B&B Italia, Cappellini and many others. Indeed, at the heart of the success of these companies' products is their artistic nature. The products leveraging aesthetic dimensions are able to interpret and communicate emotional and energetic states, which appeal to consumers. These products can be considered the result of artistic processes. Indeed, they are generated by a free-floating community of architects, suppliers, photographers, critics, curators, publishers, designers, artists and craftsmen (Verganti, 2006), who implicitly use art principles, content and processes as devices to develop new and existing products. Although the integration of art and design represents the main mode of the use of art forms as a value vector, other kinds of approaches can be identified in the business world. Consider the approach taken by some organisations that are exploiting the incorporation or association of the arts into their products. An illustration is offered by Glass, an Italian company specialising in the production of baths, shower enclosures, panels and trays, and hydromassage cubicles. In order to face the competitiveness in its industry, in 2008 Glass launched the WaterArtCollection, introducing six new portfolios of products. To define the new products a team of designers and a group of street artists were brought together.

The artists developed visual works of art with the twofold aim of inspiring designers to define the new aesthetic and functional features of the products, and delineating the image of the products. This successfully generated new products that were able to combine functional qualities with the ability to evoke emotions. A further case example is represented by Illy. This global coffee company has grounded its success, among other factors, on the ability to interpret the 'espresso' as a product incorporating artful features. The visual arts have represented a fundamental value-adding vector to create intangible value into their products. The essential idea that has inspired the union between arts and coffee has been Illy's vision of the business of espresso that Andrea Illy summarises as follows: 'Illy is in the business of the enhancement of the quality of life, looking for delivering joy, and for this reason focalises [among other initiatives] on the coffee-cup as a multisensory experiential device'.[10] The use of the arts to build an arts-based experience of espresso started in 1992, when Illy decided to launch its first collection of artistic coffee cups labelled 'Arti e Mestieri' (arts and craftsmanship). The goal was to create an aesthetic experience that would engage the customers with their emotions. Since this first experiment many artists have contributed with their artistic skills to beautify Illy's coffee cups. Today, the partnership created by Illy with the arts is more pervasive and the company has created stable relationships with arts-based organisations such as the PS1 Contemporary Art Centre in New York, Central Saint Martin's in London and Fondazione Pistoletto. Moreover, it supports international contemporary exhibitions such as ARCO in Madrid, Frieze Art Fair in London, Armory Show in New York and the Biennale di Venezia. Other ABIs involve Illy SustainArt, which has the objective of supporting artists based in the countries that produce coffee and from which the company buys the raw materials. For Illy the deployment of the arts represents a key factor contributing to the success of its products as well as raising the company's reputation around the world.

The transformational impact of ABIs focused on investments

The use of ABIs as a value vector refers not only to the incorporation of arts-based features into products, but also contemplates the employment of art forms to infuse arts-based characteristics into tangible and intangible organisation's infrastructural components. This can affect the performance of organisational processes such as new product development and information and communication processes. As an illustration, consider the case of McKann Erickson, a communications company, which was interested in shaping new approaches to communicate and share information throughout the organisation. For this reason, it was decided to adopt an ABI to be implemented during the annual company conference. Tradesecrets was brought in with the task of defining an ABI that would involve people in an innovative and imaginative way, to reflect on how to better communicate and share information. They set the annual company conference in a constantly evolving garden with aspects of creativity represented by different inspirational characters that inhabited the space. The garden grew over the course of the three-day conference, representing key aspects of the creative process and challenging delegates. This aimed at sparking reflections about change within the organisation and through this process the company identified specifications that were incorporated into the intranet structure that today allows employees to better communicate creatively across the globe. A further case example of the use of ABIs to affect the intangible assets of an organisational infrastructure is provided by the experience of the Innovation Centre at Unilever, where Sean Gogarty, head of the business unit, brought in a poet-in-residence, with the goal of spurring the creativity of his team and supporting the development of new products (Darsø, 2004). Bringing in a poet and using words as a powerful way to expand people's viewpoint was recognised as a means of developing new thinking and approaches to product development.

Networking: creating relational capital through the arts

The main goal of the organisational value-driver 'networking' is the creation of an organisation's relational capital. The ABIs adopted for this goal aim to define common ground to activate and support relationships and collaboration among people. This lays the foundation to activate and develop networking dynamics both within the organisation and between the organisation and its external stakeholders.

Implementing ABIs for networking

ABIs focused on networking are able to generate collective effects, namely a positive impact on intra- and interorganisational groups and communities. They provide means for conversation, which in turn helps to create relationships that represent the building blocks for constructing and cementing groups, community and social relations. By using art forms it is possible to bring people together and bind them, promoting community integration and interaction. Art forms can represent a very effective way to communicate across personal barriers (Lowe, 2000). They provide multiple media through which to create experiential communication based on emotive and energetic dimensions. The arts use symbols and cues representing a universal language.[11] They allow conversations to be created based on a rich communication that mixes and integrates rational information with emotive cues.[12] In addition the relevance of creating associations among elements is a core characteristic of the arts, which implies that their use fosters understanding about how to develop relationships. Indeed, all art forms are concerned with the creation of effective relations among 'parts' that constitute a whole. Whether painting, composing or playing music, writing a poem or dancing, it is critical that the different parts are integrated. Different elements have to work harmoniously together. Consequently, the arts can be used as a means to explore and understand how to see interactions, how to observe the relationships between and among parts and how to identify the qualities of the elements and the relationships constituting a whole.

Within an organisation a direct involvement of employees in an artistic process, or an experience of an artistic product, as well as the interactions with artists, can define a social platform that promotes and facilitates high quality interaction among people. This means that ABIs can be deployed as triggers and catalysers to create interpersonal bonds and to promote social interactions among community members (Griffiths, 1993; Lowe, 2000; Stern and Seifert, 2000). Art forms are able to generate unique aesthetic contexts in which people can interact in ways that make them feel connected and involved. Through the arts, social boundaries may collapse and the members of a group can be integrated and co-inspired. This brings people together, creating bonds between them, driving team-building and encouraging collaboration.

A case study illustrating how ABIs can shape the creation of relational capital of an organisation is provided by the arts-based management action labelled as 'the percussion symphony at Lafarge'. Undergoing a takeover process from the French group Lafarge, Blue Circle Industries adopted percussion workshops as a team-building exercise and as a means of getting ready for the merger with a company with a very different culture. A percussion symphony was used as a metaphor for how different parts of the organisation could work together. All the participants needed to learn to play in time together, working up to a grand finale. Rick Haythornthwaite, who was chief executive at that time, recalls: 'You can get across the message and create a new vocabulary incredibly quickly when people are playing the same drumbeat, for example. It had a very profound effect. And you get 100 per cent participation, even from those who have made a career out of sitting on the sidelines. Once you have photographed them in eager anticipation, waiting to hit their triangle, they never look back.' He adds: 'There was a moment when people had performed something very powerful, and we said they had an hour to go away and do what they wanted with their parts. They came back and this very powerful piece of music had descended into chaos; they all went away to complicate it. If ever there was a metaphor for trouble in business, that's it. From then on, people would refer to this moment when they realised they were complicating life. It was fantastic, irreplaceable. And this was a team that not long after fought off and won the first successful defence against a cash bid in fifteen years. It tells you what esprit de corps it produces.' The ABI was facilitated by the arts-based organisation tradesecrets. Sam Bond, the director of tradesecrets, played the role of a fictitious symphony orchestra conductor Gregor Timeriovich, who had an enormous ego and was obsessed with individuals. This subverted the whole procedure and he was eventually thrown out of the room. Rick then took up conducting himself. The percussion workshop helped to look at the individual's role in the whole and what part they played for the ongoing success of the group. Employees got the message across: 'you couldn't demonstrate the basic elements of teamwork better'. Everyone was aligned and focused towards a common goal and this was particularly effective as everybody started from the same base and came together.

A further case study highlighting how ABIs can improve the quality of the relationships by helping people to discover and develop the factors affecting the quality of the relations is offered by the ABI 'braver conversations' implemented at Unilever UK. This ABI aimed at stimulating and improving Unilever employees' conversations. It included a series of workshops, a live event, a sound installation and a CD. The focus was the development of people's ability to have braver conversations, i.e., conversations that are vital for organisational success and address important business and people issues with honesty, clarity and courage. In a series of workshops, Unilever employees discovered how to have honest and straightforward conversations whether talking with a colleague, getting in touch with a supplier or negotiating with a customer. As part of the arts-based project, a sound installation was created, made up of a series of private conversations, initiated and recorded by Unilever's employees. In addition, a double CD was developed for staff to use with the aim of stimulating and enabling people to continuously maintain their braver conversations.

ABIs not only play a fundamental role in building links within an organisation, but they can be exploited also to improve the customer–supplier relationship. Consider the approach taken by Sainsbury's to address the customer–supplier relationship in its supply chain, with the aim of improving the quality of the links with key suppliers. For this reason an arts-based workshop was designed. The MAP Consortium, as part of its programme 'Housework' for The Royal Opera House, with a team of artists, including a choreographer and two dancers, designed a set of movement exercises that were specifically designed to reflect the challenges of the customer–supplier dynamic, then participants had to learn, rehearse and perform the exercises under the facilitation of the artists. The workshop created a shared aesthetic-based team-building experience that facilitated reflection and understanding on issues related to the factors affecting successfully working as a group and how to improve networking relationships.

The transformational impact of networking

ABIs focusing on networking dynamics generate a wide range of benefits. They can promote greater understanding, tolerance, respect for diversity and trust between people, building cohesion and an ethic of solidarity. Arts-based experiences help people bridge interpersonal and social boundaries of age, gender, race/ethnicity and hierarchical status. This not only supports the creation of a team-building culture and orientation within an organisation, but also encourages intergroup cooperation and partnership.

One of the fundamental dimensions characterising relationships that is affected by ABIs is trust. This is an essential building block of any relationship. Arts-based experiences encourage people to reflect on the elements that characterise the development of trustful and constructive relationships in order to create better internal and external organisational relationships. Art forms create aesthetic experiences and contexts that enable people to relate to each other; share their points of view, beliefs, values and ways of seeing the world; break down their social and cultural barriers; get out of their comfort zones; and be encouraged to activate emotional and energetic ties. This affects people's social behaviours, promoting and facilitating social interactions among the organisational members. People learn how to improve the process of giving and receiving feedback as well as questioning and having conversations about important organisational issues.

ABIs spark conversations that significantly contribute to identifying the individual's role in a group and to understand what part people play in the ongoing success of the group. ABIs are a relevant device to facilitate and support the development of relational capital. They promote fluid and positive organisational networking dynamics in which people are willing and feel free to communicate with feelings and exchange feedback. Art forms engage people in relations that are energetic and joyful. The emotional and energetic dynamics characterising the relationships drive the enhancement of people's morale and motivation as well as nurture a positive sense of a community identity.

Grisham (2006) analyses the use of storytelling and poetry as methods to bridge cultural gaps between leaders in cross-cultural settings so that they develop a common understanding to connect with one another. In addition, ABIs contribute to people's sense of connectedness and belonging by generating organisational community pride and prestige (Jackson, 1998). They can be used for diversity management and to promote intercultural awareness and tolerance. For example, at Aston Business School, ABIs are adopted to improve intercultural awareness among students and teaching staff. They are deployed as a means of supporting conversations and reflections about diversity and cultural issues, breaking down barriers between people of different nationalities and encouraging them to give up their prejudices. This aids an enhancement of the relational dynamics within the business school and promotes the development of a community. ABIs play a fundamental role not only in supporting the enhancement of the networking dynamics among employees within an organisation and between the organisation and its customers or suppliers, but also in shaping relationships with external stakeholders and particularly with the community and society at large. In fact, an organisation can deploy art forms as an effective way to have a significant social and cultural impact on the community in which it operates. The impact of ABIs on the public domain can demonstrate the organisational commitment and active participation to the solution of communities' challenges and problems. Fundamentally, ABIs allow the construction or reconstruction of trust in the relationship with stakeholders in order to enhance and build relational capital. This may have positive effects on multiple competitive dimensions of an organisation.

Building relational capital through ABIs: the case of UBS

As a case study, the financial conglomerate UBS has built partnerships with arts organisations as part of its corporate social responsibility and community affairs strategy. In particular, among others, UBS has established a major relationship with Circus Space, an arts-based organisation devoted to enhancing, protecting and advancing circus art forms. Other UBS relationships with arts organisations involve the London Symphony Orchestra and the Tate Modern.

The partnership created by UBS with Circus Space began by providing assistance in achieving the necessary funding for the restoration of a Victorian power station in Hoxton at the heart of the east end of London. This initiative not only contributed to creating a unique circus creation studio, but also promoted the cultural regeneration of a traditionally degraded area and acted as a catalyst for the development of the urban area. Although the relationship with Circus Space was not planned at the outset to organically grow towards a strategic partnership, it has evolved as such over time, creating benefits for the organisation in different ways, particularly by contributing to the development of the relational capital with organisational stakeholders. Today, UBS works with and through Circus Space and different kinds of activities have been undertaken. UBS is supporting employee volunteering, with staff offering mentoring to Circus Space's graduating students as well as providing business advice to Circus Space's board. Other activities supported by UBS have included the underwriting of the development of circus programmes for the community, such as the London Youth Circus. In addition, UBS uses Circus Space's arts-based services for people learning and development as well as to run corporate events. These different formats of ABIs have produced a positive impact on the ties with the local community and provided networking opportunities for the people and for the organisation, which has strengthened relations with external clients and institutional actors.

Nowadays, the relationship with Circus Space is acknowledged as an important intangible asset that can contribute to dealing with the turmoil that has characterised the global financial market. Indeed, there is now great attention to restoring stability and, in this perspective, it seems that the attention of global banks is about recreating themselves to be fit for purpose. Recreation is strongly linked to cultural values such as transparency, trust and openness. The deployment of the arts can support the recreation of a relational capital based on these fundamental pillars. UBS sees the partnership with arts organisations as well as the use of ABIs as a key management tool to develop a common culture. In particular, UBS recognises that arts organisations are characterised by a culture that is relevant for corporate development and relationships with arts organisations can contribute to promoting cultural awareness. The partnership with Circus Space has provided UBS with the opportunity to foster people to: have an open dialogue; trust in each other; reflect on personal responsibility; and do the right things 'when no one is looking', i.e., without direct internal or external supervision. Commenting on the role of community-based activities, Nick Wright, UBS managing director of corporate responsibility and community affairs, states: 'People who have the tendency to gravitate towards volunteering programmes with arts organisations or other community-based programmes tend to exhibit the kind of characteristics that we have identified ourselves as what we want. There is a growing awareness in the organisation that ABIs and community-based activities are both pulling in the right kind of people and creating the kind of culture that promotes the relevance of looking more holistically, and taking care of our relationships within and outside the firm.' The use of ABIs acts as a platform and a device to spark and support conversations that ground the creation of relational capital. The arts ask people to make an emotional and empathetic leap and to understand the world from other perspectives. In this regard, Nick Wright points out that: 'Particularly in large organisations there is the tendency for people to become siloed in their operational activities, without actually translating the synergies between the different groups. As a consequence people tend not to sit down and have conversations. In terms of breaking down the silos the arts-based activities provide an important contribution to prompt the kind of behaviours that bring people to have conversations.' Finally, the partnership with arts organisations and the use of art forms is crucial because it creates the kind of learning context that helps an organisation to understand and focus on its fundamental purpose. This is critical in order to catalyse the emotional and energetic dynamics that are at the basis of building the relational and social capital of an organisation. On this perspective, Nick Wright comments: 'In the best arts organisations there is a sense of common purpose, which is very powerful. The sense of purpose is related to what it means to be human and the link with human life, while in many organisations the purpose is not so clearly understood. People need to feel differently about what they do in terms of making sense of their activities and how these activities are connected with life.' ABIs have the power to humanise an organisation and let people discover how to work passionately, and build enriching and enlightening relationships.

Transformation: the arts for driving organisational change

ABIs can be adopted to address the organisational value-driver 'transformation'. This means that the arts can be deployed as a management means to drive organisational change. The use of art forms within an organisation can contribute to creating a new consciousness for people that affects the organisational ability to undertake a renovation. This drives the creation of a new culture and involves the transformation of organisational infrastructure components.

Transformation occurs when people change their beliefs, attitudes and behaviours in their day-to-day working activities as well as when the organisational infrastructure components, such as workplace, culture, environment, furniture, procedures and routines, are modified. At this level of the Arts Value Matrix people are profoundly touched and involved with an inner transformation, which is aligned with the needs and wants of the organisation in terms of strategic and performance objectives. Through the arts, people are inspired and energised in order to accept and prompt changes both in their behaviour and in the reality around them. This drives organisational renewal. Thus transformation represents the convergence of people change and organisational infrastructure development.

Implementing ABIs for transformation
ABIs can be considered particularly powerful in driving the creation and absorption of new values and culture. They can support

organisations in creating and sharing a renewed organisational culture, involving all employees in the process of understanding what organisational behaviours to adopt and how to translate key organisational values into day-to-day actions. As one illustration of how ABIs can shape organisational culture, consider the case of Saxton Bampfylde. This leading executive search company in England was interested in examining and discussing the moral influence of the company after an acquisition and post-merger integration with part of KPMG who had a less intricate culture and set of values. Saxton Bampfylde was interested in examining and discussing the moral influence of the company. They used a series of workshops incorporating visual arts to help articulate and embed the mission and the strong Christian values of the company. They wanted to investigate whether everyone on the programme had the same values, and whether everyone was genuinely subscribing to these values. A manager reported that 'The ABI format showed it was fine to be different in the company, and helped us to feel like "one firm".' This resulted in streamlining people's views and feelings about the company and changed the atmosphere of the office, bringing people together.

In the sections below two key case studies of how ABIs can support organisational change are illustrated.

Transforming corporate culture at 'Television'[13]

'How can we effectively create a new culture based on accepted, understood and absorbed values and related shared behaviours, and achieve consistency throughout the organisation?' This was the issue dealt with by Television and solved by adopting ABIs.

Television had recently grown considerably in size as the result of a merger of a number of different companies, each with their own cultures and different ways of doing things. As a result, Television was looking to build a new corporate culture. It needed to create a common vision about the companies within the company in order to establish shared new values and behaviours. It was evident that the behaviours of all staff should fit the values of the organisation and that the workforce should buy into and understand these values, while accepting the related behaviours. They developed a set of values and established a common vision through questionnaires and focus groups at all levels of the organisation. However, Television recognised that simply talking about the new organisational values would be quite meaningless to people on a day-to-day basis and that they should make sure that the new values affected the way people actually behaved. Television's objective was to look for a clear definition of the fundamental values and a shared approach to work, which would remain consistent throughout the organisation.

The technical skills of Television's staff were second-to-none, but a culture had developed where staff relied on that alone and hid behind their technical expertise, ignoring the need for good relationships with colleagues. There was therefore an awareness that a common standard of behaviour and internal relationships should be developed, in order to create a better working environment and a better quality of work.

Television was very thorough in producing a set of organisational values. Moreover, the training and development manager liaised with heads of departments and their staff, asking them to write short reports containing examples of 'bad behaviour' between employees and between managers and staff. A great deal of material was produced, with examples of 'bad behaviour' ranging from mild to very serious. Starting from this material Television decided to opt for aesthetic-based techniques that would engage people through experiential processes and at the same time would be able to handle the intangible dimensions of the organisational infrastructure such as culture, values, attitudes, behaviours and climate. Thus it was decided to use the approach of the forum theatre workshops to force people to reflect on the organisations' behaviours and to absorb and apply to day-to-day activities the new set of values. Ci: Creative intelligence was brought in with the task of designing and implementing the 'Values Roadshow', a programme of forum theatre workshops to be run throughout the organisation. Starting from Television's reports on values and behaviours, Ci: Creative intelligence conducted an investigation to better understand the organisational context, interviewing staff, witnessing them at work and viewing their finished products. They then wrote a play, with three scenes, incorporating many of the behaviours which had come out of the investigation. The play was rehearsed using actors who had an understanding of the corporate sector and the cultural and behavioural issues companies faced. The scenes illustrated familiar situations and issues to which people could relate. During the forum theatre workshops the audience was asked to correct the behaviours played in the scenes. The workshops were interactive with the actors responding to suggestions from the participants and re-performing the scene. By representing all of the behaviours found in the investigation into three short scenes, as well as slightly exaggerating behaviours, they avoided stigmatising participants as perpetrators of bad behaviour and instead allowed them to discuss behaviour through proxies, without individuals having to confront each other.

The play was first presented to senior management at two levels prior to the running of twenty-one further workshops around the country, and ultimately being rolled out to the whole organisation.

The implementation of the values roadshow was followed by an assessment. The evaluation was initially undertaken by using questionnaires implemented one or two weeks after the forum theatre workshops. Afterwards a further evaluation was undertaken several months later in interviews with all Television's managers and a random selection of staff. From the overall assessment emerged that the response from the organisation to the adoption of the ABIs to catalyse organisational transformation was hugely positive. Employees' answers to the assessment questions were fundamentally consistent across the organisation. Some responses included: 'No one likes to have to think about what we do. It is quite an uncomfortable process to analyse yourself; analyse other people that is easy, analyse yourself is quite hard; a lot of people went away from the forum theatre workshop thinking and commenting "do I do that?" and you recognised a lot of other people in the actors and even yourself and then you realise how you can face somebody and be so wrong; [the Value Roadshow] put the values and behaviours out there and made them real – we could relate to them, not just read them and you could see them in action. People could collectively see what they were and why they were important – and how to apply them.'[14]

The Television case study represents an example of ABIs driving and supporting organisational transformation, particularly when a company is dealing with organisational culture and behaviour change. Using forum theatre workshops to play organisational scenarios and real situations through a humorous and exaggerated platform, with engaging and inclusive acting, Television enabled employees change and organisational infrastructure development. The transformation of the culture occurred at Television, as suggested by the Arts Value Matrix, was the result of an integrated and synergistic development of employees and organisational infrastructure. In particular, the values roadshow created a platform capable of engaging people emotionally and energetically activating self-reflection and self-assessment about the dominant values and behaviours within the organisation. The ABIs creating entertaining and energetic representations forced people to reflect on their personal and interpersonal behaviours. In addition, they also provided learning insights about how to modify and handle communication and feedback style in order to enhance the quality of relationships with colleagues. The arts-based interventions spotlighted the factors influencing and hampering the development of organisational capital both in terms of good relationships between colleagues, and of inter-group and inter-department communication and collaboration. They created a visualisation of the problems affecting the quality of the organisational climate. Employees, through the forum theatre workshops, had the opportunity to identify and analyse the 'negative attitudes and behaviours' and experiment how to improve them. This generated great benefits in terms of bonding and inspiring people. People could identify what was going on in their organisation. During the workshops they could suggest alternatives and instantly see what impact a change of behaviour would have.

The forum theatre workshops not only had the capacity to galvanise and inspire people, but also played an important role as instruments to visualise the current dominant organisational culture. This helped to make understandable some of the intangible infrastructural components affecting the quality of the working environment and the features of the internal networking dynamics. The ABI helped to define the norms, a common standard of behaviour and a shared approach to work to be consistent throughout the company. As a result of the value roadshow, as reported by the evaluation feedbacks gathered after the programme, people's behaviours within the organisation changed and relationships between colleagues improved. It was also reported that some quite dramatic changes had occurred. Once behavioural norms were established, the senior management felt legitimate in reacting strongly to inappropriate behaviour.

'Live + Direct': changing the feedback culture at Unilever

A key case study pointing out how ABIs can be deployed to affect and drive organisational transformation is provided by the in-house arts-based programme named 'Catalyst', adopted by Unilever UK, from

1999 to 2006, with the aim of radically transforming the organisational culture. The programme was originally created in 1999 by James Hill (then CEO of Lever Brothers) and Alastair Creamer (director of the Catalyst programme) for Lever Brothers and Elida Fabergé, during their merger to become Lever Fabergé, and later moved into a second Unilever operating company, Unilever Ice Cream and Frozen Foods (UICFF). Originally the programme was defined with the aim of developing and embedding a new culture within Lever Fabergé. Unilever was searching for innovative approaches to engage people and implement change management projects and decided to use arts-based activities to explore and resolve business issues.

Catalyst involved the use of an integrated set of ABIs focusing on the development of a new organisational culture, based on the encouragement of the creativity and entrepreneurship among employees. Different organisational change issues were addressed such as creativity, communication, personal expression, behaviour, culture, ways of thinking, risk-taking, mindset and consumer insights. The focus was both on employees and infrastructure. The programme supported organisational transformation impacting on five main areas as follows: mindsets and behaviours; communication and coordination; organisational creativity; design, product development and advertising; and organisational atmosphere.

The arts-based programme was based on many different arts-based projects, involving a wide ecology of artists and arts-based organisations. A number of artists, including actors, writers and directors, were brought together in the organisation to perform arts-based workshops, placements, one-to-one coaching, performances, debates, installations, workshops and events. Although the programme involved a number of ABIs, one of the largest arts-based projects undertaken by Catalyst was 'Live + Direct'. This ABI was adopted with the goal of changing the feedback culture at Unilever. The MAP Consortium was brought in and designed a programme that used rehearsal room techniques, and in particular the relationship between director and actors, to offer tools that could improve the ways of giving and receiving feedback in the organisation. The intention was to change the traditional business methods of being top-down and target orientated by using a systematic set of arts-based management actions.

Writer/researcher Julie Batty, arts consultant Andrew McIlroy and visual artist and MAP associate Martin Gent tracked and documented the programme. The MAP Consortium worked in residence for three months with Lever Fabergé and UICFF, at all levels and alongside the Unilever human resources department. The attention was fundamentally focused on promoting straightforward and direct communication among people in the organisation. Unilever wanted to introduce a language of possibilities that would make feedback more accessible to all levels of staff.

The MAP Consortium and a group of managers from Unilever UK identified recurring feedback themes to be addressed within both companies, such as short-term thinking, a constant need for increased delivery, an emphasis on quick answers rather than questions, overlooked feelings and a focus on winning. In order to raise awareness of the project several interventions were staged at UICFF, including live theatre in the courtyards at lunchtimes. A series of thirty-two feedback workshops using live rehearsal and directing skills as a stimulus were organised and attended by business teams from UICFF and Lever Fabergé, and were tailored to some extent to their specific needs. In the workshop the staff took over the roles of director and actors. In this way people were immersed in an analogical model to observe and reflect on their feedback behaviours. After the workshop each team appointed a 'feedback caretaker' who was the point of contact for MAP with the task of co-ordinating follow-up meetings after the workshops and reporting evaluation feedback. Then, seven business teams signed up to work with an arts associate, an artist member of the MAP team. The arts associate sat in on team meetings and helped each business team disseminate the knowledge gathered during the workshops, and also held one-to-one surgeries to develop the team's communication culture.

At the end of the project The MAP Consortium wrote and performed a piece of theatre, 'The Live Report', based on their experiences of working with both companies. The piece was performed in each business and to the board. Each performance was followed by a debate between staff, leaders and MAP around the issues raised. The performances acted as pieces of three-dimensional feedback that were deliberately challenging. The project had an overall positive impact on the feedback culture within and between teams. Large numbers of staff from both companies were involved in sharing and comparing knowledge and experiences as well as communicating and giving feedback, resulting in the formation of new relationships.

Keith Weed, Chairman at Lever Fabergé, reported that: 'Live + Direct helped people learn techniques, practise giving and receiving feedback and appreciate the power of conversations that can make a difference, whether they are comfortable or uncomfortable. Live + Direct helped us reclaim a little bit of the child within us.' The original business feedback culture of being primarily top-down and target-focused was influenced by one based on process and geared to creative and collaborative approaches. Sarah Sturton, Training Manager at UICFF, pointed out that: 'Whether a direct correlation or not, there appears to be a big focus on team building involving "transforma-tional" activities. So perhaps having opened up the debate, 'Live + Direct' gave people some reflection time and has led them into taking action.'

UICFF and Lever Fabergé developed a shared language on the sub-ject of giving and receiving feedback. For four months the business highlighted the importance of feedback in the context of doing better business, making it a core value and simultaneously more accessible and positive for all levels of staff.

The project pushed boundaries in terms of length, scale, participa-tion, inclusiveness and the balance struck between arts-based activity and tools for business. James Hill, Chairman at UICFF, stated that: 'The Live Report and the debates that followed were eye-opening for people. It was a risky thing to do as they could have flattened the energy in the business. Instead they focused our minds to do more. Since Live + Direct, the Board has been challenged to re-consider our role in sustaining cultural change.' The 'Live + Direct' project was followed by other ABIs. In particular, in 2004 a series of posters was designed by the artists Maria Hipwell and James Starr to remind staff of the development of language and mindset during the project.

The arts-based project 'Live + Direct' provides an example of how ABIs can be exploited to drive organisational transformation. The transformational effect has to be considered as a synergetic com-bination of effects that can be accounted in the different dimen-sions of the Arts Value Matrix. In fact the improvement of the feedback culture, in particular, can be analysed in terms of people change due both to learning and development, and to inspiration; as well as of organisational infrastructure development involving the enhancement of the organisational atmosphere and of the networking dynamics.

The polyvalent nature of the impact of ABIs

The Arts Value Matrix is a holistic framework mapping the potential organisational value-drivers that can be affected by the adoption of ABIs. It is not intended to be an analytical model to separate and evaluate the impact of ABIs. Rather, it supports the understanding of the strategic aims grounding the deployment of art forms as a management means to face managerial challenges and business problems. The underlying assumption of the matrix is that through ABIs, managers can shape organisational aesthetic dimensions and handle people's emotional and energetic dynamics that directly or indirectly influence organisational value creation. Each value dimension of the matrix has to be considered as an explanation of the organisational nature of the outcomes generated by the creation of aesthetic experiences and/or the manipulation of aesthetic properties.

The Arts Value Matrix is conceptually based on the recognition that an organisation is a techno-human system and as such people and their emotional and energetic dimensions have a central role in organisational behaviour. Accordingly ABIs can be interpreted as managerial levers to humanise an organisation and, in this perspective, the Arts Value Matrix translates the 'humanisation' of organisational components into organisational value-drivers, providing a managerial explanation for the reasons that can motivate organisations to adopt ABIs for strategic and operational purposes.

Regarding the impact of ABIs on the development of people, it is assumed that the quality of people's knowledge-based actions is based on the interweaving of the emotive and rational mind. The organisational value-drivers, mapped by the Arts Value Matrix, identify the organisational benefits of adopting the arts as a management means to create aesthetic experiences that influence people's emotions and energy. The deployment of ABIs allows the creation of emotive knowledge in people, both at individual and group levels, that provides them with soft skills fostering adaptability, resilience, and imagination. The Arts Value Matrix's categories define the effects on people of the emotive knowledge created through ABIs and help to distinguish how managers can engage people's human nature. It is fundamental to stress that the boundaries between these categories are fuzzy. Therefore the impact of ABIs on people has to be understood in a composite way. In other words, the value categories have to be integrated, recognising both their scalability, i.e., the different levels of intensity of the impact of the arts-based experiences on people's attitudes and behaviours, and their additional nature, i.e., the possibility to have a synergetic combination of effects.

Regarding organisational infrastructure, the impact of ABIs is grounded in the recognition that any tangible and intangible organisational element can be seen as a human artefact, i.e., the product of people's knowledge actions. As such, it projects and embeds human knowledge that is made up of emotive and rational dimensions. ABIs allow the manipulation of the aesthetic properties of organisational artefacts, so they are capable of affecting the emotional and energetic features characterising the tangible and intangible organisational elements. The Arts Value Matrix conceptually recognises the power of art forms to shape and influence the emotional and energetic characteristics of organisational artefacts that, consequently, generate aesthetic experiences for people both within and outside an organisation. The manipulation of the aesthetic properties of organisational infrastructure contributes to humanising the organisation, i.e., to making the organisation both a better place where people can express and put into action their passions, and a system that recognises that its real mission is the generation of wealth for people.

The Arts Value Matrix translates the impact of ABIs into organisational benefits. In analysing these benefits, it is important to take into account that each organisation is a complex system made up of tangible and intangible artefacts that are linked to each other by bundles of dependent and interdependent relationships. Thus, it is likely that the manipulation of one organisational dimension affects other elements of the system. This means that, although an ABI can specifically address one focused tangible or intangible organisational asset, the effects can spread to other components. Then, when tracking the effects on the development of organisational infrastructure it is important to take into account that ABIs can generate multiple benefits. Then an ABI can simultaneously activate different organisational value-drivers as mapped in the Arts Value Matrix. This means that the nature of the impact of ABIs tends to be polyvalent. Hence, an ABI does not produce a straightforward impact and benefit, but rather it has a polyvalent impact on people and infrastructure. Accordingly, the Arts Value Matrix supports the identification of the strategic intents grounding the adoption of ABIs so that managers can understand what value-drivers they want to affect.

Which impact, or combination of impacts, is best for an organisation? That depends on the strategic and operational goals motivating the adoption of ABIs. Ideally, starting from the origin of the Arts Value Matrix's axis and moving along its two sides, the impact of an ABI on people and infrastructure tends to be more intense and broad. The polyvalent nature of ABIs means that, though the adoption of an ABI can be essentially focused on a specific objective, it tends to generate multiple spill-over benefits. Moreover, the benefits related to people and to the organisational infrastructure are likely to converge. In that instance, an ABI can primarily benefit the organisational infrastructure, and subsequently have an impact on people; vice versa it can generate, at the beginning, a benefit for people and then have an impact on the tangible and/or intangible organisational infrastructural components. Therefore the nine categories of the Arts Value Matrix have to be considered as not mutually exclusive.

The polyvalent impact of ABIs: the case of 'RE:creation' at PricewaterhouseCoopers

A case study illustrating the importance of recognising the polyvalent nature of ABIs is provided by 'RE:creation', an arts-based management action designed and delivered by The MAP Consortium for PricewaterhouseCoopers (PwC). This addressed 750 staff of PwC Financial Services Assurance's (FSA's) Southwark Towers base. The company had multiple objectives associated with the ABI. They wanted to ensure that the organisational environment would transform in such a way to be able to attract and retain the right people. They wanted to unlock their employees' creative energy and inspire and challenge people to think and act differently, during a period when accounting regulations were changing and staff were required to adapt to new working practices. They wanted to build a climate of communication that was open and honest. The arts were identified as a management instrument to support the organisational transformation mainly impacting on people's attitudes, behaviours and skills. The MAP Consortium was brought in to devise an integrated set of ABIs that took place during one year through three main projects. One project aimed at changing their approach to client team meetings. The goal was to improve the efficiency and effectiveness of the meetings. Client teams represent a crucial dimension of PwC FSA's operation, but team members generally operate in different office buildings and mainly communicate virtually. The client team meeting is the time when the whole team comes together to share information and assess progress. With a crowded agenda and with up to fifty people attending, the challenge is to ensure that everyone's contribution is heard during the meetings, and that the event would remain positive and forward looking. The MAP Consortium used rehearsal room techniques to encourage collaboration and concise expression and the team was also taken 'off-site' and into an arts environment. The arts-based interventions basically operated as instruments to achieve a twofold objective. On the one hand, using the rehearsal technique, people were trained on how to provide and receive concise feedback in order to enhance their communication skills. On the other hand, the arts-based experiences created an opportunity to bond people and reflect the deep human nature of their relationships and of the organisation. In this regard one of PwC's partners commented: 'I know it sounds strange but I think the significant thing is that we have become more human with each other. We spend most of our daily lives in each other's company; it's very powerful to begin to have a sense of the full resource of the team in human terms.' Thus the arts-based project, though focused on client team meetings, produced benefits that can be accounted in four dimensions of the Arts Value Matrix: learning and development, networking, galvanising and inspiration.

Another project was defined with the aim of creating a sense of identity. PwC FSA operates on the basis of a group system that aims to connect people on an administrative, social and support level. So everyone at PwC, from partners to new joiners, belongs to a group led by a senior manager. The challenge was to create cohesive units of these groups whose members have busy schedules and are often out at client offices. The MAP Consortium placed artists as associates in six of the groups to explore how to transform these groups and create a sense of identity. Artists worked with their groups in different ways by creating bespoke ABIs based on visual arts, film-making and visits to galleries to aid communication and strengthen connections within the group. The activities culminated with the ABI named 'Re:play festival' where groups could share some of their work, including musical performances and a giant 'PwC Pollock' action painting. The 'Re:creation' team of artists also gave a performance that reflected their findings and experiences of working in the building, and thus a sense of identity with PwC FSA staff. The benefits produced by this project can be mapped in the Arts Value Matrix at three main dimensions as follows: networking, environment and transformation. The ABI helped to break down the barriers between the different groups by stimulating a better interactive and communication capacity. In addition the arts-based activities fostered the creation of a positive organisational atmosphere, changing and nurturing the sense of identity. Further, the project was energising and provided an opportunity for self-reflection and self-assessment.

The third arts-based project was focused on leadership awareness. The focus was mainly on learning and development with the purpose of transforming good managers into leaders. The MAP Consortium devised ABIs aimed at providing practical experience of leadership. In particular every participant gained experience of leading a team of their peers, revealing the areas that needed to be changed and developed. This project provided benefits in terms of skills development for leading a group, but also contributed to assess and enhance the organisational team-building culture with a positive impact on organisational renovation.

The above examples show how an ABI can generate benefits that can be mapped simultaneously in different categories of the Arts Value Map. Therefore the Arts Value Matrix has to be adopted as a framework to identify and analyse the strategic intents for the managerial implementation of ABIs. It can help managers and arts providers to understand how ABIs can impact on organisational value-drivers that activate cause-and-effect chains, ultimately impacting on business performance.

Strategic intents of ABIs: the four value zones of the arts

The intersection of the intensity of ABIs' impact on people and on organisational infrastructure defines the strategic intents of the management adoption of the arts for organisational development purposes. Measuring the intensity of the impact of ABIs on people and infrastructure as simply 'low' and 'high', it is possible to define, as shown in Figure 3.4, a framework that identifies four main strategic reasons underpinning the management adoption of the arts for business

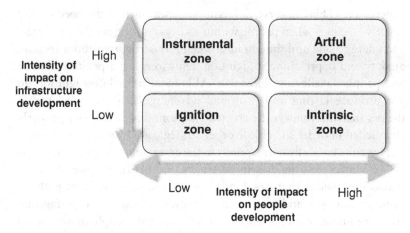

3.4 The four value zones of the arts

purposes. The framework is built on four quadrants representing strategic value zones that can be defined as follows: 'ignition zone', 'intrinsic zone', 'instrumental zone' and 'artful zone'. These value zones overlap with the organisational value-drivers mapped by the Arts Value Matrix, though they offer a different kind of understanding of the role and relevance of ABIs. The goal of the four value zones of the arts is to denote the fundamental strategic intents at the basis of the adoption of ABIs in organisations. They explain the utilitarian role of the arts in management and denote the main strategic focus of ABIs. According to the framework, organisations can adopt the arts as a management means to deal with business issues having in mind four fundamental strategic goals. Managers can implement ABIs with the strategic intent to ignite emotions and energy in and around the organisation. Alternatively, they can adopt ABIs as a means to create instrumental value or intrinsic value. When the focus is on the transformation and development of the organisation by levering the properties of art forms, then the adoption of ABIs responds to an artful strategic intent.

Ignition zone – ABIs in the ignition zone have a low level of impact both on people and infrastructure. Their strategic goal is to activate an organisation's interest around an issue or simply to entertain the organisation's employees. ABIs defined with the strategic intent of igniting are aimed at triggering feelings in people. They fundamentally aim to spark emotions and energy that create pleasurable and joyful experiences. This can serve different purposes, such as the need to face negative feelings when people within an organisation set their passions and energy aside and the organisational infrastructure echoes tedium, anxiety and depression. So, ignition helps to spark a positive climate and people's wellbeing. However, ABIs focusing only on ignition do not produce lasting and profound advantages for either people or the organisation, unless the created emotions and energy are properly channelled in order to achieve other strategic goals besides ignition.

This zone basically corresponds to the entertainment area of the Arts Value Matrix and denotes those effects of ABIs that ignite emotions and energy states that are fundamentally positive, such as enthusiasm, passion, joy and happiness. However, it is worth stressing that ABIs are unconventional and the involvement of people in arts-based experiences can put them in a new and different context, encouraging them to get out of their comfort zone. This means that ABIs can be challenging and may provoke uncomfortable feelings.

Generally, for organisational purposes in order to be successful an ABI has to be an enjoyable experience. This means that it has to be able to engage employees primarily at an emotional and energetic level. Successful ABIs show this common denominator. Ignition is therefore a starting point from which to progress and move people's experiences towards the intrinsic and/or artful zone. For example, the engagement of people at Television, for absorbing new values and building a new culture, was based on the ignition of energy. Indeed, the forum theatre implemented to create and share a new culture was able to capture people's interest and attention because it was, as underlined by all the participants, first and foremost pleasant and enjoyable. Employees reported that 'the acting was hilarious and very inclusive. The forum theatre approach was very engaging. The way it was presented was funny and thought-provoking'. A further example of the ignition power of ABIs is the use of the percussion symphony workshop at Blue Circle Industries. Even if the ABI addressed a traditional human resource management development activity, i.e., team-building and communication, participants found the overall experience deeply different, unusual and unique, with a fundamental underlying feature: the percussion sessions were fun, humorous, invigorating, enjoyable, lively, physical and active. As stated by a participant: 'I really liked the metaphorical use of the arts to convey a message, it was fun, it was engaging.' Thus ignition is fundamentally a common feature of all

ABIs that by their very nature are capable of triggering emotional and energetic dynamics.

Intrinsic zone – ABIs in this zone have a high intensity impact on people, while their influence on organisational infrastructure development is marginal. Their strategic intent is to engage people and nourish their emotions and energy. At this level ABIs lever personal pleasure, and create a sense of satisfaction and inner value. They are able to arouse personal emotional and energetic dynamics that modify people's perception of the reality, galvanising and inspiring them. The adoption of ABIs as an intrinsic management means allows organisations to stimulate and marshal personal positive emotions and mental energy that drives good moods and enhances the ability to think in a more flexible and complex way. ABIs create intrinsic value by affecting the development of people's psychological traits. In particular, four main dimensions of the personal psychological strength can be positively influenced by ABIs, they are: *self-efficacy*, which stands for the belief that one has mastery over the events of one's life and can meet challenges as they come up – this drives hope and optimism; *self-awareness*, which corresponds to the awareness of one's own emotions and to be able to recognise emotional mood; *emotional display*, which represents the ability to shape emotions by adopting different strategies based on the minimisation, exaggeration or substitution of emotions; and *flow*, which represents the particular state of mind during which excellence becomes effortless and the person is absorbed in the moment. Each of the above personal psychological traits affects people's attitudes and behaviours with an impact on their propensity and capacity to take decisions, perform actions, and cope with the complexity of the reality around them and with difficult times.

Instrumental zone – ABIs in the instrumental zone have a high level of impact on the organisational infrastructure, while the direct influence on people tends to be low. This zone mainly denotes the strategic use of art forms to increase the value incorporated into tangible and intangible assets of an organisation. ABIs are deployed as a tool to raise the reputation of the organisation, or to produce economic benefits in terms of increasing the value embedded into products. The benefits related to the adoption of ABIs for sponsorship and investment goals, as identified in the Arts Value Matrix, fall into this value zone.

Artful zone – ABIs in the artful zone have a high intensity impact on both people and organisational infrastructure. In this zone the generated benefits are the result of a convergence of the impact of art experiences on people and on organisational infrastructure. This zone denotes the impact of those ABIs which allow an organisation to absorb and show arts features through its tangible and intangible structural components. In addition, it encourages people to open up to and expand upon, a new awareness and understanding of themselves and of the reality around them on the basis of a deep personal experience grounded in the arousal and development of emotional and energetic states. ABIs mapped in the artful zone are able to integrate people change and organisational infrastructure development, which drives the organisation's transformation. The benefits related to environment, learning and personal development, networking and transformation are included in the artful zone. Among others, some of the effects of ABIs mapped in the artful zone are: change in the organisational environment and atmosphere; enhancement of people's skills and attitudes; modification and improvement of people's behaviours; development of relationships and of a networking approach; recognition, absorption and sharing of an organisation's new values and ethics; development of social processes; and more generally an evolution of the organisation.

In Figure 3.5 the overlapping of the above four value zones with the Arts Value Matrix is depicted. This associates the strategic intent of the use of the arts with the organisational value-drivers characterising the adoption of ABIs.

Conclusion

The managerial use of the arts can help management to transform organisations. By managing aesthetic dimensions ABIs can develop people and organisational infrastructure. This can produce a wide range of benefits that have an impact on the organisational value-creation capacity. In order to help managers to understand the potential benefits of the use of arts in organisations, the Arts Value Matrix classifies the potential effects of ABIs. It identifies the organisational value-drivers that can be affected by the managerial deployment of ABIs. They explain the management reasons grounding the adoption of ABIs, providing a conceptual basis for managers to clarify the value purposes that can be addressed by arts-based management actions. On the other hand, the four value zones delineate the strategic intents of

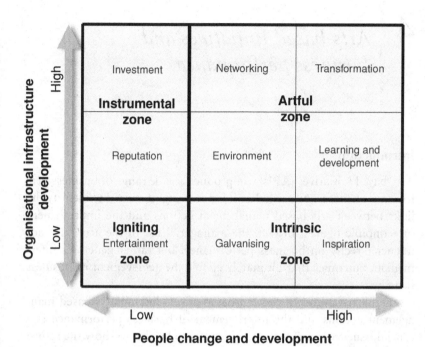

3.5 Overlapping the four value zones of the arts with the Arts Value Matrix

ABIs. An ABI can act as an instrument merely to ignite positive feelings within and around an organisation, or can be deployed to support the creation of intrinsic benefits for people or instrumental advances of organisation's structural assets; or it can address an artful development of organisational components. The understanding of the value purposes of ABIs for business defines the informative background to identify and assess the links between the adoption of ABIs, the enhancement of organisational value-creation capacity and the improvement of business performance.

4 | Arts-based Initiatives and business performance

Introduction

Arts-based Initiatives (ABIs) can produce a wide range of business performance benefits. Nevertheless it is not straightforward to identify the links between arts-based management actions and the improvement of economic figures. In fact, the managerial use of the arts does not impact directly on business performance, but rather generates intermediate outcomes that ultimately enable the achievement of business benefits.

The identification of the cause-and-effects linking arts-based management actions and the improvement of business performance is a crucial issue for management, which has to be able to show the return on investment in ABIs. For this reason, it is essential to provide an answer to the following question: *How is it possible to assess the impact of ABIs on the improvement of business performance?* This is a key question in proving the value of using the arts for business purposes and accounting for the benefits of adopting ABIs in management.

The starting point for understanding the influence of ABIs on business performance improvements is the recognition of the transformational power of art forms. As illustrated in Chapter 3, the managerial deployment of the arts allows the development of organisational components. By managing aesthetic experiences and properties, ABIs can support the development of employees and organisational infrastructure, activating cause-and-effect chains that ultimately produce impacts on business performance.

The focus of this chapter is the investigation of how ABIs are linked to business performance. In order to explain how ABIs produce business benefits, a knowledge-based view is adopted, assuming that ABIs produce positive effects on the achievement of operational and strategic objectives because they affect the features and content of organisational knowledge domains. Through ABIs it is possible to handle people's aesthetic experiences and to manipulate the aesthetic properties of organisational infrastructure in order to catalyse and create emotive knowledge. ABIs can act either as a learning platform and a device to spark and nourish emotive knowledge in people, or as a vector to incorporate emotive knowledge into organisational infrastructure. This means that the deployment of ABIs changes the knowledge characteristics of an organisation and activates organisational learning and knowledge management processes that allow the synergetic integration of emotive and technical knowledge.

The core mechanism translating the implementation of ABIs into business performance improvements is the development of organisational knowledge assets that in turn affect organisational capabilities. The enhancement of organisational capabilities is the intermediate outcome of improving business performance as they enable an organisation to better deliver value to organisational stakeholders.

This chapter analyses the links between ABIs and knowledge assets, outlining how the arts can transform the characteristics of organisational knowledge domains and stimulate the creation of emotive knowledge. The organisation's knowledge asset categories related to people and organisational infrastructure are identified, and a knowledge-based taxonomy for their analysis is proposed. This taxonomy defines the conceptual basis of the Arts Benefits Constellation: a model to assess the impact of ABIs on organisational knowledge dimensions. The goal of this model is to provide managers with a framework for understanding how to measure the effects of ABIs on organisational components, taking into account that they represent the building blocks of organisational capabilities. The transformational effects of ABIs on people and organisational infrastructure are then identified as a 'trigger' to activate organisational development dynamics that ultimately have an impact on business performance. The analysis of the cause-and-effect chains activated by ABIs that have an impact on business performance is carried out through the Arts Value Map. This model adopts a mapping visualisation technique to assess the business performance benefits generated by ABIs. Most importantly, it allows an integration of ABIs in the operation and strategy of an organisation, and can be adopted as a descriptive and/or normative framework.

ABIs and organisational knowledge assets: emotive knowledge and artful workers

As discussed in the previous chapters, with the adoption of ABIs managers can affect the aesthetic dimensions of an organisation. Art forms can be deployed both to activate people's aesthetic experiential dynamics and to shape the aesthetic characteristics of tangible and intangible organisational infrastructure. By harnessing aesthetic dimensions, ABIs are capable of generating emotive knowledge, stimulating and affecting the working mechanisms of the personal emotive mind. This knowledge is related to the human senses and denotes the emotive and energetic dimensions of knowing. Emotive knowledge can be considered opposite to technical knowledge, though they work in an integrated and synergetic manner.

Emotive knowledge

Emotive knowledge is the result of the emotive mind and stands for how people feel, their emotions and energy levels in what they do; while rational knowledge is seen as attached to the rational mind and represents the logical and analytic way of performing actions.

From a managerial point of view, emotive knowledge has a twofold relevance. First, it is a crucial factor affecting the quality and productivity of people's actions, because it is a factor having an effect on the passion that people put into their actions. Second, emotive knowledge is a fundamental dimension in building the intangible value incorporated into organisational products and infrastructure. This considers that any organisation's tangible and intangible infrastructural artefacts can be defined so that they are able to provoke emotional arousal. Consequently, emotive knowledge, from a practical standpoint, when related to artefacts corresponds with the attributes that form and characterise an organisation's infrastructure from an emotive point of view. It is fundamentally what moves people's feelings.

At the people level, the use of art forms as a management means creates aesthetic experiences that can activate and lever people's emotional faculties affecting the creation of knowledge that pertains to their senses. This can, in particular, help people to discover and develop their inner reality, affecting the nature of their involvement in everyday work activities. Through ABIs people can learn how to perform actions as a result of a synergetic combination of their emotive and rational faculties. ABIs can support people to find out how to carry out working activities by deploying know-how, i.e., the best logical way of doing things, and what can be labelled as 'know-feel', that is, the ability to be positively in touch with feelings and capable of deploying emotions when performing actions and activities.

By experiencing art forms, people can appreciate and learn the energy and benefits of employing in an integrated manner rational thinking and emotional abilities in order to better deal with challenges, solve problems and make decisions. People can learn not only how to put their emotions and energy into practice, but also the intrinsic personal advantages of doing so. This means that by merging know-how and know-feel, people can be centred in what they do (Richards, 1989). This makes them highly efficient, happy and engaged.

In practice, the balanced combination and integration of the rational and emotive mind gives people the competence to be adaptable, imaginative and resilient. This is the essence of a new kind of worker that can be labelled as the 'artful worker'.

Artful workers

The concept of the artful worker is proposed with the intent of denoting a new 'species' of employee that better meets the twenty-first century organisation's need to navigate the new complex and unpredictable business landscape. Artful workers are knowledgeable as assumed by the concept of knowledge workers (Drucker, 1999), but at the same time are also engaged in what they do and are capable of engaging others through their actions. They are people who are able to combine and deploy rational and emotive knowledge in their jobs. They are proficient in knowing how to do activities, but also how to feel when performing activities. Although different factors may contribute to turning ordinary employees into artful workers, the thesis here is that ABIs are fundamental instruments to help people and organisations to discover and apply the ingredients and actions that create an artful worker.

Embedding emotive knowledge into organisational infrastructure

At the infrastructure level, ABIs can act as a vector to incorporate emotive knowledge traits into organisational assets that in turn have an influence on people's experiences. In fact, ABIs can manipulate the aesthetic properties of organisational infrastructure components shaping their emotive facets. In this case, the arts are adopted as a management device to embed emotive and energetic attributes into organisational structures, so that they are able to touch, engage and evoke people's feelings. Emotive knowledge can be embedded in both tangible and intangible assets. Indeed, unless considering natural resources, any organisation's structural component can be interpreted as a cognitive artefact. In other words, any dimension of an organisation can be seen as the output of an individual or collective application of knowledge and/or as made of a knowledge substance.

The knowledge features incorporated into organisational infrastructure components can be essentially distinguished, on the basis of people's knowledge traits as follows: rational/technical and emotive knowledge. As a result, I propose an interpretation of an organisational infrastructure as a collection of cognitive artefacts incorporating knowledge features resulting from the application of know-how and know-feel. The 'know-how' denotes the knowledge characteristics related to explaining how an organisational asset, from an analytical and systemic standpoint, works and is made in order to perform a function or a task. Instead, the latter represents the knowledge associated with the emotional features of an organisational asset and defines its capacity to spark and nourish emotional and energetic dynamics in people. Thus, an organisation's infrastructural assets can be characterised in terms of their rational and emotive knowledge dimensions.

The identification of the existence and relevance of emotive knowledge attributes a strategic role to ABIs that represents the main instruments to create and affect the emotive and energetic attributes of organisational assets.

The importance of emotive knowledge and the role of the arts

During the twentieth century, the principles of the industrial era pushed the focus of attention onto rationality, disregarding the arts as a possible production factor. Progressively the arts have been seen as something to enjoy, but not useful in industrial manufacturing and business activities (Richards, 1995). The arts were separated from work and products. The recognition of emotive knowledge as an important facet characterising both people's working activities and the properties of organisational infrastructure points out that art forms have a critical role to play. The deployment of the arts can improve both knowledge domains grounding how employees work in organisations, making their working activities engaging, fulfilling and joyful, and the knowledge dimensions characterising an organisation's infrastructural components, particularly developing their incorporated intangible value dimensions. In other words, the arts can be deployed as a strategic management means to develop organisational knowledge assets domains. This means that the analysis of the impact of ABIs on business performance can be investigated adopting a knowledge-based view.

A knowledge-based interpretation of the impact of ABIs

The explanation of how ABIs can enhance organisational value-creation capacity is related to the power of art forms to develop organisational knowledge domains characterising an organisation. In particular, the creation of emotive knowledge allows a transformation of the organisational knowledge assets grounding the competencies and capabilities of an organisation that in turn affects the organisational value-creation (Amit and Schoemaker, 1993; Hill and Jones, 1992; Hitt *et al.*, 1999).[1] This interpretation is grounded on insights from strategic management literature, suggesting that organisational resources can be distinguished between traditional resources and strategically valuable resources. This distinction can be traced back to two fundamental micro-economic strategic approaches: the resource-based view and the competence- or capabilities-based view. These approaches argue that institutions searching for a sustainable competitive position have to control and develop resources characterised by heterogeneity and immobility. In particular, the resource-based view stresses that resources are a source of sustainable competitive advantage if they are hard to transfer and accumulate, rare, not substitutable, idiosyncratic in nature, synergistic and not consumable because of their use (Barney, 1991; Peteraf, 1993; Teece *et al.*, 1997; Wernerfelt, 1984). Thus, an organisation can strategically differentiate itself, in the competitive arena, both by the inimitability and imperfect substitutability of its specific resources and by its competencies and capabilities (Amit and Schoemaker, 1993; Davemport and Prusak, 1998). The underlying assumption is that organisational value-creation capacity is derived from organisational competencies and capabilities that are strictly idiosyncratic and accumulated over time (Dierickx and Cool, 1989). They are rooted into knowledge and learning processes taking place in organisations (Iansiti and Clark, 1994; Leonard-Barton, 1995). On this track of research, the competence- or capability-based view stresses that an organisation can be interpreted as a portfolio of specific specialised know-how and abilities and its value-creation capacity is based on the development of core competencies, absorptive capacity and dynamic capabilities (Prahalad and Hamel, 1990; Stalk *et al.*, 1992). Therefore organisations that want to improve their value-creation capacity have to focus on the development of distinctive competencies and capabilities that can differentiate the organisation in the competitive arena.

The resource-based view and the competence-based view are two integrated strategic approaches and can be summarised by the knowledge-based theory of an organisation (Grant, 1996a, 1997; Spender, 1996; Spender and Grant, 1996). This more comprehensive strategic view suggests that knowledge is the critical source for organisational growth and competitiveness. Knowledge is both a resource and a source of organisational value creation, and represents the building blocks of organisational competencies and capabilities.

Adopting the knowledge-based approach, the relevance of an organisational resource is related either to its embedded knowledge or to its role of stimulating and sustaining knowledge process dynamics. Hence, the strategic organisational resources can be interpreted and analysed as entities embodying critical knowledge and/or as catalysts of cognitive dynamics. This means that the assessment of organisational knowledge resources provides twofold information. On the one hand, the accounting and understanding of organisational knowledge resources, as a stock of assets, contributes to defining the value of an organisation. On the other hand, the assessment of organisational knowledge domains provides information about the potential organisational capacity to use resources to perform tasks and activities, i.e., the organisational capabilities and competencies that define the pillars of value-creation mechanisms.

To denote the strategic organisational knowledge resources grounding the organisational capacity to create value, the notion of knowledge assets has been used in the management literature (Boisot, 1998; Marr and Schiuma, 2001; Nonaka *et al.*, 2000a, 2000b; Teece, 1998, 2000). It stands for those strategic organisational knowledge resources driving and defining the value of an organisational system.[2] Accordingly, the notion of knowledge assets denotes any strategic organisational resource made of or incorporating knowledge that grounds competencies and capabilities to carry out and/or review a process or a function with the aim of creating and/or delivering value.

The adoption of the knowledge-based approach has two main implications for the rationale of this book. First, the impact of ABIs on organisational components can be assessed in terms of their effects on the development of organisational knowledge assets. Second, ABIs affect business performance through their capacity to develop knowledge assets that in turn drive the enhancement of organisational value-creation capacity and the organisational ability to achieve business performance improvements. Therefore, recognising that ABIs represent a management means of developing organisational knowledge assets, the assessment of their impact corresponds with understanding the knowledge assets dimensions that are affected by the managerial adoption of art forms. For this reason, in the next section, first an analysis of the main categories of organisational resources is introduced, and then adopting a knowledge-based view of organisational components, a taxonomy of the knowledge assets characterising an organisation, is proposed.

The organisational resources

ABIs can affect the development of employees and organisational infrastructure. In order to discern the impact of ABIs on the elements of an organisation, it is worth identifying the main categories of organisational resources characterising an organisation. According to Barney (1991), organisational resources can be conveniently classified into three categories: physical capital resources, which include the physical technology used in an organisation, the organisational plant and equipment, its geographic location and its access to raw materials; human capital resources, which include the training, experience, judgement, intelligence, relationships and insight of individual managers and workers in an organisation; and organisational capital resources, which include formal reporting relations among groups within the organisation and between the organisation and those in its environment. Moving from this classification, on the basis of a systematic review of the key outlets of scholarly research in the management field, four main categories of organisational resources can be distinguished (Carlucci and Schiuma, 2007); they are: human capital, social capital, stakeholder capital and organisational or structural capital. Below, each category is introduced addressing its main content.

Human capital

The concept of human capital is derived from human management theory (Becker, 1964; Schultz, 1961). The focus of this theory is the individual within the organisation. Leana and Van Buren III (1999) define human capital as people's knowledge and technical ability. DeFilippi and Arthur (1998) describe human capital as people's skills. Dess and Picken (2000) and Youndt et al. (2004) state that human capital consists of organisational people's capabilities, knowledge, skills and experiences. Pennings et al. (1998) argue that the human capital of an organisation is the knowledge and skills of its professionals. Bolino et al. (2002) argue that human capital is reflected by education, training or experience of people, while Burt (1997) interprets human capital as the quality of individuals. In summary, it is possible to assume that human capital is a holistic concept that represents those abilities that are related to employees. It includes the knowledge, skills, intellect, attitudes, talents and behaviours of people working for an organisation. Some of the main components of human capital are people's dimensions such as: know-how, expertise, problem-solving capability, innovation aptitude, teamwork propensity, productivity, formal training and education, learning competence, leadership and management ability, and generally the ability to accept and manage change. These resources represent fundamental factors affecting the value-creation capacity of an organisation.

Many scholars have stressed that an increase in employees' skills, knowledge and abilities most likely translates into an improvement in organisational performance (Berg, 1969; Dutta et al., 2002). When people possess high levels of knowledge and skills they can perform work activities in an effective and efficient way; can generate new ideas and techniques that can be embodied in production equipment and processes; initiate changes in production and service delivery methods; and improve their relational capabilities both internally to the organisation and externally.

Social capital

The concept of social capital was popularised by Putnam (1993, 1995), and recently has been applied to denote a broader range of social phenomena (Fischer and Pollock, 2004). This conceptual category was originally used by social theorists to denote relational resources embedded in cross-cutting personal ties for the development of individuals in communities (Jacobs, 1961; Loury, 1977). With specific reference to micro-organisations, the concept of social capital has been interpreted in accordance with an inner and an outer perspective. Leana and Van Buren III (1999: 538) propose a conceptualisation of social capital 'as a resource reflecting the character of social relations within the firm. Organisational social capital is realised through members' levels of collective goal orientation and shared trust, which creates value by facilitating successful collective action. Organisational social capital is an asset that can benefit both the organisation (e.g., creating value for shareholders) and its members (e.g., enhancing employee skills)'. While, from an outer perspective, Pennings *et al.* (1998) interpret social capital as the relationships supporting the creation of ties between the organisation and other economic actors, and particularly potential customers. So, social capital can be interpreted as the network of relationships between people within and outside an organisation.

The role of social capital as an important factor affecting organisational value-creation capacity has been already addressed in the management literature (Anand *et al.*, 2002; Tsai, 2000). In this regard, Nahapiet and Ghoshal (1998) highlight that social capital increases the efficiency of organisational actions, while other scholars have pointed out the position of social capital in improving people-related dimensions affecting organisational value-creation mechanisms (Adler and Kwon, 2002; Leana and Van Buren III, 1999).

Stakeholder capital

Stakeholder capital fundamentally represents a subset of social capital. Consistent with the stakeholder-based view, stakeholder capital denotes the relationships between an organisation and its stakeholders (Donaldson and Preston, 1995; Jawahar and McLaughlin, 2001). In the management literature it is often considered equivalent to relational capital (Ireland *et al.*, 2002), customer capital (Bontis, 1998; Pennings *et al.*, 1998) or external social capital (Chung *et al.*, 2000; Fischer and

Pollock, 2004; Koka and Prescott, 2002). On the basis of the conceptualisations offered in the management literature, stakeholder capital can be considered as the network of relationships linking an organisation to its external actors. It is complementary with the notion of social capital and together represents all the possible networking relationships characterising an organisation.

Organisational and structural capital

Consistent with the management literature, organisational capital and structural capital can be considered, essentially, as interchangeable concepts. Bontis (1998) refers to structural capital as all mechanisms and structures that can help employees to better deploy their cognitive resources and improve organisational performance. Other scholars point out that structural capital consists of organisational know-how that is incorporated into routines or rules embedding tacit knowledge as well as culture (Ambrosini and Bowman, 2001; Nelson and Winter, 1982). In particular, routines act as the 'glue' for organisations and contribute to enhancing cooperative working for the creation of new knowledge (Rumelt, 1984), while culture identifies the way of interpreting and approaching things within an organisation. It represents the beliefs, attitudes of mind and customs, language, values, learning mechanisms, habits of behaviour and thought, to which people are exposed within an organisation (Bontis, 1998; Hall, 1992). Winter (1987) refers to structural capital as the 'intellect of the organisation'. Youndt *et al.* (2004) state that organisational capital represents institutionalised knowledge and codified experience stored in databases, routines, patents, manuals, structures and the like. On the basis of the different interpretations, organisational or structural capital can be conceptualised as the overall tangible and intangible organisational resources that build the infrastructure of an organisation in order to perform its business processes. It mainly includes: routines, procedures and rules, patents and licences, organisational facilities, operating systems, equipment and machinery, information and communication technologies, software, systems for resource acquisition, development and allocation, performance measurement systems, organisational culture, image and identity, leadership and management philosophy and, more generally, business models.

Structural capital is a key dimension of organisational value-creation capacity. It defines the platform for an organisation's working actitivities to take place and forms the essential sub-stratum for the growth and exploitation of human capital, social capital and stakeholder capital.

The identification of the above organisational resource categories represents the conceptual background to defining a taxonomy of organisational knowledge assets that can map and assess the impact of ABIs on the development of organisational knowledge dimensions.

The Knoware Tree: a taxonomy to map organisational knowledge assets

In order to define a taxonomy of organisational knowledge assets, it is important to start from the acknowledgement that, in accordance with a knowledge-based view, organisational resources can be interpreted and analysed on the basis of their knowledge-based nature. The underlying premise is that knowledge represents the fundamental discriminating dimension characterising any organisational resource. Indeed, whatever an organisation uses or produces can be considered as the result of the application and/or codification of knowledge, or that it is made of knowledge, i.e., information endowed with interpretation and function.[3]

In order to denote the knowledge-based nature of organisational knowledge assets, the notion of 'knoware' is adopted (Schiuma *et al.*, 2008a). This notion aims to highlight that any tangible or intangible organisational component can be interpreted as an artefact made up of and/or embodying knowledge, resulting from individual or collective cognitive activities. Adopting this conceptual category and sharing the basic hypotheses of the frameworks introduced in the management literature to classify knowledge-based resources, the Knoware Tree is proposed as a framework for classifying organisational knowledge assets (Schiuma *et al.*, 2008a, 2008b).[4] As depicted in Figure 4.1, the Knoware Tree proposes a taxonomy of organisational knowledge assets. It is grounded in the knowledge-based view and, accordingly, considers both intangible and tangible assets as organisational resources incorporating knowledge. This is a distinguishing feature of

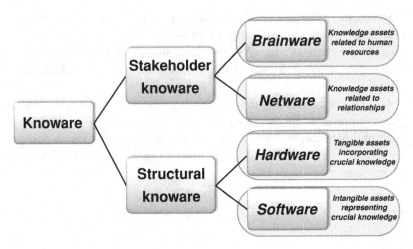

4.1 The Knoware Tree

the framework because most of the management literature identifies knowledge resources with intangible assets. This represents a limitation not only because the tangible assets significantly contribute to defining the competencies of an organisation, but also because they strongly affect the intangible assets through a web of interdependencies linking the overall organisation's resources.[5] Of course not all the tangible assets should be considered knowledge assets. The attention has to be focused on those that have an important interplay with intangible resources. Tangible assets affect the characteristics of intangible assets, and vice versa. The intangible assets influence both the employment and the development/acquisition of tangible assets.

The Knoware Tree distinguishes two essential strategic dimensions in building an organisation: organisational people, or stakeholders, and the organisation's infrastructural components, or structural resources. According to a knowledge-based view, these two dimensions correspond to two macro-categories of knowledge assets defining an organisation and its working mechanisms, as follows: the knowledge assets related to organisational stakeholders, named 'stakeholder knoware', and the knowledge assets associated with organisational infrastructure, named 'structural knoware'. These two knowledge assets macro-categories can be further divided into other sub-categories, specifically: 'brainware' and 'netware' for stakeholder knoware, and 'hardware' and 'software' for structural knoware. It is here proposed the use of these four categories to provide a classification of organisational knowledge resources. Below, the characteristics of each typology are outlined.

The notion 'brainware' is a conceptual category denoting the knowledge assets that are related to the human capital resources of an organisation. It intends to represent the knowledge resulting from people's brain capacity. Some of these knowledge assets include: innovation capability, imagination and creativity, experience, teamwork propensity, leadership, flexibility, tolerance of ambiguity and uncertainty, motivation and satisfaction, learning capability, loyalty and commitment, skills and expertise, and problem-solving capability.

Brainware characterises all possible knowledge assets that are embedded by organisational people and are manifested through their actions and behaviours. Traditionally, organisations have mainly focused their attention on rational capabilities, i.e., on people's know-how that drives the development and application of technical knowledge. The specialised know-how of people is fundamental for the success of an organisation, but in today's business landscape it has to be integrated with people's emotional capabilities. People's attitudes and behaviours are strictly influenced by people's know-feel that denotes people's ability to engage emotions and energy in what they do. Therefore, the brainware category essentially gathers two typologies of people's knowledge assets: those related to the specialised know-how or technical knowledge, and those associated with soft abilities or emotive knowledge.

The 'netware' category represents the set of knowledge assets associated with the social and the stakeholder capital of an organisation. It stands for the knowledge incorporated and/or related to the relationships of an organisation. In particular, netware denotes the networking dynamics activated by organisational people both within and outside organisational boundaries. The internal networking dynamics involve the interactions between employees and managers as well as the relationships between teams and internal communities, while the external relationships represent all the possible ties linking an organisation to the actors in the economic, production and socio-cultural environment. In particular, the external relationships include the networking dynamics with customers, suppliers, institutions, local community and society at large.

Netware not only accounts for the nature of the relationships, but also their traits. It also includes dimensions such as the quality, content and density of relationships. For example, important traits of the networking dynamics are: the quality and content of the information channelled into the relationships, the stability of the relationships, the level of coordination and mutual understanding between the actors involved in the relationships and the trust embedded in the relationships.

The 'hardware' category includes all structural assets that embed strategic knowledge and/or represent important organisational instruments for knowledge management processes, which includes in particular, knowledge development, acquisition, codification, transfer and application. The fundamental idea at the basis of this knowledge asset category is that tangible assets are physical artefacts that are made of knowledge. Thus, tangible assets not only significantly contribute to defining the organisational knowledge domains, but they also play an important role in stimulating and supporting knowledge creating processes in organisations. Hardware gathers all organisational tangible assets that significantly contribute to defining organisational competencies. It embraces dimensions such as operation technologies, facilities, structural layout, information and communication technologies, equipment and any other context specific tangible assets. A further typology of organisational knowledge assets that can be put in the hardware category is the set of localised territory-specific tangible assets that generate positive externalities and, most importantly, incorporate social knowledge and represent and shape a community's culture and behaviours.

Finally, the 'software' category represents the structural assets having an intangible nature. They indicate the intangible artefacts incorporating critical knowledge for the organisation. Some important knowledge assets included in this category are: routines, internal practices, procedures and rules, operating systems, processes and task design, decision processes and information flows, incentives, management systems, culture, leadership, climate and management style. Other fundamental strategic knowledge assets accounted in software are: patents, copyrights, trademarks, brands, registered design, trade secrets, brand reputation and identity. It is important to point out that some important knowledge-based dimensions of the software capital are significantly influenced by the 'cognitive and cultural flows' taking place between the organisation and socio-cultural system in which the organisation geographically operates. Indeed, an organisation is not an isolated and closed system, but is characterised by conversations with the socio-cultural context in which it is situated. This particularly has an influence on some key organisational knowledge-based dimensions such as: values, behavioural and social norms, culture, organisational atmosphere, symbols and codes.

The Knoware Tree provides an interpretative framework to discern the organisational knowledge assets characterising an organisation. Figure 4.2 shows the hierarchy of the knowledge dimensions characterising the Knoware Tree. It can be considered as a 'lens' through which to analyse the key organisational knowledge assets that are potentially affected by the management adoption of ABIs in order to support both individual and organisational learning, and enrich organisational knowledge domains with the creation and infusion of emotive knowledge.

The Knoware Tree can be adopted as a taxonomy to distinguish the organisational knowledge assets that can be developed by implementing ABIs, recognising that art forms operate as a platform and/or a device to catalyse and maintain organisational learning and knowledge management mechanisms. The Knoware Tree provides the conceptual basis on which to discern the effects of ABIs on organisational components.

The Arts Benefits Constellation: assessing the impact of ABIs on knowledge assets

The first and foremost impact of ABIs is on the transformation of the knowledge characteristics of organisational assets. ABIs act as a trigger and catalyser to develop emotive knowledge in people and/or in organisational products and infrastructure. They are a management means to manage aesthetic experiences and properties that in turn stimulate and develop emotional and energetic mechanisms affecting people's attitudes and behaviours as well as the intangible value incorporated into products and infrastructure. This is the core mechanism activating the enhancement of organisational value-creation capacity. Indeed, ABIs produce an improvement of business performance by developing the organisational knowledge assets that in turn affect organisational

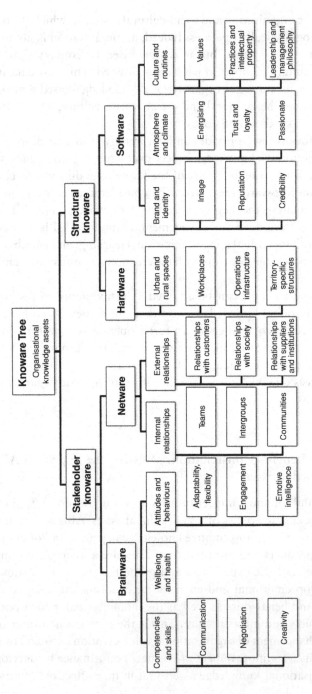

4.2 The hierarchy of knowledge dimensions of the Knoware Tree

competencies and capabilities, and then the capacity to achieve operational and strategic objectives. This is based on the hypothesis that organisational competencies and capabilities can be seen as a combination of all knowledge assets enabling an organisation to carry out and enhance its business processes (Miller, 2003; Montealegre, 2002; Pehrsson, 2000). Such a combination of knowledge-based resources depends upon the basic characteristics of knowledge and knowledge flows. The 'engine' of knowledge flows is the organisational learning mechanisms and knowledge management processes. Dosi *et al.* (2000), focusing on organisational learning mechanisms, assume that they produce the coordinated performances of organisational capabilities. Iansiti and Clark (1994) point out that an organisation's ability is based on its competencies and capabilities, which in turn are based on the organisational knowledge base, and that problem-solving, as a learning mechanism, is the key driver in generating new competencies and capabilities. Kogut and Zander (1992) also state that organisations have the possibility to create new capabilities by a process of trial-and-error learning. Therefore the knowledge flows activated and supported by organisational learning and knowledge management processes drive the development of knowledge and their incorporation into organisational competencies and capabilities (Rouse and Daellenbach, 2002; Schroeder *et al.*, 2002). In this perspective ABIs represent both a platform and a device supporting learning mechanisms and knowledge management processes aimed at developing the content and nature of organisational knowledge domains. Hence, the understanding of how ABIs contribute to the improvement of organisational business performance has to start from the assessment of the transformational effect of arts-based management actions on the knowledge dimensions associated with employees and organisational infrastructure.

In order to assess the impact of ABIs on organisational knowledge assets the Arts Benefits Constellation is proposed. As shown in Figure 4.3, this framework is built on the categories of the Knoware Tree and identifies four assessment perspectives as follows: brainware, netware, software and hardware. The fundamental idea underlying the Arts Benefits Constellation is that the assessment of the impact of an ABI has to be carried out, first by identifying in each perspective what typology of knowledge assets is affected by the managerial deployment of art forms, and second by defining indicators to track the effects of ABIs on the targeted knowledge assets.

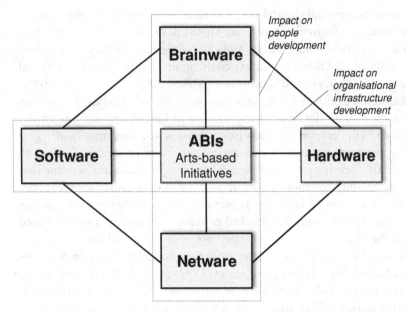

4.3 The Arts Benefits Constellation

The use of the notion 'constellation' is meant to highlight that the assessment has to take into account that an ABI can generate multiple impacts. This is due both to the polyvalent impact of ABIs, and to the interconnectivity of organisational knowledge assets, i.e., the acknowledgement that they depend on each other, building the organisational capabilities as a bundle of knowledge resources (Barney, 2001; Peteraf, 1993; Wernerfelt, 1984).

The Arts Benefits Constellation is consistent with the Arts Value Matrix. In fact, the brainware and netware perspectives stand for the potential impact of ABIs on organisational people; while the software and hardware perspectives denote the possible impact of ABIs on organisational infrastructure. The two models are complementary and offer different managerial information. The Arts Value Matrix provides a holistic understanding of the value purposes of ABIs in terms of their potential development influence on people and organisational infrastructure. It supports the classification of the organisational value-drivers that can inspire management to adopt ABIs. These value-drivers can be considered as operational mechanisms activated by ABIs to transform and grow organisational competencies and capabilities, which in turn operate as enablers for the organisational capacity to achieve business performance improvement outcomes. The Arts Benefits Constellation provides complementary information to the Arts Value Matrix and, particularly, supports the assessment of the effect of ABIs on organisational knowledge assets. It helps managers to both understand how ABIs develop the building blocks of organisational competencies and capabilities, and account for the benefits of implementing art forms as a management means to deal with management challenges and business problems. The two frameworks are integrated. Their integration is rooted in the recognition, as postulated by the knowledge-based view, that organisational value-creation capacity is based on the development of organisational knowledge assets that shape and affect organisational competencies and capabilities (Carlucci *et al.*, 2004).

The deployment of the Arts Benefits Constellation allows the assessment of the impact of ABIs on the growth of organisational knowledge assets from two fundamental value-based perspectives. As addressed in Chapter 1, the organisational value-creation capacity can be analysed adopting a stock or flow standpoint. Accordingly, the assessment of the development of organisational knowledge domains provides useful information to define both the value incorporated by organisational components and the potential ability of the organisation to generate value. This also means that the assessment of the growth of knowledge assets can be approached according to a static or a dynamic perspective (Schiuma *et al.*, 2007a). According to the static viewpoint, the knowledge assets owned by an organisation contribute to defining its value in the market. This means that the improvement of the content and quality of organisational knowledge domains aims to increase the market value of an organisation and its components. This mainly represents an economic-based perspective and it is useful in cases where it is important to take into account the evaluation of an organisation in the financial market. On the other hand, the flow or dynamic perspective focuses the attention on the functional value of knowledge assets as enablers and drivers to support organisational value-creation mechanisms. The knowledge assets are seen as the fundamental factors for performing organisational actions. They are the pillars of the working mechanisms of the organisational business model. Therefore, the development of knowledge domains contributes to the continuous advance of the quality and productivity of organisational processes.

The managerial adoption of the Arts Benefits Constellation, like the Arts Value Matrix, can respond to interpretative and normative purposes. It can be used to assess the impact of an ABI, or can be employed to identify the knowledge assets that an organisation wants to develop through the adoption of an ABI. Therefore, the Arts Benefits Constellation is not simply a four-box model to drive the assessment of the impact of ABIs, but rather a management framework to support strategic decision-making about the definition of the key strategic knowledge assets to be addressed through the managerial exploitation of art forms.

From an operative point of view, the use of the Arts Benefits Constellation is based on the understanding of the impact of an ABI in each organisational knowledge asset perspective. Even if an ABI can be designed focusing the attention on the development of a specific knowledge asset dimension, considering that knowledge resources in organisations interact and are interrelated by means of a dense network of direct and indirect relationships, the assessment of the impact of ABIs has to be carried out taking into account the four perspectives of the Arts Benefits Constellation at the same time. Below, the main characteristics of each knowledge-based assessment perspective are introduced.

The brainware perspective accounts for the impact of ABIs on people development. All ABIs that are focused on the development of knowledge traits related to people fall into this category. These are essentially the ABIs that work by activating learning dynamics with the aim of having an impact on the improvement of people's abilities, competencies and behaviours. In this perspective, those art forms that are employed as a management means to provide a learning platform that can spark and develop people's technical and emotive knowledge can be fundamentally accounted for. The fundamental question to address in this perspective is: *How do ABIs impact on people's knowledge?* The answer to this question corresponds with the identification of the competencies and behaviours of people that ABIs can affect and transform.[6] This also corresponds with the understanding of how the implementation of ABIs contributes to developing people's abilities and ways of being in the workplace. In Box 4.1, some of the main possible dimensions of people's capabilities and behaviours that can be affected by ABIs are identified. This list of people's possible knowledge assets is not intended to be comprehensive, but rather to

Box 4.1   Dimensions of the brainware perspective that can be
affected by ABIs

Brainware

People's attitudes and behavioural traits	*People's capabilities*
Confidence; curiosity; emotions and feelings; empathy; engagement; flexibility; mental focus; individual energy; instinct; intelligence; mindset; passion; readiness; reflection; self-esteem; empowering; sensitivity; vitality.	Appreciating others' skills and abilities; being in the present and being centred; caring; coping with nerves; creative thinking, imagination and inspiration; driving team-working; empowerment; encouraging yourself within yourself; listening and advising; influencing and negotiating; leadership; managing presentation and personal impact; realising potential; risk-taking; moving out of personal comfort zone; utilising personal energy; using language and writing skills.

denote what kind of people-related knowledge dimensions managers can address by implementing ABIs. Therefore, on the basis of the specific organisational and business issues to be faced, it is a management task to identify the focus of the brainware components.

As a case study of how ABIs impact on people's knowledge assets, consider the experience of Pret A Manger, which wanted to enhance the capabilities of front-of-house managers to deliver better customer service. Using a theatre-based workshop, shop managers were immersed in scenarios that helped them to understand how customers were treated. Using role play scenarios addressing issues such as queue management, clearing tables, team members' behaviour, displaying merchandising and workplace dress, the team managers could directly experience the kind of service offered in their shops through the eyes of customers and gain insights for the management team. In addition, ABIs to develop people's capabilities appeared the most effective way to put Pret's vision into action and encourage their shop managers to 'lead', rather than just run the day-to-day working activities. This required the development of people's abilities on the basis of a passionate commitment that could not be inspired using traditional training and development approaches.[7]

The netware perspective takes into account the impact of ABIs on people's networking dynamics. ABIs can support the development of relationships both within an organisation and between an organisation and its external stakeholders. They can play a twofold role. ABIs can act as a role model, allowing people to better understand how to manage fruitful conversations. Otherwise, they can play the role of a device to facilitate the creation of relations and improve the process of giving and receiving feedback. The fundamental question characterising the netware perspective is: *How do ABIs facilitate and improve people networking dynamics?* Addressing this question, management can identify, on one hand, the typology of organisational relationships they want to improve, and, on the other hand, the relationship traits that can be developed. Box 4.2 lists some of the possible typologies of relationships and relational traits that can be addressed by ABIs. Potentially ABIs can be adopted to shape and affect any kind of relationship between two actors. The focus is the development of the factors that mainly pertain to the empathetic dimensions of the interaction and distinguishing the relationship. From a practical point of view, the identification of the key emotional and energetic aspects affecting a relationship is a management task. Managers clarifying the business issues to deal with the need to define what relationship-related factors they want to enhance. It is worth noting that very often key aspects concern the features of communication and the creation and strengthening of trust. This dimension, in particular, is a fundamental factor affecting the quality and performance of organisational networking dynamics. The arts and artists can show business people how to communicate effectively, focusing not only on the information processing dimensions, but also and specifically on the emotive features. In addition, artistic products and processes require trust in many different ways and organisations can learn how to build relationships that are grounded on trust.

Box 4.2 Dimensions of the netware perspective that can be
affected by ABIs

Netware

Typology of relationships	*Relationship's traits*
Communities of practice; team-building; inter-personal relationships; relationships with local communities and society at large; relationships with suppliers; relationships with institutions; relationships with customers; inter-group cooperation and multi-functional groups; virtual networks; mergers and acquisitions.	Giving and receiving feedback; dialogue and conversation; trust and cooperation; friendship; openness and transparency; integration and coordination; meaningfulness; honesty and solidarity; team spirit; harmony and cohesion; collaboration and cooperation.

As one illustration of how ABIs can be deployed to develop knowledge assets related to the netware perspective consider the case of public sector workers in Wales who wanted to develop their leadership skills and improve their performance management and feedback practices. The improvement of the feedback culture and approaches was addressed by involving managers in an arts-based workshop, delivered by the Welsh National Opera (WNO), in which they explored the practices of how an opera director inspires and manages a range of performers by tailoring the feedback process and considering the nature and personalities of the performers. By watching a live rehearsal with two different performers, the workers witnessed how a director enhanced the singers' performance according to their ability and experience, and explored the different ways in which he worked with them in order to get the best out of them.

ABIs can improve networking dynamics in many different ways. They can address the improvement of the relationships in a team or between teams. For example, using the rehearsal process to illustrate and investigate how people can better work together in order to produce a high-quality performance, WNO, levering the analogies between the world of opera and the world of business, uses the rehearsal practices of the opera to let people understand the role of an individual in a team, how to develop feedback styles, and how to manage constructive conversations in which people listen to one another and develop trust in team members to deliver performance.

The hardware perspective reports all ABIs impacting organisational tangible infrastructure that can have an influence on organisational capabilities. The ABIs that fall into this category are aimed at managing the aesthetic properties characterising the tangible assets both internally and externally to the organisation. They act either as a device to inject aesthetic properties into the organisational infrastructure or as a vector to increase the value of an organisation's infrastructural components and, particularly, products. Management addressing the impact of ABIs in the hardware perspective should consider the question: *How can ABIs shape and enrich tangible organisational infrastructure with aesthetic properties?* Addressing this question, it is important, first, to distinguish between the impact on external infrastructure, i.e., the tangible assets that mainly pertain to the public domain; and the impact on internal infrastructure, i.e., the tangible assets within the organisation. This recognises that ABIs can be deployed as a management means to influence the aesthetic characteristics either of public spaces both in urban and rural areas, for example, by sponsoring art installations or the arts-based renovation of buildings and gardens, or of office spaces and facilities, for instance, by combining arts and design to define engaging workplaces.

The ABIs adopted with the goal of impacting hardware fundamentally tend to correspond to the adoption of artistic products either in the form of organisation artworks, or of artworks from the artworld. Organisation artworks can be characterised both by works of art made by artists for the organisation and by a mixed application of arts and design in order to shape and beautify tangible organisational assets. On the other hand, the use of artworks from the artworld essentially corresponds to the use of works of art identified as such by art experts. A key example is represented by the creation of art collections that can be shown in office spaces and exhibitions, or even in an organisational museum.

When assessing the impact of ABIs on tangible organisational knowledge assets it is important to clarify the fundamental aim inspiring the

---

Box 4.3 Dimensions of the hardware perspective that can be affected by ABIs

Hardware

External infrastructure	*Internal infrastructure*
Urban and rural elements that an organisation can affect by the deployment of art forms, some possible dimensions are: gardens or a court (e.g., sculpture garden); squares (e.g., arts exhibitions and installations); buildings; public facilities; and so on.	Tangible organisational assets that can be shaped and designed through art forms, some possible dimensions are: products; workplaces; office spaces; office buildings; facilities; equipment; furnishings; information and communication technological infrastructure.

---

management adoption of art forms. It can be the improvement of the aesthetic features of tangible assets or to increase the value stock of the organisation. The former is mainly aimed at creating intangible value by enabling tangible assets to evoke aesthetic experiences, while the latter focuses on the use of the arts as an economic lever, for instance, in the creation of a corporate art collection. Box 4.3 identifies the two fundamental typologies of infrastructure that can be affected by ABIs. Potentially any tangible asset can be affected by the managerial use of art forms when the intention is to design and shape its working mechanisms in such a way that it incorporates emotive knowledge that is capable of generating and affecting emotional and energetic dynamics in people. The effect of ABIs can be interpreted both in terms of enhancement of the aesthetic properties of the organisational tangible assets, and of the increment of the value incorporated by the organisation.

A case study of how the mix of art forms and design can support the development of organisational tangible assets is provided by Ducati's turnaround (Schiuma *et al.*, 2008a). During the period between 1997 and 2004 Ducati Motor Holding, one of the leading world brands in sportive motorcycle manufacturing, engaged in a turnaround programme that aimed at driving a significant improvement in the company's performance. The overall turnaround strategy was summarised by Federico Minoli, who was the company's CEO at the time, with the vision 'of transforming the company from a mechanic to an entertainment firm'. This vision was integrated with the message that Ducati is producing works of art rather than 'machines'. Different initiatives were launched to put this vision into practice. In particular great attention was focused on the transformation of the factory, considered as a fundamental component of Ducati's know-how, as well as on the creation of a museum as an integrated component of the factory. The creation of a museum dedicated to the company's history had a clear objective. It aimed at providing a tangible sign of the culture, identity and tradition of the company. The creation of the museum and its integration into the factory focused on the creation of aesthetic experiences that would capture the emotions of people both within and outside the organisation. With the idea of incorporating, into the tangible knowledge infrastructure, the passion and culture characterising the company, the overall factory was redesigned. However, rather than organising the layout as it normally would have been done, focusing only on the optimisation of the internal logistics, it was thought of as a 'theatre'. The factory's space was designed so that workers would act as if they were on stage. The idea was to allow external people to visit the company and give them the opportunity to see the places where the 'works of art' and objects of their admiration are assembled. Today, the company is visited every day by hundreds of people, such as fans, students and customers. Moreover, the conceptual idea of putting organisational people on stage has created an engaging atmosphere, contributing to a rise in people's pride and passion for what they do. The design of the factory included the combination of the arts, interior design and architecture. The use of colours and images scattered all around the workplace contributes to generating an energising atmosphere. Today, the company's tangible infrastructure seems to incorporate the passion of the people working in Ducati. The factory evokes an involving energy and when visiting the company it is hard not to feel its emotive and energetic atmosphere.

The software perspective considers the impact of ABIs on the intangible dimensions of organisational infrastructure. ABIs can transform

---

Box 4.4 Dimensions of the software perspective that can be affected by ABIs

Software

Intangible assets that can be affected by ABIs

Atmosphere; collegiality; commitment; connectivity; cooperative mindset (reciprocity, connectivity, collegiality); culture; energy; identification; intimacy; excitement, interest and engagement; good place to work; involvement; mutuality; reciprocity; routines and practices; supportive, safe, comfortable and idea-rich environment; values; work practices.

---

the intangible assets of an organisation so that they are able to create aesthetic experiences that can spark and nourish positive emotional and energetic dynamics. The fundamental question that management has to address in this perspective is: *How do ABIs influence the intangible organisational infrastructural assets so that they can evoke aesthetic experiences?* In addressing this question it is important to understand what intangible assets can be developed through the arts. Box 4.4 identifies some of the main possible intangible organisational assets that can be affected by ABIs. Possible impacts of ABIs can refer, for example, to the development of traits such as sense of belonging, pride of being part of an 'organisational family', awareness of contributing to an ongoing history of an organisation, recognition of and attachment to organisational values, and more generally the creation of an engaging organisational atmosphere in which people feel energised and passionate about what they do. Again the intangible dimensions listed in Box 4.4 represent only a possible set of knowledge assets that managers can develop by implementing ABIs. From a practical point of view, it is a management task to define what the organisation's key intangible infrastructural components are to be developed.

An illustrative example of how ABIs can contribute to shaping intangible organisational infrastructure is represented by the initiative implemented by Unilever UK with the goal of celebrating the organisation's mission to 'add vitality to life'. The goal of the ABI was to develop some important intangible knowledge infrastructure, as follows: to strengthen brand awareness, to raise the company's identity among people, to galvanise organisational people and to build the image of the company around the new brand message. For the implementation of the ABI tradesecrets was brought in. They designed a movement workshop with a set of choreography to be first rehearsed by employees and afterwards collectively performed. So, people were first trained in physical exercises animated by professional artists with the twofold aim of involving them in energising activities, and of instructing them in how to perform the designed group choreographies. Then the employees enacted the word 'vitality', using their bodies on a football pitch and the 'performance' was filmed from above by a helicopter. This was then shown to the company during a conference and the individual company members could see how they were, symbolically, part of the bigger picture of the company and its mission. The overall ABI was galvanising for the people, and highlighted the power of the brand proposition, which was visually demonstrated internally and externally.

The Arts Benefit Constellation provides managers with a framework to support the assessment of the impact of ABIs on organisational knowledge assets. This is based on the interpretation of the assessment as a knowing process that involves three main sub-processes: identification, classification and measurement. The assessment process starts with the identification of the objects to be evaluated. It aims to recognise and discern the organisational knowledge assets that are affected by ABIs, while the classification process aims to define the categories to group the organisational knowledge assets, taking into account that different categories can be defined on the basis of different classification criteria.[8] Identification and classification are strictly interrelated serving each other. The identification aims to screen an organisation in order to reveal its knowledge assets, while the classification is intended to distinguish the different typologies of knowledge assets. Both processes represent a prerequisite for measuring knowledge assets within an organisation. The measurement of knowledge assets can be defined as the collection process of qualitative and quantitative information concerning the characteristics of knowledge assets.[9] From an operative point of view the measurement is carried out by a system of indicators and metrics (Bourne, 2001; Kaplan and Norton, 2008;

Neely, 1998). The indicators and metrics can be defined adopting measurement units which can be of a monetary or non-monetary nature. In the first case, the indicators and metrics essentially aim to provide economic and financial information in order to support the negotiation, the transaction and/or the transfer of knowledge assets in the market, while non-monetary metrics allow us to define and describe, both from a qualitative and a quantitative point of view, the properties and the specific features of organisational knowledge assets. Due to the difficulty in quantifying knowledge assets in economic and financial terms, non-monetary indicators and metrics tend to be more frequently defined and adopted in practice.

Figure 4.4 shows a schematic representation of the Arts Benefits Constellation indicating that each assessment perspective has to be populated with key measures and related development targets.[10]

The assessment perspective of the Arts Benefits Constellation allows the identification and classification of the impact of ABIs on organisational knowledge assets. In order to perform the measurement each perspective has to be populated with indicators and metrics. To support managers in this task, in the next section some fundamental guidelines for the definition of measures are introduced.

Criteria for defining indicators and metrics to measure the impact of ABIs

Once the knowledge assets to be developed are identified in each perspective of the Arts Benefits Constellation, a set of key indicators and metrics to carry out the measurement of the impact of ABIs has to be defined. The definition of the measures is not a straightforward process. Recognising that the adoption of ABIs responds to context-specific business issues, managers have the task of defining the set of measures that are able to provide the appropriate information for their decision-making processes. Therefore, the selection of the qualitative and/or quantitative measures to be employed has to be approached as a management design process in which managers are engaged in understanding what kind of information they need in order to support their actions and how they can gather this information by deploying a measurement system. From an operational point of view, the definition of indicators and metrics can be based on two fundamental

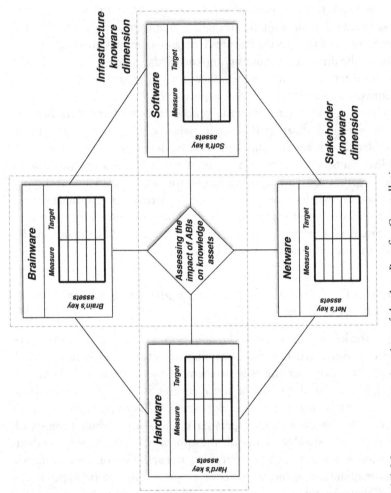

4.4 Measurement perspectives of the Arts Benefits Constellation

approaches. They can be identified among the indicators and metrics forming the organisation's 'basket of measures'. In this case, management can screen the existing organisational performance measurement system in order to identify available and meaningful measures that might be deployed to track the effects of ABIs. Alternatively, management has to design specific indicators to perform the measurement. For this reason, different approaches can be adopted. Neely *et al.* (1996) propose the 'Performance measure record sheet' as a simple and effective template to support managers in the designing of measures. In any case, in choosing the indicators and metrics, managers have to keep in mind some important criteria to make sure that they define a robust and meaningful measurement system. In particular, four important criteria can be identified for the selection and/or design of measures as follows: relevance, reliability, comparability and clarity (Carlucci and Schiuma, 2010). The relevance is related to the quality of the information provided by the measure to the end-user. It is important that the selection or design process of the measures is always based on a clear definition of the end-users and on a prediction of the use and value of the measures for the end-users. In addition, the information provided by the measure not only has to be meaningful, but it also has to be timely, i.e., available before it loses its capacity to influence decisions. This means that the measures have to be simple enough to be implemented. The reliability refers to the quality of a measure and it is related to its capacity to measure the object it intends to measure as closely as possible. This means that the measure has to clearly address the targeted organisational knowledge asset it intends to assess. The comparability refers to the possibility of comparing two sets of the information gathered through the measures. Finally, clarity is related to the meaning and format of the information provided by the measure. A measure has to be as simple as possible and easy to understand and communicate for the organisation, both internally and externally. Possibly it has to be built on existing data streams and has to be practical and manageable.

Knowledge assets, value-creation and business performance

The fundamental mechanism at the basis of the impact of ABIs is represented by their capacity to develop organisational knowledge assets. This in turn produces an improvement in business performance.

Indeed, the knowledge assets constitute the foundations of organisational capabilities. Hence, ABIs acting as a catalyst both to transform the knowledge characteristics and to support the learning mechanisms and knowledge management processes aid the evolution and enhancement of organisational value-creation capacity.

Gathering insights from the management literature, this section seeks to delineate the theoretical framework explaining the links between knowledge assets, value-creation and business performance. This provides the conceptual background to propose a management model to support managers in the understanding of the relationships linking ABIs to business performance improvements.

Two perspectives of business performance

The business performance of an organisation can be explained as the result of two major dimensions: exogenous market factors and internal organisational resource endowments (Cockburn et al., 2000; Wiggins and Ruefli, 2002). In particular, McGrath et al. (1995) argue that there are two major paradigms for explaining superior organisational performance. First, traditional industrial organisation economics emphasises the barriers to competition, and takes the position that industry effects explain the greater part of persistent above-normal returns (Bain, 1956; Caves and Porter, 1977; Porter, 1985). Specifically, Bain (1956) argues that industry structure determines a firm's conduct, which in turn determines economic performance. Second, the resource-based and competence-based view assumes that organisations accumulate unique combinations of resources and capabilities that allow them to achieve performance benefits on the basis of their organisational capabilities (Barney, 1991; Grant, 1991; Peteraf, 1993). The two perspectives are different, but can be considered as strictly complementary in explaining organisational competitive advantage (Peteraf and Bergen, 2003). As a result, the role of management is to match the external business opportunities with what an organisation is capable of doing at an acceptable level of risk, while safeguarding the weaknesses of the organisation from the threats of the same business environment. The understanding of the value of arts for business is here fundamentally considered related to the role of the arts as a management means to develop internal organisational resources and capabilities.

The knowledge-based view and the position of ABIs

To explain the role and relevance of ABIs as a management means to improve business performance, a knowledge-based view of the organisation is proposed.

The knowledge-based view postulates that an organisation can be interpreted as a bundle of knowledge resources (Barney, 2001; Dierickx and Cool, 1989; Peteraf, 1993; Wernerfelt, 1984). When these resources are strategic they denote organisation-specific knowledge assets forming and affecting organisational capabilities (Helfat and Raubitschek, 2000; Lei *et al.*, 1996; Nonaka *et al.*, 2000a; Teece, 1998, 2000). Organisational knowledge assets are dynamic in nature and are enhanced, renewed and developed over time through knowledge flows (Conner, 1991; Kaplan and Norton, 2003; Roos and Roos, 1997; Schiuma *et al.*, 2007b). This suggests that organisational knowledge assets can be interpreted in their twofold nature as knowledge stocks and knowledge flows. Knowledge stocks characterise the overall knowledge assets controlled by an organisation at a specific time. They evolve over time through knowledge flows that are activated and supported by organisational learning mechanisms and knowledge management processes (Dierickx and Cool, 1989). They are essentially the result of people's ability to create and handle knowledge. People learn thanks to their cognitive abilities, leveraging the rational and emotive mind, which they use and renew through reciprocal interaction. Then knowledge is created both as an individual construct and a social construct in the form of collective knowledge resulting from social networking dynamics. People learning dynamics become organisational learning when individual and collective knowledge is captured and incorporated into an organisation's infrastructural components and/or deployed in business activities (Kim, 1993; Loermans, 2002). This means that the knowledge created through organisational learning is integrated into organisational capabilities (Grant, 1991, 1996a, 1996b; Rouse and Daellenbach, 2002; Schroeder *et al.*, 2002). The knowledge-based view allows the interpretation of ABIs as mechanisms to develop the knowledge contents and characteristics of an organisation. In particular, ABIs can be seen as instruments to spark and support organisational learning mechanisms and knowledge management processes that create and infuse emotive knowledge into organisational knowledge assets, which in turn contribute to making the organisation more adaptable, resilient, innovative, agile and intuitive. They provide management with approaches and tools to manage the organisational aesthetic dimensions that activate learning mechanisms and knowledge processes concerning the organisation's emotional and energetic dynamics. Specifically, they promote the development of people's knowledge by harnessing emotions and energy. Thus, the deployment of art forms allows the creation of emotive knowledge that is incorporated, converted and organised into organisational components shaping organisational capabilities and defining organisational socio-technical processes.

How ABIs affect organisational capabilities

The transformational mechanisms activated by ABIs are based on the recognition that an organisational capability can be seen as a combination of all knowledge assets and cognitive processes that allow an organisation to carry out its business processes (Miller, 2003; Montealegre, 2002; Pehrsson, 2000). According to Amit and Schoemaker (1993), capabilities can be abstractly thought of as intermediate goods generated by the organisation to provide enhanced productivity of its final product or service.

Organisational capabilities can be classified as either operational or dynamic and are related to two sorts of organisational activities: those that perform individual tasks and those that coordinate the individual tasks (Helfat and Peteraf, 2003; Winter, 2000; Zollo and Winter, 2002).

Zollo and Winter (2002) define operational capabilities as organisational activities geared towards the operational functioning of the organisation including both staff and line activities. Winter (2003) considers that operational or ordinary capabilities are 'zero-level' capabilities that are exercised in a stationary process or in a hypothetical 'equilibrium', in which an organisation keeps developing by producing and selling the same product, on the same scale, and to the same customer population over time, while, dynamic capabilities relate to the organisational ability to create and sustain competitive advantage through the capacity of managing change (Teece, 2007).

Dynamic capabilities, like operational capabilities, arise from learning and they constitute the organisational systematic methods for modifying and shaping operational capabilities (Zollo and Winter, 2002). While capabilities are at the basis of the execution of organisational activities, the dynamic capabilities are focused on the continuous improvement of organisational effectiveness through reconfiguring organisational abilities, resources and functional competences in order to face changes in the business environment (Teece *et al.*, 1997; Zollo and Winter, 2002).

In the management literature many scholars have outlined how organisational capabilities generate business performance achievements. Adner and Helfat (2003) recognise that managerial dynamic capabilities impact on business performance by making heterogeneous managerial decisions. Aragon-Correa and Sharma (2003) stress the role of proactive environmental strategies, considered as dynamic capabilities, in enhancing organisational performance. Rindova and Kotha (2001) demonstrate how continuous morphing, enabled by organisational dynamic capabilities and strategic flexibility, generate competitive advantage. Porter (1996) also argues that competitive advantage comes from the way organisation's activities fit and reinforce one another and the operational effectiveness. Finally, Verona (1999) and Brown and Eisenhardt (1995) show how organisational capabilities are a first important driver of product development outcomes which in turn affect economic benefits. There are also many empirical studies that show the positive cause–effect relationships between organisational capabilities resulting from various knowledge dynamics and superior organisational performance. For example, Collis (1991) shows how organisations' core competencies and implementation capabilities determine product market position and global competition in the bearings industry. Henderson and Cockburn (1994) also find out that the research productivity in different pharmaceutical firms depends mostly on differences in research strategy, in organisation and programme-specific resources and in organisational capabilities, and that the right combination allows firms to explore product development strategies that are not available to their competitors. Similarly, Zander and Kogut (1995) identify how the ease of codifying and communicating a manufacturing capability affects not only the time to its transfer, but also the time to imitate the new product. McGrath *et al.* (1996) also found out that the antecedents of achieving rent-generating innovations are causal understanding,

innovative proficiency, emergence and mobilisation of new competencies and creation of competitive advantage. On the other hand,
Lorenzoni and Lipparini (1999) show how relational capability (i.e.,
the ability to interact with other companies) accelerates a firm's knowledge access and transfer, how this affects organisational growth and
innovativeness in the packaging machine industry and how managers
can deliberately shape and design the inter-firm network to develop
the capability to integrate knowledge residing both internally and
externally to the firm's boundaries. Finally, Afuah (2000) identifies
how post-technological change performance decreases with the extent
to which the technological change makes competitors' capabilities
obsolete.

The above theoretical implications represent the conceptual basis
to propose an interpretative framework exploring the links between
knowledge assets, organisational capabilities, value-creation and business performance. This framework defines the conceptual platform
to clarify why and how ABIs impact on business performance. As
shown in Figure 4.5 business performance and organisational value-
creation can be ultimately considered as the final outcome of a set of
transformational mechanisms that are centred on the development of
organisational knowledge assets.

Knowledge assets represent the strategic resources and sources
of organisational capabilities. The development of organisational
knowledge assets through organisational learning mechanisms and
knowledge management processes influences operational and dynamic
capabilities. Then, organisational capabilities are translated into performance consequences when they are leveraged into products and
services that in turn generate value for organisational stakeholders.
This means that the quality of organisational capabilities grounds
the effectiveness and productivity of organisational business activities. Hence, business performance improvements are the result of
cause-and-effect chains activated by the development of organisational
knowledge assets.

The above considerations highlight that ABIs impact on business
performance by developing the organisational knowledge domains.
Accordingly the assessment of the impact of ABIs on business performance improvements has to be carried out by understanding how
their transformational effects on organisational knowledge assets are

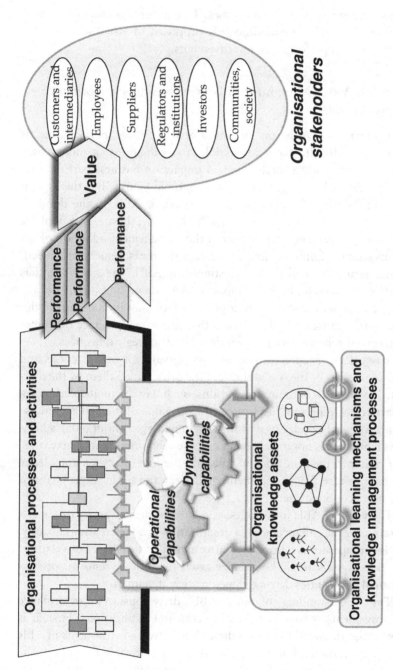

4.5 A representation of the links between knowledge assets, organisational capabilities and business performance translated in performance outcomes. To explore this issue in the next section, a mapping methodology is proposed to visualise how ABIs drive business performance improvements.

The Arts Value Map: how ABIs drive business performance improvements

The impact of ABIs on organisational business performance is extremely difficult, if not impossible, to evaluate using money as a measurement unit. ABIs do have an impact on business performance and particularly on organisational economic figures, but this is fundamentally the indirect result of the effect of ABIs on the development of organisational components. In this view, the assessment of the business performance benefits from the management adoption of art forms cannot simply be defined through the measurement of the economic returns related to the investments in ABIs. The assessment has to take into account how the impact of ABIs on organisational knowledge assets activates the development of organisational capabilities and sparks cause-and-effect chains that ultimately produce outcomes in terms of achievement of operational and strategic objectives.

Artworks can represent relevant investments for organisations and their value can be measured through the price put on them by the market. However, economic transactions, such as the commercialisation of artworks, represent just a proxy of the value of the managerial use of art forms. The relevance of the arts in management in today's business landscape is not merely related to the economic value of artworks, but rather to the fundamental role that the arts offer as a knowledge domain to face the management challenges and business problems of the new economic age.

The value of ABIs for business is related to their capacity to act as a catalyst for the enhancement of organisational value-creation capacity. ABIs can operate as a learning platform and/or as a device or vector to develop organisational knowledge assets that in turn renovate organisational capabilities driving value-creation dynamics.

The understanding of how ABIs drive business performance improvements is based on two fundamental implications. First, it is not straightforward to draw a direct line between investments in ABIs and organisational bottom-line results. It is unfeasible to evaluate the adoption of art forms directly in terms of economic returns, except in those cases in which ABIs either correspond to specific business activities in the cultural sector aimed at generating cash flow, or equal real estate investments. Second, ABIs tend to satisfy different organisational wants and needs that are idiosyncratic, context-specific and time-related. They operate at multiple levels impacting on people and/or organisational infrastructure. So, the benefits of ABIs for the improvement of business performance have to be fundamentally investigated in terms of their positive impacts on organisational value-drivers. This means that the understanding of the business performance improvements has to take into account the virtuous knowledge assets development dynamics activated by ABIs.

ABIs, by managing organisational aesthetic dimensions and handling emotional and energetic dynamics, support the development of organisational knowledge domains with an influence on operational and dynamic capabilities that in turn affect the execution of organisational processes and the achievement of performance and strategic objectives. This ultimately drives the organisational ability to deliver the targeted value propositions and generate wealth.

The Arts Value Map is proposed with the aim of providing a framework that can support management in the understanding of how ABIs drive the improvement of business performance. It provides a mapping-based assessment methodology to understand how ABIs can be converted into business performance improvements. In Figure 4.6 the key conceptual dimensions characterising the Arts Value Map are schematically depicted showing the fundamental logic at the basis of the framework. It offers a visualisation of the relationships between the adoption of ABIs with the transformation of organisational components and their potential business performance outcomes.

Mapping the links between ABIs and business performance

The understanding of how ABIs can drive business performance improvements is based on their alignment with organisational performance and strategic objectives. An ABI can have a relevant impact on organisational performance only if it is integrated in the organisational strategy and/or responds to the achievement of operational objectives that are consistent with the strategic intents. It is very unlikely that the implementation of an ABI that is not aligned with an organisation's

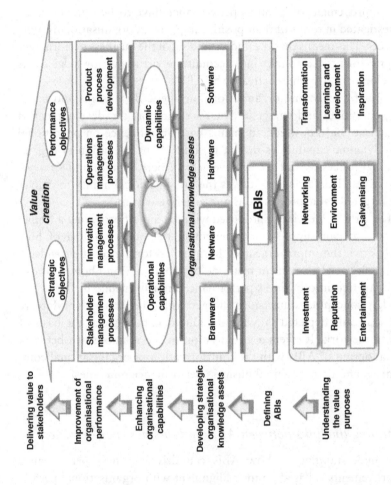

4.6 The conceptual dimensions of the Arts Value Map

wants and needs can generate significant and sustainable benefits for the organisation.

The relevance of aligning management initiatives to operations and strategy has been largely addressed by the performance management literature. Management initiatives to support organisational value-creation have to be integrated into the strategic plan and have to respond to specific operational performance problems. This is the fundamental assumption of the models proposed to support organisational strategic performance management (e.g., Balanced scorecard by Kaplan and Norton, 1996; Performance prism by Neely *et al.*, 2002).

The Arts Value Map takes into account the crucial importance of aligning and integrating ABIs with the strategic and business performance objectives and adopts a mapping visualisation of the cause-and-effect relationships explaining how ABIs impact the achievement of performance improvements and strategic objectives. The Arts Value Map provides a visual assessment of the pathways through which the adoption of ABIs affects the development of the knowledge-based, competence-based and process-based dimensions of an organisation and improves business performance.

Figure 4.7 shows the template for the Arts Value Map. It represents the relationships linking ABIs, organisational knowledge assets, organisational capabilities, process and performance improvements objectives, strategic objectives and value propositions. The fundamental assumption at the basis of the framework is that the growth of knowledge assets operates as a key driver to activate value-creation dynamics (Carlucci *et al.*, 2004; Carlucci and Schiuma, 2007). The development of organisational knowledge domains improves organisational capabilities enabling a better execution of business processes that in turn allows an improvement of organisational performance and more generally the achievement of business and strategic objectives.

The Arts Value Map provides a visual representation of the cause-and-effect relationships linking ABIs to business performance, sharing some of the fundamental hypotheses of other similar frameworks proposed in the strategic management literature such as the Strategy map and the Success map.

The Strategy map was initially introduced by Kaplan and Norton (2000, 2003) as a tool to provide a visual representation of the critical objectives of a company and the relationships among

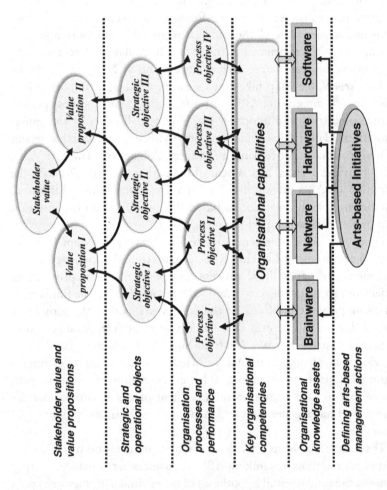

Stakeholder value and
value propositions

Strategic and
operational objects

Organisation
processes and
performance

Key organisational
competencies

Organisational
knowledge assets

Defining arts-based
management actions

4.7 Template for the definition of the Arts Value Map

those that drive organisational performance. The Strategy map aims to show 'how an organisation will convert its initiatives and resources – including intangible assets such as corporate culture and employee knowledge – into tangible outcomes' (Kaplan and Norton, 2000: 168). The Strategy map is proposed as an architecture that provides an integrated view of strategies and operations (Kaplan and Norton, 2003, 2008). It allows the explanation of organisational value-creation processes, describing the logical causal relationships among the four balance scorecard perspectives: 'financial', 'customer', 'process' and 'learning and growth' (Kaplan and Norton, 1992, 1996). The Success map is conceptually similar to the Strategy map. It is a framework aimed at visualising the relationships between management actions and business performance outcomes. However, it is based on the five perspectives of the performance prism: 'stakeholder wants and needs', 'organisation wants and needs', 'strategies', 'processes' and 'capabilities' (Neely *et al.*, 2002). It is a useful managerial technique to help managers align a company's strategy, processes and capabilities with the delivery of stakeholders' satisfaction and contribution. Both the Strategy map and the Success map provide a visual representation of the organisational strategy, and clarify how an organisation intends to achieve its strategic outcomes. They are frameworks particularly useful for promoting greater clarity and commitment to the strategy within an organisation. In fact, they define a platform for identifying, understanding, implementing and reviewing the strategy, its components and the related links.

In the management literature the adoption of visualisation approaches to assess the linkages between management initiatives and organisational value objectives has been further extended. In particular, great attention is focused on the application of mapping methodologies to assess the role and relevance of knowledge assets to achieve performance objectives. In this regard, the adoption of the mapping methodology is particularly useful to visualise and assess both the importance of knowledge assets and the interdependences among knowledge assets against the achievement of specific performance objectives.[11]

The Arts Value Map is based on the use of conceptual maps as a powerful approach to visualise, describe and understand the dynamic relationships that convert ABIs into business performance improvements. It is built on two fundamental dimensions. On the one hand, it adopts the logical architecture of the strategic mapping frameworks introduced in the management literature. The mapping visualisation methodology allows the identification of the strategic and performance objectives and of the processes and capabilities an organisation needs to manage in order to deliver value. On the other hand, it recognises that organisational business performance is the result of bundles of organisational knowledge assets. They represent the foundations of organisational capabilities. By developing knowledge assets, organisations can support the enhancement of their value-creation capacity. The management of the aesthetic experiences and properties contributes to shaping and developing the knowledge features of organisational domains. So the Arts Value Map is proposed as a managerial framework both to define ABIs that are aligned with organisational strategy, and to assess how ABIs have an impact on the achievement of the strategic and performance objectives of an organisation.

The template depicted in Figure 4.7 represents a general chart. It has to be tailored to the specific organisational needs and contexts. From a practical point of view, the framework can be adopted either as a descriptive tool or as a normative approach. As a descriptive tool, it can support the interpretation and assessment of an ABI. In this case, the Arts Value Map is used as a lens to explain the 'what', 'how' and 'why' an ABI has generated value for business. The 'what' corresponds to identifying the organisational knowledge assets that have been affected. The 'how' explains the impact of organisational knowledge assets development on the organisational value-drivers, as well as on the enhancement of organisational competences and processes. Finally, the 'why' codifies the reasons for the implementation of the ABI and identifies the achieved benefits. From a normative point of view, the definition of the Arts Value Map has to start with the definition of the organisational value propositions. The main framework's assumption is that the value generated by an organisation is the result of the organisational capability to satisfy key stakeholders. Accordingly, ABIs are relevant when they contribute to improving organisational business performance that in turn satisfies the wants, needs and expectations of organisational stakeholders. The definition of the value propositions has to be translated into strategic objectives. They can be cascaded into business performance targets and can be associated with organisational processes. The quality of the execution of the processes affects the performance and ultimately the capacity of the organisation to achieve the targeted performance improvements. In order to effectively manage organisational processes and improve their productivity it is crucial to develop organisational capabilities that are rooted in organisational knowledge assets. Thus on the basis of the organisational processes to be developed, the key knowledge assets affecting their productivity and improvements have to be identified, and then, the most appropriate ABIs to develop the organisational knowledge assets have to be defined.

Conclusion

The management adoption of art forms activates and supports organisational value-creation that produces different positive business performance outcomes. In this chapter it has been suggested that the understanding of the mechanisms converting ABIs into the enhancement of organisational value-creation capacity can be approached by adopting a knowledge-based view of the organisation and of its components and working functions. Accordingly, knowledge assets are the building blocks of organisational capabilities and knowledge characteristics affect the function, productivity and value of organisational components.

The ability of an organisation to deliver value to its stakeholders and to accomplish continuous business performance improvements is the result of organisational capabilities. They affect the effectiveness of operations and managerial actions, and the capacity to renew existing know-how and develop new abilities. This means that the improvement of organisational value-creation is strictly related to the advancement of organisational capabilities. In this perspective ABIs operating as a learning platform and a device to manage aesthetic organisational dimensions stimulate and support learning mechanisms and knowledge management processes. Particularly, they contribute to the development of emotive knowledge to be synergistically integrated with technical knowledge. Therefore, first and foremost, the impact of ABIs has to be assessed in terms of their impact on the development of organisational knowledge domains. Arts-based management actions advance both people's knowledge and the infrastructure's knowledge characteristics. To provide managers with frameworks to assess the effects of ABIs on knowledge assets and to understand the relationships linking arts-based management actions to organisational value-creation mechanisms, the Arts Benefits Constellation and the Arts Value Map are proposed. They can support management from both an interpretative and a normative standpoint, providing effective frameworks to define and account for the links between ABIs and business performance improvements.

5 | *Managing Arts-based Initiatives to improve business performance*

Introduction

Arts-based Initiatives (ABIs), like any other management initiative, have to be properly aligned and integrated with organisational operations and strategy, in order to produce positive and significant benefits for the improvement of business performance. The arts in management contribute to developing the emotive and energetic dimensions of organisational functions and working mechanisms that modern management has fundamentally disregarded. However, to make sure that the managerial uses of art forms respond to business purposes, ABIs have to be combined with traditional management approaches. ABIs are instruments used to manage the aesthetic organisational dimensions that in turn allow managers to create and affect organisational emotive knowledge, both in people and infrastructure. Through art forms management can handle emotions and energy states in and around organisations. However, the emotional and energetic dynamics sparked and nourished by art forms need to be channelled towards strategic and business objectives. For this reason, ABIs have to be managed and assimilated within the management system of the organisation.

In this chapter, attention will be focused on how management can integrate ABIs into the organisation's management system, by clarifying the arts-based strategic approaches grounding the adoption of art forms. In particular, the focus will be on how to run arts-based management actions so that they are structured consistently with the design and implementation of other management actions aimed at driving business performance improvements. Finally, acknowledging that ABIs, as instruments impacting on the features of organisational life and processes, can also produce detrimental effects if not properly designed and implemented, some managerial insights are discussed to identify some important factors affecting the successful implementation of arts-based management actions.

Arts-based strategic approaches for organisational value creation

ABIs can be implemented to address a wide range of management challenges and business problems. Managers approaching the use of the arts in organisations need to have a clear understanding of the arts-based strategic approaches at the basis of their adoption in order to make sure that they contribute to business performance improvements. Organisations that successfully implement ABIs have a clear understanding of how ABIs can strategically contribute to developing organisational components and drive value creation. To bring the arts into organisations is always a pleasant initiative because art forms have the power to generate joyful experiences. However, to avoid an ABI simply becoming a temporary amusing experience, rather than a management means to enhance organisational value-creation capacity, arts-based management actions have to be defined with a clear strategic intent in mind.

The definition of the main strategic intents for the adoption of the arts in organisations is provided by the framework introduced in Chapter 3 and labelled as the 'four value zones of the arts'. According to this framework, managers can use art forms to create intrinsic value for people, and/or intangible value that can be incorporated into the organisational infrastructure. It considers ABIs as critical levers and catalysers that can be deployed to handle emotional and energetic dynamics in order to create and affect arts-based experiences and contexts that can transform an organisation. The strategic intents identified by the four value zones of the arts allow the definition of three main arts-based strategic approaches that managers can follow when adopting ABIs to improve business performance. They are based on the fundamental distinction existing between the development of people and the transformation of organisational infrastructure.

Figure 5.1 shows conceptually the arts-based strategic approaches and the logic behind their definition. Fundamentally ABIs start from the igniting zone and can move towards the intrinsic zone or the instrumental zone. This is based on the assumption that art forms first and foremost have the capacity to spark and trigger emotions and energy.

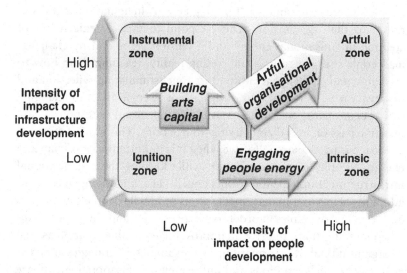

5.1 Arts-based strategies

The contact with the arts and artists is generally a pleasant and joyful experience. So, from a strategic point of view, ABIs represent an approach to entertain and to create happy experiences and contexts. However the real strategic relevance of ABIs is related to their capacity to transform organisational components so that they can act as value-drivers.

ABIs for engaging people's energy

As the initiatives move from the igniting to the intrinsic zone and progress from the entertainment to the inspirational zone, in accordance with the Arts Value Matrix, they respond to a people management strategy. A strategy that is inspired by the strategic intent of generating intrinsic benefits in terms of impact on an organisation's people development can be labelled as a strategic approach that 'engages people's energy'. In this case, ABIs are implemented with a focus on people and with the strategic goal of engaging their emotions and energy. This activates and nourishes the creation of emotive knowledge that is capable of driving individual change, or the improvement of people's ability to take better knowledge-based actions. ABIs that are implemented with the strategic approach of engaging people's energy are aimed at bringing energy, imagination and inspiration to the organisation. They respond to the strategic intent of creating organisational energy and a tension for action by challenging people's way of seeing and feeling reality, teaching them how to recognise and challenge their comfort zone, stimulating reflection and observation on personal and business issues, enlarging and changing their perspectives, enhancing emotional and intuitive responses and injecting passion into their activities and actions. This kind of strategic approach is particularly effective when it is important to motivate and energise people in an organisation while keeping the organisational infrastructure fundamentally unchanged. The underlying idea is to adopt art forms as a management means to handle people's emotional and energetic dynamics in order to create emotive and energetic organisational states that can drive an improvement of value creation as well as organisational transformation. Two examples of strategies aimed at engaging people's emotions and unleashing organisational energy are provided by Bruch and Ghoshal (2003). They adopt two metaphors to highlight the relevance of harnessing emotions and energy in organisations: the 'slaying the dragon' strategy and the 'winning the princess' strategy. The authors adopt this distinction to identify different leadership styles aimed at engaging people and unleashing organisational energy. They point out the importance of defining strategies inspired by the strategic intent to spark, channel, nurture, drive and manage people's emotional and energetic dynamics. The first strategy, 'slaying the dragon', is aimed at focusing and channelling people's attention, emotions and efforts towards an imminent threat such as bankruptcy, a new winning competitor's solution, or a disruptive technology, for example. This kind of strategy can be made operative by adopting ABIs aimed at galvanising people, creating a tension for action. The second strategy, 'winning the princess', seeks to engage people's dreams, emotions and energy to achieve challenging organisational objectives that require people's engagement and passion. In this case ABIs can be adopted with the goal of inspiring people, driving self-assessment that triggers change.

ABIs for building arts capital

ABIs don't necessarily have to be directly focused on people. When ABIs are defined with the strategic intent to generate effects related to the instrumental zone, they fundamentally respond to an infrastructural management strategy. In this case, the focus of arts-based strategies is to affect the aesthetic properties of organisational infrastructure in order to generate instrumental benefits. These kinds of strategies follow the strategic approach that can be labelled 'building arts capital'. They are particularly useful when it is necessary to increase either the intangible value incorporated into the organisational infrastructure, or to transform tangible and intangible organisational structural components so that they better support organisational value-creation dynamics. Some examples of strategic objectives related to this strategic approach include: the improvement of organisational identity; the development of brand reputation and awareness; the creation of socio-cultural values for communities; a better management of the communication of the organisational image; the adoption of alternative marketing approaches; the incorporation of art collections in the organisational portfolio of assets; and the creation of intangible value to be incorporated into organisational products.

ABIs for artful organisational development

When ABIs are adopted with the strategic intent to develop both people and organisational infrastructure, they move into the artful zone. In this case the managerial use of art forms can be focused on the transformation of tangible or intangible organisational assets and/or on the development of people's abilities or networking processes. The essential goal is to enable a transformation of the organisation. The strategies that employ ABIs to stimulate and support organisational transformation respond to a strategic approach that can be labelled as 'artful organisational development'. The focus of the strategies aligned with this strategic approach is to exploit and lever the properties of art forms in order to catalyse and drive change both at a people and infrastructural level. This can generate benefits in terms of growth of key organisational dimensions such as values, culture, mindsets, skills, workplace, routines, procedures, internal and external relationships and products. The definition of 'artful organisational development' strategies is at the core of the adoption of the arts to create value for business. In the twenty-first century business landscape, the value and the capacity to create value is increasingly tied to the organisation's ability to manage aesthetic experiences both internally and externally.

Internally, organisations need to create contexts in which people are keen to put passion into what they do. Externally, organisations need to create impacts that are aligned with the people's wants and needs to experience positive feelings. This sets the challenge to handle and harness people's emotions and energy states. They are key factors in creating value in the new business age. In this perspective, art forms are the instruments for management to understand how to spark and govern emotional and energetic dynamics. The artful organisational development strategies recognise the managerial relevance of the arts and the importance of integrating the use of art forms in management systems. As for how this integration can be performed, it is possible to identify two main approaches. On the one hand, arts-based management actions can be adopted as approaches and tools on the basis of specific needs related to management challenges or business problems to deal with. On the other hand, arts-based practices can be fully incorporated into the business model of the organisation. The former considers ABIs as strategic management actions to be brought into organisations every time it is necessary. The latter assumes that ABIs can become part of the everyday organisational life, and that the arts can be absorbed in the organisational DNA. Many examples of organisations that have adopted ABIs as a management means to face specific business issues have been already addressed in this book. In the following section the case study of Spinach, an organisation that has fully adopted arts in its business model, is presented. Spinach is a marketing research company that has integrated the arts into its organisational life, making ABIs a component of the management practices and the arts the foundation of the management philosophy.

Integrating the arts into organisational life: the case study of Spinach

Spinach represents an example of the adoption and absorption of the arts into day-to-day organisational business activities. The arts are integrated into the organisational business model and into everyday business activities as a way to be creative and to handle complexity, turbulence, uncertainty and ambiguity. While most companies tend to experience the arts and adopt ABIs on an occasional basis, Spinach underpins its strategy, operations and organisational activities with the arts.

Spinach is a marketing research agency established by Tom Conway and Lucy Morris, both with previous professional experiences in the marketing research industry. They both used to work for companies adopting traditional approaches to human resource management, operations management and product development. In the act of establishing their own company, they aspired to create an organisation with imagination at its heart, both in the way they run the company and in the way they approach project work and generally any other business issue. Their original inspiration was to create an organisation that would be able to work in a creative way.

Shaping the business model of Spinach, Tom Conway and Lucy Morris were interested in building an organisation which would not only be proficient in achieving high business performance, but also in generating a working context and atmosphere capable of keeping them interested in what they do, as well as to continuously and positively challenge them and the people working in the organisation, in order to support their growth as individuals, as a community and as a business organisation. Thus, the original idea was to develop an inspiring enterprise by working with creative people, in order to craft a creative atmosphere and 'osmotically' transfer to employees the abilities to creatively and enthusiastically harness business challenges. This led to the decision to involve artists in the organisational life and to adopt artistic products and processes as a key component to support and inspire everyday activities. To bring the arts in and to continuously generate an organisational context in which arts-based experiences shape a positive emotional and energetic organisational atmosphere was not a straightforward task. Spinach's top management, looking for possible approaches to integrate the arts into the company's business model, decided to opt for bringing an arts champion in the organisation, i.e., someone with the task of acting as a catalyser to create a continuous tension between daily rational-based business activities and emotive-based artistic experiences. The position of creativity director was defined and a professional artist with experience in business was appointed. However, in order to guarantee that the creativity director could continue to keep their creative life as an artist and be able to bring in refreshed emotive and energising ideas and stimulus, it was decided they should be independent of the company, to give them the freedom to decide how to arrange and manage arts-based management actions within the organisation. Martin Gent, a conceptual artist with a wide range of expertise at the intersection between arts and business, was appointed. His responsibility was defined as the role of defining and managing ABIs which could trigger, develop, maintain, renew and flourish a creative organisational environment, pervaded by positive emotional and energetic dynamics.

The role of creativity director is to guarantee that the arts in all their possible forms can continuously pervade the organisational environment and activities. The strategic intent of his role is to make the organisation as artful as possible, making sure that the traditional rational-based toolbox adopted by the organisation is blended with the intuition and aesthetic characteristics of the arts. Indeed, Spinach relies on traditional marketing research techniques, but there is a fundamental understanding that these rational-based management tools need to be enriched and integrated with aesthetic- and creative-based approaches. The fundamental assumption is that the arts can help the organisation not only to be more productive, but most importantly to be more resilient, adaptable, agile and intuitive. Therefore bringing the arts into the organisation is not meant to transform employees into artists, and neither to necessarily adopt the arts as an instrument to carry out day-to-day organisational activities, nor to force the use of the arts into organisational processes such as new product development or marketing and communication. The arts in business are aimed at creating a more human-centred organisation which values the strategic importance of the aesthetic experiences, emotions and energy to enhance organisational wealth and value-creation capacity.

The task of the creative director is to guarantee that the organisation is immersed in the arts so that they can shape the aesthetic properties of organisational infrastructure and engage people in aesthetic experiences. Therefore, the adoption of ABIs is not an occasional event that responds to specific management needs, but it is rather a constant facet of organisational life. ABIs are adopted with the aim of creating a positive tension between rational and emotive thinking. The goal is to spur people's imagination, creativity and emotions, and to create organisational contexts and dynamics that significantly contribute to people feeling fully alive and centred, i.e., engaged in their working activities. ABIs represent, for Spinach, the approaches and tools to continuously contaminate the organisational life with arts-based experiences and properties. Today, they are an integrated aspect of organisational activities and can be more or less aligned with the achievement of business objectives.

The strategic approach adopted by Spinach to integrate the arts in business implicitly reflects a vision of the organisation as a techno-human system recognising the importance of aesthetics and emotions in shaping organisational life and activities. In Spinach there is a strong acknowledgement of the centrality of people. In this perspective the use of the arts represents the approach to shape the organisational infrastructure and to influence employees' attitudes and behaviours with the scope of creating and maintaining the organisation as a living organism capable of adaptive and proactive innovation capacity.

The ABIs at Spinach

At Spinach, some ABIs can be defined to face specific business issues such as the presentation of a marketing research to important clients, or the design of a creative approach to start a marketing investigation. Other ABIs can be defined not necessarily targeting a specific business problem, but just with the aim of creating aesthetic experiences, or to shape the aesthetic properties of tangible and intangible organisational assets. In this case, ABIs appear to be independent from the organisational business objectives. Nevertheless they affect the day-to-day business activities, creating an ideal space and atmosphere where employees can find emotive and energetic refreshment able to simply help them to feel better, or to inspire them to find creative solutions or different approaches to the tasks they are dealing with. In any case, the use of art forms is fully integrated in the organisational context and workplace. The ultimate objective is to make them a characteristic of Spinach's modus operandi, and to make sure they are absorbed into the organisation's business model and management philosophy.

The contents and features of ABIs adopted in Spinach are very wide ranging. All the possible working mechanisms of ABIs are basically leveraged. Both artistic products and processes are adopted, and people can be involved in both hands-on and hands-off initiatives that take place mainly, but not exclusively, in the organisational workplace. Employees are involved in 'making aesthetic artefacts' in order to explore their deep understanding of the business challenges and problems to be faced, or simply just to express their feelings about themselves in the organisation. The arts are brought into the organisation creating situations that allow employees to 'attend artworks'. This catalyses aesthetic experiences and generally has an impact on people's emotions and energy. People can also be involved in 'artful creation'. In this case employees are engaged in an art-making process aimed at awakening their passion and commitment for what they do. Finally, ABIs are also used in order to make possible the 'absorption of the artistry' in order to improve business processes. This means that the art-making process is analysed as a role model with the aim of extracting insights to be incorporated in daily work activities such as, for example, how to manage time and space when performing a creative investigation or when it is necessary to find inspiration and exercise imagination.

In order to ensure that employees are continuously exposed to new art expressions and can be stimulated by new emotional and energetic experiences, ABIs change over time and involve different artists.

Although the adoption of the arts in Spinach can present different facets and can respond to different organisational value-drivers as mapped in the Arts Value Matrix, there is a constant attention to keeping ABIs aligned with the organisational strategic objectives. Therefore, the arts in Spinach do not represent just something nice to have because they can make people happy and differentiate the company in the market, but they are considered a key dimension of the value-creation capacity of the organisation. The alignment of arts-based management actions with strategic objectives and business performance targets is assured by strategic meetings between Spinach's top management and the creativity director, in which the strategic intents of ABIs are outlined on the basis of a discussion of the management and business challenges to be faced. Experiential days are planned in advance with Spinach's top management and the creativity director to bring the team together and work on particular issues and/or needs that it is felt the company needs, both on an individual and an organisational level. These days are held 'off-site' and involve working with arts-based practices and processes in order to highlight, explore and experience new and different ways of dealing with organisational needs and issues. The aim of the experiential day is to guarantee that the arts and business become interwoven. This does not mean that ABIs are consequently implemented only to solve pragmatic and contingent business problems. They have a wide-ranging focus addressing employees and infrastructure development. The adoption of ABIs is essentially aimed at creating and maintaining an organisation climate in which people are continually engaged to reflect on what they do, recognising the importance of their actions for the creation of sustainable value. So, most ABIs involve people in experiences that are not necessarily directly linked to the business activities. In this regard Tom Conway, Spinach's chief executive officer (CEO), states that ABIs 'make people wonder "why do we dedicate time and resources to experiential activities, rather than simply chase after business which is what basically pays our salaries?" Questions like this one move people to see their job and their organisation differently and most importantly to develop a better awareness of themselves, of the organisation and of the world around them.'

For Spinach the meaning of the arts in the organisation is to create a continuous creative tension that permits the development of what they label as the 'right side of the brain', that is the emotive and energetic dimensions of the organisation, in order to foster adaptability, imagination, creativity and intuition.

The arts-based strategic management actions implemented by Spinach fundamentally respond to the artful organisational development strategic approach. This means that if ABIs are adopted focusing on people or on infrastructure, they are recognised as levers to support the continuous renovation and evolution of the organisation. The ABIs implemented in Spinach address all the organisational value-drivers mapped by the Arts Value Matrix. Below, in particular, three main arts-based strategic management actions are outlined.

ABIs for creating an emotive and energetic workplace

Spinach's workplace setting is structured in order to synergistically combine open spaces with private corners and areas in which people can do some 'heads-down' work when they need concentration that the open space cannot assure. In the office space, music is played and artworks hang on the walls. Each work desk is a 'hot-desk' specifically designed so that anyone can use it on the basis of his/her own specific needs. The open space with an espresso coffee-machine corner and a meeting area facilitates and supports knowledge-flow dynamics, and creates a pleasant area where people can relax and have conversations.

At the same time, two colourful creative cubicles, specifically designed as creative 'war rooms', allow people to have at their disposal a private space to either exercise their creative activities and conversations, or manage business activities that require confidentiality. Thus, Spinach dedicates great attention to the design and setting of the organisational environment. It is recognised as a platform for igniting people's emotions and energy and as a device to inspire people's imagination and creativity as well as to support people's networking dynamics. By shaping the environment with arts-based features Spinach is able to foster the creation of an engaging organisational atmosphere. This, as suggested by the Arts Value Matrix, encourages employees to feel free to express themselves.

Many ABIs are adopted by the organisation to shape and beautify the workplace. The office space is considered not only as the area in which business activities take place, but also as a physical 'container' to be filled with art forms. The office space is periodically made available as an open gallery in which artists, organisational people and other guests can meet, discuss and have a glass of wine in a convivial, informal and social atmosphere. Every three months a different artist is invited to set an art exhibition in the workplace. Usually artists are invited to work in-residence contributing to create a context in which people can be entertained, but most importantly energised and inspired. Through the implementation of arts exhibitions, events and performances, Spinach values the workplace as a relevant organisational tangible asset permeated with emotive knowledge.

The ABIs aimed at shaping the organisational environment are considered a key factor in sparking and nourishing a creative and energetic atmosphere. The underlying organisational vision is to create and maintain a workspace that incorporates art manifestations and related aesthetic properties, so that it is able to evoke aesthetic experiences. Then the arts are used both to beautify all the possible facets of the workplace and to shape organisational contexts. This contributes to the development of organisational knowledge assets, the effects of which can be accounted for in the four perspectives of the Arts Benefits Constellation. In fact, people's capacity for dealing with business issues (brainware) is maintained positive; the networking dynamics in the organisation as well as between the organisation and external stakeholders (netware) are kept effective; the culture and identity of the company (software) are continually strengthened; and finally, the physical space of the workplace (hardware) is systematically managed in order to be engaging.

ABIs for people development

Spinach as a marketing research agency needs people with sensitivity and well-developed collaborative skills. Business projects start from a client brief outlining their objectives and requirements from the agency. The brief internally represents the basis for a creative conversation aimed at defining and proposing possible solutions to the client. Once the proposals have been approved, the agency's researchers conduct appropriate fieldwork with the target audience of consumers. The team of researchers then collaborate in analysis sessions, looking not just to summarise the key findings but also to find deeper, more fruitful insights that can create added value for their client. The last phase is a debrief presentation to the client.

Spinach recognises that the process is far more effective and productive when the research team possesses and develops the right combination of abilities over the time. The capabilities that are identified as crucial for the performance of the organisation can be summarised as follows: being supportive and empathetic; being able to realise and identify critical business issues; feeling more comfortable to speak to each other; being sufficiently and properly equipped to cope with and solve the proposed client's issues; being comfortable with proposing and sponsoring one's own ideas and standpoints; having a collaborative approach; feeling active without negative tension; feeling more confident; reducing personal fear; being more comfortable in dealing with complex situations; managing the fear of failure; and being able to accept and deal with uncertain and ambiguous situations. In order to develop the above people's capabilities, the top management of Spinach considers the adoption of unconventional learning and development approaches of fundamental importance. With this target, ABIs are deployed as arts training and professional development instruments. They are recognised by the organisation as an essential learning platform to support positive changes in people's mindsets and behaviours as well as to expand specific people's skills, particularly in the area of communication and creativity.

Having an artist as a creative director and exposing everyday employees to artists-in-residence and/or to artistic products and processes generates different benefits for Spinach in terms of people development. First and foremost, this poses a challenge to people's preconceived ideas about what the work activities might be. People get to understand the artistic process, seeing the hard work and the intellectual act grounding the creation of an artwork.

The fact of being immersed in the art creation process and being part of this process by making connections and sharing ideas with the artist, gives Spinach employees the valuable opportunity to share and understand the arts-based work dynamics, the complexities of the artistic work and the inspiration grounding the artistic creation process. Through the ABIs' working mechanisms of 'artful creation' and/or 'artistry absorption', people can respectively understand the importance of being fully engaged in what they do and/or discover how to perform their activities differently. Working in an organisation infused with the arts allows people to develop emotive knowledge and tune their 'know-feel' abilities. This is further facilitated when the ABIs are based on artists-in-residence, in which case the social interactions between artists and employees activate socialisation processes and empathetic communications that support the transfer of tacit knowledge. The people observing and sharing artistic working practices have not only the opportunity to reflect on the creative process, but also to borrow approaches and techniques to use in their daily activities. As accounted for by the Arts Value Matrix, the employees involved in ABIs can develop their own soft skills which in turn help them to be more productive and self-confident.

ABIs for organisational transformation

The integration of the arts in the organisational business model and in the management philosophy has significantly contributed to developing Spinach's capabilities of being adaptable and innovative. The industry in which Spinach operates requires high flexibility and agility due to both its intrinsic complexity and its knowledge-intensive nature. In Spinach, ABIs are adopted as a management means to generate creative tension and an emotional energy that encourages a change-oriented organisational culture. This, today, allows the company to grow according to both an adaptive and a proactive approach. Arts maintain a set of values that promote esprit de corps, collaboration, risk taking, respect of standpoints and ideas and an organisational culture based on loyalty and integrity.

ABIs are continuously deployed as a means to sustain strategic transformation. This is achieved on the basis of a stakeholder-oriented view that recognises the company's focus on creating value by balancing the economic dimension with other value scopes and particularly with the wellbeing of people in the organisation.

ABIs are used to shape a positive atmosphere that creates a spirit within the organisation. This reflects the soul of the company that is focused on people and wants to create value for them, rather than, as stated by Tom Conway: 'being another productive context focused on making money'. The adoption of art forms creates joyful experiences for people, making them happy, excited and fulfilled. In addition, the full integration of the arts into organisational life drives the definition of new products and a better search for new opportunities. In this regard, the ABIs produce benefits in terms of 'investment' as accounted for in the Arts Value Matrix. Indeed, they are also used as an instrument to add value to Spinach's products.

An interesting example of how ABIs are implemented in Spinach to support transformation is the creation of a collaboration with an artist in order to stimulate conversations and thoughts around the key strategic objective of rebranding the company. An artist was invited to make a proposal of what he would do in the Spinach space, as the company was in the process of rebranding. It was agreed that the artist worked 'in-residence' for a week, and 'rebranded' the company every day, on the basis of his observations and feelings. The artist worked in close proximity with employees, interacting with them, but at the same time in parallel and independently from their daily business activities. The fundamental idea at the basis of the ABI was to encourage a reflection around the rebranding, focusing on the development of Spinach's logo. The artist explored many ideas in a short space of time and responding to his daily experiences in the office. Through words, conversations and images raised by the interactions between the artist and the organisation's people, at the end of the week, five works of art were produced. They were then displayed in Spinach's workspace as an exhibition for the next few months. The artist did not have a direct involvement or say in the design of the actual new branding, but his engagement at that time helped to highlight and support the change process taking place with regard to the rebranding. The outcome of this ABI was not only the production of inspiring works of art, that ultimately contributed to defining the new branding of the company, but also the creation of conversations that sparked many transformational reflections such as, in particular, a better understanding of how to experience the inspiration that starts from ideas and as a reaction to inner instincts.

The arts as a key dimension of Spinach's DNA

Today, the arts represent a key dimension of Spinach's DNA. The company has fully absorbed the arts into its business model. The member of the organisation responsible for maintaining and developing the relationships with the arts is the creativity director, who acts as a gatekeeper between two realities: the arts and the business. He works in close coordination with the top management, sharing the strategic intents to adopt ABIs. As a result the arts are part of Spinach's organisational life and they are employed to support enhancement of the organisational value-creation capacity both internally and externally. From an internal point of view, the arts are exploited as a management means to develop organisational knowledge assets and particularly, among others, the organisational culture and atmosphere capable of guaranteeing an emotional and creative ability to cope with changes and business complexity. This also allows an organisational environment to be created in which people are engaged with their emotions and energy in daily working activities. From an external point of view, the management integration of the arts in Spinach's business model contributes to defining and communicating the organisational identity and raising brand awareness.

Managing ABIs: deploying the arts to improve business performance

ABIs contribute to creating value for business only if their adoption is linked and aligned with the organisational operations and strategy. Indeed, simply bringing art forms and artists into an organisation does not produce positive impacts on business performance. Contaminating organisational life with art forms is energising and beneficial in many ways. However, in order to make sure that ABIs are addressed so as to enhance organisational value-creation capacity and to respond to strategic management purposes, their adoption must respond to a structured management process. This represents an important condition to ensure that ABIs produce impacts capable of developing organisational value-drivers.

Before exploring the stages characterising the management process of ABIs, it is important to address a preliminary question: *Who is responsible for managing ABIs?* The responsibility for defining and managing ABIs aimed at producing business benefits is attributed to two fundamental integrated organisational functions that can be defined respectively as: the 'arts architect' and the 'arts management team'. They are, conceptually, two different organisational functions, although they are interdependent and in some cases they may overlap each other. In the next section the role of these organisational functions is elaborated.

The arts architect and the arts management team

Today, business and the arts are still two different realities. In order to bridge the gap between them, it is important that organisations have in place specific functions operating as an interface facilitating the deployment of art forms for organisational and business development purposes. The arts architect and the arts management team play this essential role.

The arts architect operates as a gatekeeper with the goal of both understanding the management challenges and the business problems to be faced, and defining the most appropriate art forms to be adopted by the organisation to enhance its value-creation capacity.

The position of the arts architect, which can be held by an artist or a group of artists and business consultants, is responsible for five fundamental functions. First, the arts architect is in charge of analysing and understanding the context in which the art forms are going to be deployed. This entails a thorough investigation of the nature of the business problems that will have to be faced through the managerial use of art forms. For this reason it is critical that the arts architect build igniting and fruitful conversations with the management of the organisation. The aim of establishing conversations is to clarify how the arts can be employed to address the specific business problems the organisation is dealing with. The conversation represents a fundamental method to explore the issues that are hampering organisational value-creation dynamics. They respond to the second fundamental function of the arts architect, corresponding to the diagnosis of organisational problems. In this regard, it is very important to point out that although the organisation's management can have a clear understanding of the challenges and issues to be faced, very often it is not fully capable of recognising the emotive and energetic factors affecting the organisational capacity to face and solve the business problems. The third function is related to the designing of ABIs. This corresponds to shaping the most appropriate art forms to adopt and exploit in order to achieve the targeted organisational development objectives. This is a precondition for the implementation of ABIs. The coordination of the implementation of ABIs represents the fourth function of the arts architect, who has to exploit the aesthetic power of art forms making sure they create aesthetic experiences and/or manipulate aesthetic properties that spark and nourish positive emotional and energetic dynamics in and around the organisation. Finally, the arts architect contributes to the assessment and revision of the impacts of the arts-based management actions in order to prove the generated benefits and to explain the causes enabling or hampering the successful achievement of business targets.

The professionals in the position of arts architect generally are proficient artists who have developed the competences of a facilitator to plan, implement and assess ABIs with the aim of creating value for an organisation. In some cases, particularly when ABIs address complex business issues and take the form of projects and programmes, the artist(s) can work in cooperation with business consultants.

It is worth highlighting that the arts architect's role requires that this function cannot be simply occupied by an artist or a consultant who has acquired some familiarity with arts-based techniques. The managerial use of the arts for business purposes does not simply mean to bring artists or art forms into an organisation. ABIs are purposely management actions using art forms to deal with business issues that require emotive and energetic understanding. The exploitation of art forms for management purposes requires an understanding both of the ABIs' capacity to address business issues and of the techniques used to design and implement art forms able to create and transfer emotive knowledge. For this reason, an arts architect has to be proficient in both the artistic and the business language. They have to be able to understand the characteristics of the arts and the challenges of business, as well as to bridge the gap between business and the arts, so that the application of art forms drives the management of aesthetic dimensions to handle emotional and energetic dynamics in the organisation. It is worth noticing that in most cases the position of arts architect is held by conceptual artists. They are skilled at shaping art forms to address conceptual issues, and can more easily understand how to employ the arts to face business problems once they have developed experience in managing organisational arts-based experiences, as well as in embedding the arts into business assets to enhance organisational value-creation capacity.

To make sure that ABIs are properly adopted to improve business performance within organisations, the arts architect needs to work in close collaboration with managers. The team formed by the arts architect and the organisation's managers can be named the 'arts management team'. Organisations can approach the adoption of art forms in very different ways. An ABI can be adopted simply as a 'one-off' intervention to address a specific operational task. At the same time other organisations may approach art forms as a management means to achieve more strategic objectives. In any case the adoption of an ABI involves the running of a management process in order to make sure that it produces the expected outputs and outcomes. Therefore, it is fundamental to understand who the owners of the adoption of an ABI are and who is responsible for its running and its impact on organisational performance. The arts management team is the organisational function responsible for the adoption of ABIs. With regard to the scale of the initiative, the arts management team can present different characteristics in terms of size, nature and function. However, it essentially includes at least two important actors: the manager and the arts architect. For successful adoption of ABIs, the organisation's managers have to be directly involved in the definition and implementation process. They bring knowledge about the management challenges and the business problems the organisation is facing, as well as a thorough understanding of the organisational strategic and operational objectives to focus on. In addition, they ensure that ABIs are implemented in order to produce the highest possible benefits for the organisation. At the same time, the arts architect is in charge both of defining the most appropriate ABIs that meet the organisation's wants and needs, and of putting ABIs into action. The arts management team is ultimately responsible for the success of the adoption of ABIs. It has to ensure that ABIs are defined and implemented in such a way as to enhance organisational value-creation capacity, and its impacts can be accounted for. For this reason it is essential that ABIs are linked and aligned to organisational operations and strategy. In this regard, in the next section a structured management process is discussed.

The management cycle of ABIs

Organisations can approach the adoption of art forms in very different ways. They can either be seen simply as a tool to address a key operational task aimed at solving a narrow business problem, or they can represent approaches and techniques integrated into the management system in order to support the continuous improvement of business performance, as well as the sustainable renewal of organisational capabilities. In the first case, an ABI can simply represent a 'one-off' intervention to address a specific operational task, while in the second case, organisations distinguish the use of the arts as a strategic management means and embrace ABIs to address strategic objectives. In this perspective, the adoption of the arts in management can significantly contribute to the transformation of organisations, impacting on critical facets such as: management's and people's mindsets; organisational life and processes; organisational business model; products; and relationships with external stakeholders.

Therefore, the implementation of an ABI can be aimed at solving a very well-defined organisational problem or at supporting the development of key strategic organisational value-drivers. In both cases, the successful adoption of an ABI and its positive effects on business performance are significantly related to the management process of the arts-based management actions. An ABI, as any other management initiative, has to be successfully integrated into the organisational management system. The integration makes sure that ABIs are linked and aligned to operational improvement programmes and organisational strategy. Specifically, the incorporation of ABIs into organisational operations ensures that they are tailored to solve specific operations performance problems the organisation is dealing with. At the same time, linking and aligning ABIs with strategy allows the understanding of how they contribute to the enhancement of organisational value-creation capacity, both by developing organisational value-creation

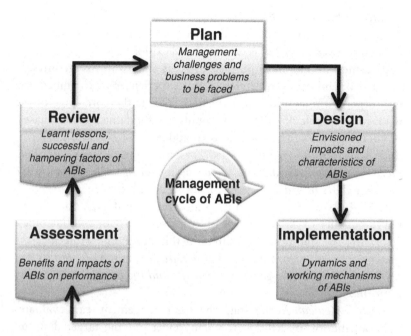

5.2 The management cycle of ABIs: a closed-loop process

mechanisms and/or by increasing the value stock embedded in organisational components.

A structured management process that can support managers as they integrate and align ABIs to organisational operations and strategy is shown in Figure 5.2. This framework is based on a closed-loop managerial process including five major stages that denote the management cycle of ABIs.

Stage 1: Plan. The arts management team defines the strategic intents and the organisational value-drivers to be addressed with the adoption of ABIs. During this stage, an organisation has to address two main questions: *What are the management challenges or business problems to be faced? What are the expected results and outcomes of ABIs?*

Stage 2: Design. Once the managerial and business reasons grounding the adoption of ABIs have been clarified, the arts management team has to define the action plan. In this stage, three important questions have to be addressed: *What are the envisioned impacts of ABIs? What are the traits characterising ABIs? How can ABIs be implemented?*

Stage 3: Implementation. The implementation stage corresponds to the process of putting ABIs into practice. In this management stage, the aesthetic power of an ABI is disclosed and exploited for organisational and business development purposes. Artists and art forms are brought into the organisation to catalyse artful experiences or to embed arts into organisational and business assets. This is the core stage of the management cycle of ABIs and it entails five fundamental sub-phases. At this stage the critical questions to address are: *How do we introduce ABIs into the organisation? What are the dynamics and working mechanisms that characterise the development of ABIs? How do we facilitate ABIs in order to extract learning insights?*

Stage 4: Assessment. This stage is aimed at identifying and accounting the quality of ABIs in terms of processes, outputs and outcomes. Typically, the questions to address in this phase are: *How was the quality of the implemented ABIs? What are the main ABIs' results and features? What are the generated benefits and the impacts on business performance?*

Stage 5: Review. At this stage the arts management team evaluates the contribution of ABIs to the achievement of the targeted strategic and performance objectives. Additionally, the main managerial insights related both to the implementation process of ABIs and to the organisational absorption of ABIs' aesthetic dimensions are identified and codified. This allows for both an understanding of the value generated by ABIs and the identification of the lessons learnt, in order to drive the management towards the implementation of further ABIs. The fundamental questions characterising this stage are: *How have ABIs contributed to the accomplishment of the strategic objectives and to the delivery of organisational value propositions? What are the main lessons learnt from the implementation of ABIs? What are the successful factors and, contrastingly, the causes that have hampered the success of the implemented ABIs?*

The management cycle of ABIs can help the management to run the adoption of art forms in order to address business value-creation objectives. The stages outlined in the framework allow the definition of ABIs as a means of driving the improvement of business performance. In addition, they allow executives to incorporate the use of art forms into their organisational management systems. In the next sections, the five stages of the management cycle are discussed.

Plan: defining the strategic value objectives of ABIs

The management cycle of ABIs starts with understanding the organisational value propositions and the organisational strategic and performance objectives. These are derived directly from the organisation's strategy. Even if an ABI can be adopted simply as a tool to carry out a very well-defined practical task, it is important to clarify its position in the organisational strategic plan.

The strategy of an organisation can be considered as given, although organisations can approach the strategy definition in very different ways. Thus, it is possible to assume that an organisation has always a more or less explicit definition of its development directions and strategic objectives. This concerns an awareness of the value propositions targeted by the organisation, and the definition of the main strategic objectives as well as of the most important performance targets that an organisation wants to accomplish. The formal definition of the strategy is essentially a practice and a facet characterising medium and large business organisations, whereas it is not necessarily the case for small business organisations that tend to adopt informal and emergent strategies. Considering the strategy to be formal or informal as given, it is possible to translate it in terms of the definition of the organisational strategic value objectives and business priorities.

In the planning stage, the arts management team has to define the business problems to be addressed. They are derived from the organisational strategic objectives and they need to be aligned with the targeted value propositions. The identification of the business problems clarifies the fundamental reasons motivating the use of ABIs. Generally, due to the unconventional nature of ABIs, it is difficult for organisations to articulate and formalise the reasons underpinning the adoption of art forms in management in order to face business challenges and problems. This is particularly true for those organisations that have never experimented with the use of art forms to address business issues. In addition, there might be a tendency to put ABIs in narrow boxes; assuming that they are mainly tools for human resource management, social responsibility and community affairs and client relationship management.

The Arts Value Matrix can be used as a framework to speculate on and explore the organisational value-drivers that can be developed through the implementation of ABIs. It supports the arts management team to investigate the purposes of ABIs, disclosing the value dimensions related to the development of people and organisational infrastructure. The Arts Value Matrix represents a possible pattern to support managers in thinking about why art forms should be used to deal with business issues. Most importantly, it provides a platform to fuel a conversation between executives and the arts architect and artists. An igniting and fruitful conversation among the members of the arts management team is at the core of the planning stage. There are two fundamental reasons explaining the crucial importance of developing a proper conversation around the adoption of ABIs. First, it allows a mutual understanding to be built between managers and arts architects about what ABIs are primarily for. This, in turn, is also a critical factor for building a trustworthy partnership between arts and business. In fact, for a successful implementation of an ABI there has to be an implicit agreement on the relevance of the arts. This is grounded in the acknowledgement of the fundamental human nature of the organisation. The adoption of the arts in management is based on the presupposition that an organisation is made of people and works for people. The deployment of art forms recognises that people are not machine-like components, but human beings whose productivity depends on the full engagement of their technical and emotive knowledge. An open conversation allows the position of the organisation's managers to be understood and if they share the embedded core principle of the artworld, i.e., the centrality of human beings and of their emotional and energetic dynamics. Of course, ABIs can be adopted by an organisation as just another tool to deal with business issues, without really considering and recognising the centrality of people. In this case, art forms can become one of the possible dimensions of an organisation; but it's very unlikely they will have a positive impact as catalysers for organisational and people development. Second, through a conversation, an arts architect can understand which organisational issues ABIs should focus on. The conversation is aimed at identifying and spotlighting the problems that block and constrain the organisational value-creation capacity. Conceptually, the conversation can be associated with a therapeutic diagnostic approach. The arts architect sustains a conversation by asking questions with the aim both to understand the issues concerning the organisation, and to identify the main problems' symptoms, particularly in terms of people's attitudes and behaviours. From a practical point of view, a conversation may involve different kinds of activities including multiple interviews with key people in the organisation, qualitative evaluation questionnaires, direct observations, accessing and analysing organisational documentation, induction and testing of hypotheses by prototyping arts-based experiments or investigations. The analysis of the strategic intents at the basis of the adoption of ABIs has to be possibly integrated with a performance gap analysis in order to define the position of the organisation in terms of performance and the possible desired achievable performance improvements.

Once an organisation has clarified the reasons for bringing in artists and art forms, and has understood the potential value of ABIs, the explanation of how ABIs might impact the development of organisational dimensions and on the accomplishment of targeted performance objectives has to be addressed. This corresponds, essentially, to defining the expected results and outcomes of an ABI. For this purpose, the Arts Value Map can be used. The definition of the presupposed cause-effect relationships linking together the adoption of ABIs, the development of organisational components, the impact on organisational processes, and the achievement of strategic objectives, provides a visualisation and an understanding of how ABIs can contribute to the improvement of business performance and generate wealth. The Arts Value Map helps the arts management team to define an integrated picture of the value of the arts for business. It can be adopted in accordance either with a top-down or a bottom-up approach. In the first case, once the strategic and performance objectives at the basis of the delivery of value propositions are defined, the key processes and capabilities affecting their achievement need to be identified. Then the critical knowledge assets forming and affecting the targeted capabilities have to be understood paying particular attention to the relevance of emotive knowledge and to the role that the management's use of art forms can play for the development of organisational knowledge domains. In case the ABIs to be implemented are already defined, the bottom-up application of the Arts Value Map helps to describe the organisational components that can be affected and the outcomes of their development on organisational processes and strategic performance objectives.

In summary, the planning stage requires that the arts management team clarifies the organisation's strategy and defines the position of the organisation. The goal of this stage is to clearly identify the key strategic value objectives that the organisation aims to address through the adoption of ABIs. Although the implementation of art forms can be focused on the development of specific organisational components, it is fundamental to clarify how they are linked and integrated with the organisational strategic performance objectives. For this reason, managers need to identify the cause-effect relationship grounding the assumption that the adoption of ABIs can drive value creation. This means that the definition of the Arts Value Map can be considered as the main managerial output of this stage.

Design: defining the characteristics of ABIs

At this stage, the arts management team formulates the action plan to be executed. It provides information about the 'why', 'what' and 'how'. The 'why' corresponds to a clear definition of ABIs' purposes. It is essentially the output of the planning stage. The aim is to list the main expected outputs and outcomes. This provides an understanding of the final result of the adoption of ABIs. By leveraging aesthetic experiences and properties, ABIs activate development dynamic effects on organisational knowledge assets. The final result of these dynamics can be envisioned, but it is unlikely to define ex-ante the detailed features of this result because it mainly involves human-based dimensions that can only be fully identified and understood ex-post. In other words, it is possible to assume that the definition of ABIs' purposes, metaphorically considering the implementation of ABIs as a journey, is likely to sketch the 'final destination' rather than provide the detailed specifications of the 'coordinates' precisely describing the arrival point. The 'what' defines the characteristics of an ABI. This involves the definition of the focus of an ABI, i.e., the organisational knowledge asset to be developed, together with an understanding of the related aesthetic actions, i.e., generation of aesthetic experiences versus manipulation of aesthetic properties. It also includes the decision on the ABIs' content and working mechanisms to be exploited. Furthermore, it aims to clarify the nature of ABIs, distinguishing short-term interventions from medium- and long-term initiatives. The 'how' regards the definition of the implementation process of an ABI. This corresponds to defining the modalities for putting an ABI into practice. In this regard, it is important to highlight that ABIs are not standardised, but are idiosyncratic and context-specific arts-based management actions. Therefore, although the arts architect can adopt a defined toolbox of arts-based instruments, the peculiarities of the specific organisational context have to be taken into account. The definition of how ABIs can be implemented has to consider their influence in the specific organisational life evolution dynamics. This means that any ABI has to be conceived and defined as a bespoke arts-based management action and it has to be tailored to the specific organisational needs. In addition, since an organisation is a living system and ABIs are aimed at impacting on and interacting with organisational life dynamics, the agenda describing the modalities for the implementation of ABIs has to be considered mainly as an outline, rather than as a structured detailed programme. This is because, to release control and leave space for experiential dynamics to take place is a peculiar dimension of the implementation of ABIs, and particularly of those actions addressing people learning and development. The implementation of an ABI has to be artful in itself. This means that the design process is not to bridle ABIs' activities with the risk of undermining the development of emotional and energetic flow dynamics.

Therefore, the main focus of the design is concerned both with the definition of the vision and the sketch of the implementation process flow of ABIs. The former provides the cardinal direction of the ABI. It corresponds to projecting the desired results and outcomes of an ABI. The latter defines the agenda to follow when implementing ABIs. This involves the definition of the techniques and tools to be used as well as of the time frame for the implementation of ABIs, though this is not to be considered a tight schedule. Finally, like any other management initiative, the design process involves a budgeting activity aimed at defining and allocating the budget resources.

Implementation: putting ABIs into practice

In this stage, the designed ABI is put into practice. The characteristics of the implementation of an ABI are strongly affected by its specific traits. By focusing the attention on how the implementation process involves people in the organisation, it is possible to identify the main building blocks characterising the implementation of ABIs. As shown in Figure 5.3 the implementation of an ABI involves five major sub-processes that are functionally related to each other. The process starts

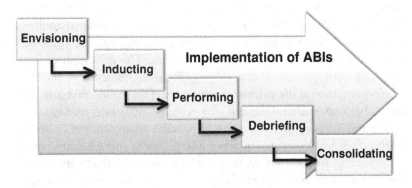

5.3 The stages of the implementation of ABIs

with envisioning the positive effects that ABIs are able to generate, and finishes with actions aimed at making sure that the learning insights of ABIs are absorbed by the organisation and produce the expected positive impacts.

Envisioning – this process is aimed at letting people understand the value associated with their involvement in ABIs. At this stage, the arts management team communicates the expected positive results and outcomes of ABIs to the organisational employees. It is also clarified who will be involved in the arts-based management actions and if this will take the form of a direct or an indirect involvement. Therefore, the envisioning is aimed at projecting the value and the positive impacts of the experiential dynamics activated by ABIs. Its goal is to create the commitment for a full involvement of people in the art-based management action.

Inducting – in this phase people are instructed about three essential traits of ABIs: the designed modalities characterising the implementation of ABIs; the role of artists as facilitators and/or of the adopted art forms; and what people need to do in order to get the most from the direct or indirect arts-based experiences. People need to understand ABIs' contents and aims. The explanation of the ABI helps both to raise people's attention and to clear up any misunderstanding. For example, it is important to instruct people in the kind of attention they would need to put both on what happens during the implementation of an ABI, and on what happens inside them as they experience art forms. People are also introduced to the agenda of the implementation of ABIs and the kind of activities they will perform or in which they will be involved. At this stage it is very important to create a safe perception of the initiative in order to overcome any possible scepticism or resistance from people.

Performing – this is the process of translating an ABI into practice. It fundamentally corresponds either to the creation of an arts-based experience engaging people into aesthetic dynamics, or to the manipulation of the organisational infrastructure's aesthetic properties, so that organisational infrastructural components can in turn resonate with aesthetic features that influence people's aesthetic experiences. Therefore, the goal of this stage is to handle organisational aesthetic dynamics in order to directly or indirectly engage people's senses so that they can live an experience that speaks to their emotive mind. This touches feelings and catalyses energies. At this stage, in order to effectively implement an ABI, it is important to understand the working mechanisms grounding its impact.

The practical approaches adopted to perform ABIs can vary greatly. Each arts architect adopts different arts-based instruments and practices. They involve a wide range of works of art, games and artistic processes and, most importantly, the deployment of artists' charisma and artistic competences. This involves understanding that there is not a fixed recipe to perform an ABI, but rather there is an art universe from which an arts management team can draw techniques and approaches. They are employed on the basis of artists' sensibility, personality and competencies. This recognises the uniqueness of ABIs. However, they are characterised by an important common facet that, independently from the specific set of techniques adopted to shape an ABI, has to be properly focused on and managed. This facet is made up of the emotional and energetic features characterising the ABI. Indeed, a fundamental characteristic of performing an ABI is the level of joy and energy that is created and sustained. For a successful implementation of an ABI, it is critical that the arts-based management action is pervaded by emotional and energetic forces that engage people and are able to evoke passion within them. This means that the arts architect needs to pay great attention to the emotional and energetic flows taking place during the ABI's development. These are dimensions that are very difficult to monitor during the performance phase. They are fundamentally handled through the development of personal empathetic awareness and communication.

Debriefing – the debriefing is the process of gathering insights from the ABI experience. It is essentially based on three sub-processes strictly intertwined. They are: reflection, contextualisation and externalisation. The debriefing starts with giving people time to reflect on their arts-based experience, i.e., the reflection process. This can be carried out in different ways. For example, people can be invited to reflect by writing their thoughts on some fundamental questions or by drawing figures that represent their thoughts; or even – when an ABI is based on a live performance such as a theatrical or a dance performance – by watching a recorded video of the performance. In order to spark reflection and activate conversations, it is essential to define the proper set of questions. They have to be able to ignite reflection and deep personal involvement in the process of extracting meaning from the arts-based experience. The questions are formulated by the arts architect and are aimed both at encouraging self-consciousness and self-awareness, and at disclosing thoughts about the addressed business issues. Richards (1995) suggests that during the debriefing two fundamental typologies of questions should be addressed: one related to the ABI's task – i.e., 'What did we do?' and the other related to the process used to attempt the achievement of the task – i.e., 'How did we do it?' Further questions could be: 'What thoughts, feelings, memory or ideas surfaced in your mind as you experienced the ABI?' or 'What kind of emotions and energies did you experience during the ABI and how do you feel now?' These kinds of questions are aimed at stimulating reflection and helping people to be centred with their rational and emotive mind. Then, people are invited both individually and as a group to connect their thoughts with their day-to-day working and business activities. This is the process of contextualising the experience. It is essentially aimed at making sure that the experiential process is significant for people's everyday activities and it is able to activate change in people's attitudes and behaviours. At this stage, it is critical to animate conversations among people, making sure that they share their perspectives and debate about the development of further ideas. Finally, people can be asked to externalise and visualise the main insights they got through the process and present them to other people. The goal is to guarantee a kind of sedimentation of the experiential learning insights and to make sure that they are kept alive once ABIs have been implemented. The codification can be performed in many different ways ranging from more traditional rational approaches, such as formally outlining the key learning insights and associating possible actionable activities, to artful methods, such as using drawings, photos, art installations, stories or poems that have the power of communicating rational and emotional messages. The latter methodology is usually fully integrated into reflection and contextualisation.

Consolidating – an ABI can create a lot of fun and excitement among people during its implementation. It can create a number of learning insights that can potentially change how people perform their work activities. However, in order to translate the experiential learning into day-to-day practices it is important to create the conditions to facilitate the application of the lessons learnt. The consolidating process is aimed at settling the learning insights so that they can drive the development of people's attitudes and behaviours.

The process of consolidation is important for any ABI. However, it has a particularly great relevance when an organisation adopts arts-based interventions. This is because arts-based interventions tend to be 'one-off' or 'stand-alone' initiatives. The process of consolidation permits to keep the insights generated during the arts-based experience alive. Indeed, arts-based interventions can be galvanising and spark learning, but they tend to be affected by the syndrome of 'hard act to follow'. Thus, particularly when it comes to arts-based interventions implemented with the goal of supporting learning and development or transformation, it is critical to put in place management actions aimed at supporting consolidation, i.e., recall and maintaining of the learning insights developed through the ABI. From a practical point of view, in order to consolidate the arts-based experience the adoption of metaphors is particularly effective. Actually, an ABI can be defined and implemented around the creation of a work of art that acts as a metaphor and/or as an analogical model. This finally encapsulates and externalises the learning insights both from a rational and an emotional point of view. For example, the creation of a group painting, an art installation, a mask, a group storytelling, a drawing, or a performance (such as a theatrical, dancing or musical show) that has been recorded, acts as a memory to recall the aesthetic experiences, and sustains reflection and learning.

Assessment: understanding the impact of ABIs

The assessment is aimed at providing an informative basis to support interpretative and normative management actions relating to the organisational reality under investigation. Its aims are the identification, classification and measurement of the main dimensions characterising the object evaluated. Therefore, the assessment of ABIs has essentially a twofold goal. On the one hand, it supports the planning of ABIs making sure that they are integrated and aligned with the organisational value strategy. On the other hand, the assessment allows the quality and the impact of an ABI to be understood. The main ABIs' dimensions to take into account in the assessment are: processes, outputs and outcomes.

The identification and classification of the organisational knowledge assets to be developed through the implementation of art forms is at the basis of the assessment of an ABI. In this regard, the Arts Benefits Constellation represents the assessment framework to support the arts management team in the decision on what organisational components are affected by ABIs. It allows the identification and classification of the knowledge assets that can be developed. At the same time, the use of the Arts Value Map explains the kind of dynamic effects activated by the adoption of ABIs, providing a visualisation of the enabling factors that in accordance with the arts management team drive the achievement of the targeted strategic value objectives.

There are different managerial reasons to perform the assessment process. A first fundamental aim is the understanding and accounting of the benefits related to the implementation of an ABI. The assessment allows the justification of the adoption of ABIs as a management means to sustain organisational development and performance improvements. In addition, it defines an informative basis to better plan and design further ABIs. From a practical point of view, the assessment of ABIs involves an integrated combination of measures.

Regarding the methodologies for data collection, different approaches can be adopted. A widely used approach is based on a feedback session. By means of questionnaires and/or interviews, self-evaluation of the people who have been involved in ABIs is carried out. People are asked to rate a list of Likert-scale statements or to answer to a set of structured or semi-structured questions. The self-assessment can also be supported by arts-based approaches such as storytelling and writing diaries. This latter approach is particularly effective where ABIs are focused on people change. The inherent difficulty in assessing personal changes makes the writing of a diary a good methodology to perform self-assessment. Usually, the writing starts when, at the beginning of an ABI, people are asked to state what they want to learn and

what is important for them. The diary works as an individual assessment tool useful for understanding the value of the initiative in terms
of personal change and achievements. Finally, alternative assessment
methodologies can be based on an external peer evaluation, in which
a third party is in the position of evaluating the effects of ABIs on the
organisational knowledge assets.

Review: extracting learning insights

Once ABIs have been implemented and assessed, the arts management team has to examine the transformational impact of ABIs on
organisational components and reflect on how the organisation has
absorbed the aesthetic dimensions related to the art forms. At this
stage, the positive benefits on the achievement of the targeted operational and strategic objectives, as well as the problems that have arisen
during the implementation of ABIs, are addressed. The arts management team discusses the indicators and the initiatives, and evaluates
the progress of the organisation in terms of value creation and the
barriers that have hampered a successful impact. The review allows
the understanding of the contribution of the arts in management to
face and solve the challenges and the problems that have motivated
the adoption of ABIs. The successes and failures of the implementation of ABIs are addressed and the reasons explaining these outcomes
are investigated in order to gather managerial insights. Reviewing the
arts-based management actions and their contribution to the improvement of business performance, it is possible to test whether the fundamental assumptions grounding the deployment of ABIs are valid.
For this reason, the arts management team has not only to analyse
the information collected from the assessment stage and to check
the benefits and barriers related to the ABIs, but very importantly
it has also to clarify how the arts in management are supporting the
progress of the organisational strategy and the delivery of value to
stakeholders. This requires the organisation's top management to be
involved, at some point, in the review process and participate in investigating how ABIs would contribute to improving the strategy or how
they would highlight some pitfalls challenging the assumptions at the
basis both of the strategy and of the adoption of the arts for creating business value. The review outlines information and lessons that
will feed the planning of further ABIs, and it provides opportunities

to see the organisation's strategy from a different perspective, exploring the role and relevance of organisational aesthetic dimensions that can call for an adaptation of the strategy. The review stage, evaluating the contribution of art forms to the enhancement of the organisational value-creation capacity, closes the loop of the ABIs' management cycle.

Management implications for the successful implementation of ABIs

Different organisational and managerial factors can hamper the successful adoption of ABIs. In order to help managers to avoid the possible shortfalls related to the managerial use of art forms to deal with business issues, it is possible to define a set of management implications for the successful implementation of ABIs.

Sharing the underlying assumption that inspires the adoption of ABIs

Although an ABI, in order to be successful, has to be considered like any other management initiative within the organisational strategic plan, its successful adoption requires the acknowledgement of a fundamental underlying assumption. There has to be a deep motivation encouraging organisations to use ABIs as a management means. In order to embrace ABIs management has first and foremost to acknowledge and respect the universal role of art forms as an instrument to express, represent and enrich human life. This subtle tacit premise stands for the credo that there is a link between the arts and the life of organisational systems. In virtue of this fundamental assumption, executives recognise and value the relevance of setting an agenda to experiment with the use of ABIs. Consequently, the deployment of art forms in management represents not only an innovative management means to deal with business challenges and problems, but also an essential lever to humanise organisations. This means that the adoption of ABIs requires as a precondition the recognition that an organisation is a techno-human system in which people have a central role. ABIs are aimed at enhancing the quality of organisational life, and at celebrating and developing people's human nature and abilities. If ABIs are not aligned with this understanding and are adopted as a way to manipulate people's experiences, they could not only end in failure, but – even worse – they could undermine the spirit and image of an organisation.

The management commitment

Unless ABIs are adopted as an entertainment means, in which case the use of art forms fundamentally fulfils a recreational purpose, the arts-based management actions are aimed at sparking and support- ing organisational transformation. In the latter case, the commitment of the top management in the adoption of ABIs is fundamental. The successful adoption of an ABI as a management means to address oper- ational and strategic issues requires the involvement and commitment of the executives who have to promote the adoption of the arts in management on the basis of their acknowledgement of and trust in the transformational power of art forms. In this regard, members of the top management are responsible, first, for the creation of the organi- sational contexts in which ABIs can catalyse emotional and energetic states that can activate the development of organisational components; second, they have to play an active role in the review of the benefits of ABIs, in order to get insights into both their assumptions regard- ing the value of arts for business, and the progress and validity of the organisational strategy on the basis of the lessons gained from the implementation of ABIs. Therefore, it is crucial that the adoption of ABIs is accompanied by support from the top management. If ABIs are adopted as isolated initiatives promoted by an organisational func- tion to address an operational or business issue, they can still produce benefits, but it is unlikely they will have a strategic significance and a capacity of impacting, in a sustainable way, the enhancement of organisational value-creation capacity.

A clear definition of the business problem to be faced

The implementation of an ABI has to be clearly aimed at helping management to deal with specific challenges or to solve well-identified business problems. Those initiatives that are implemented as 'some- thing nice to have' or 'something to try because it is different and unconventional' do not produce a sustainable impact and, even worse, they can have a detrimental effect on the organisation. The frameworks presented in this book can help organisations to understand the reasons grounding the adoption of the arts to support the enhancement of their value-creation capacity. What matters is the acknowledgement that the use of the arts in management is not a naïve methodology to entertain people, or simply a commodity to invest in (as in the case of art collections), or something that an organisation has to support as a patron because it is increasingly becoming an aspect of the company's social responsibility culture. The arts in management represent a fundamental way to transform the management system and to blend the rational-based management models with emotive-based approaches and techniques. For a successful implementation of ABIs, the management needs to understand that art forms represent powerful devices capable of creating emotive and energetic organisations where people can be fully engaged and intangible value can be created for all stakeholders. For this reason, to make sure that ABIs successfully impact on business performance, they have to be integrated and aligned with organisational operations and strategy. The implementation of ABIs has to be grounded in the formulation of a set of managerial hypotheses that link the management of aesthetic dimensions to the development of organisational knowledge assets and capabilities, and to the improvement of the quality and productivity of organisational processes that ultimately drive the achievement of operational and strategic objectives, with positive impacts on business performance as well as on the delivery of value propositions to stakeholders. Therefore, in order to avoid ABIs ending in failure, organisations need to make sure that they are linked and aligned with the organisational strategic and performance objectives.

The quality of the organisational functions managing ABIs

At the basis of a successful definition and implementation of an ABI resides the quality of the organisational functions managing the ABIs. The arts architect and the arts management team play a crucial role in making sure that ABIs address business issues and drive the development of organisational value-creation capacity. Simply bringing the arts and artists into organisations is a necessary condition, but not sufficient to generate arts-based value for the organisation. For this reason, it is fundamental that ABIs are tailored to address the specific organisation's business challenges and problems. The arts represent a fundamental knowledge domain for inspiring management, but they can play a role in transforming organisations only if they are applied and/or shaped to respond to the managerial instrumental goals. The arts architect and the arts management team are in charge of detecting the organisational problems, and of designing and implementing the appropriate ABI that really meets organisational wants and needs. Therefore, the success or failure of an ABI is strictly affected by the experiences and capabilities of the arts architect and arts management team. To make sure that the arts in management create value for business, it is essential to select art facilitators and business people who have the necessary expertise and charisma to run the management cycle of ABIs.

Building trustful relationships

The success of the managerial use of the arts in management is significantly affected by the creation of a trustful relationship between the company and the artists. This is a precondition to ensure an organisation can absorb the aesthetic dimensions of the arts and let them act as catalysers for the development of organisational components. A trustful relationship sets the right basis to allow artists' actions to fully work in the organisation. The lack of standards and procedures describing the artistic processes and activities means that those organisations interested in bringing in the arts and in absorbing the artistic processes need to trust the artistic experiential approaches and to create an organisational context able to accept the arts and the artists. Artists cannot be curbed in their act of enabling arts-based experiences to release their powerful galvanising, inspirational and catalysing energy, but they have to be free to express themselves so that their tacit abilities can be osmotically transferred to the organisational components. However, on the other hand, to build such relationships, artists need to speak the business language and understand the business issues. This is essential both to develop initiatives which are capable of meeting the organisation's wants and needs, and to understand how to channel the emotional and energetic dynamics sparked and nourished by art forms towards the achievement of business performance improvement targets. Therefore, in order to guarantee the production of positive benefits for the organisation, artists and business people have to shape a mutual trustful relationship.

Overcoming organisational diffidence about ABIs

The adoption of the arts as management means can be hampered by the diffidence and scepticism of the employees. People can see ABIs as a waste of time and resources, and as a consequence they can be resistant to ABIs. Particularly at the management levels, resistance to the arts can be dictated by a rational-based mindset and a managerial philosophy. A successful implementation of ABIs has to take into account that people can be profoundly uninterested in undergoing an arts-based experience. In some cases, they could even become hostile to ABIs. The reasons for the lack of interest or hostility can be related to different individual and organisational factors. Therefore, it is crucial to analyse the organisational context and to identify eventual difficulties. Then, ABIs should not be forced on the organisation, but the participation has to be on a voluntary basis. They should not be perceived by employees as something 'over their heads'. This requires that ABIs have to be properly introduced and explained to people, clarifying why to use them, the benefits that can be captured both at individual and at organisational levels, and the challenges that the involvement in the arts-based experience can raise for them.

Creating a 'safe' arts-based experience

ABIs can run into resistance from an organisation's employees. Indeed, people might feel initially stretched by being involved in art forms, especially when their hands-on participation is requested. This happens because people are generally concerned by being involved in arts activities in which they have limited talent. In addition, people who have physical or general health problems might feel uncomfortable and negatively challenged. The definition of a successful ABI has to take into account all these dimensions. Furthermore, it is fundamental to understand that ABIs are not amateur psychological tools. Therefore, recognising their potentially powerful impact on people's interior life, the ABIs have to be carefully designed and implemented particularly when aimed at addressing physiological traits of the organisational behaviour. ABIs are aimed at catalysing people's emotions and energies acting through their sensory system involving personal psychological dimensions. If an ABI does not consider this important aspect, it can turn into a detrimental personal experience. For this reason, it is critical that the definition and implementation of an ABI take into account the creation of a safe arts-based experience in which people can feel challenged and even provoked, but not threatened or hurt. In order to guarantee the creation of a fruitful and fulfilling arts-based experience, a clear understanding of the specific tensions characterising organisational life has to be defined. Both group dynamics and people's basic traits have to be understood. These are issues to be addressed in the planning stage of the management cycle of ABIs and explored through deep conversations between the arts architect and the management of the organisation. Then the arts management team has the task of monitoring the implementation of ABIs ensuring that it fulfils expectations.

The management process of ABIs

An ABI like any other management initiative has to be carefully managed in order to be successful. For this reason, each stage of the management cycle of an ABI has to be addressed. The capacity of an ABI to generate value for business is the result of a structured approach that defines the contents and features of art forms against the outstanding management challenges and business problems. It is possible to identify four main causes of the failure of ABIs related to a deficiency in the management process, as follows: a poor understanding of ABIs' purposes; a lack of deep understanding of the specific characteristics of the organisational context in terms of business and organisational dynamics; poor design of the implementation process; and lack of a proper assessment and review of the impacts. To reduce the risk of ABIs missing the improvement of the performance targets, the arts management team has to make sure that the adoption of the arts is properly planned, designed, implemented, assessed and reviewed. Moreover, this is the mechanism at the basis of the creation of virtuous cycles that facilitate the stable absorption of the arts into the organisational business model.

Information flow about ABIs

It is very important to keep the level of information flow about ABIs high before, during and after their implementation. The information flow is aimed both at making sure that the people directly involved in the art forms clearly understand the purpose, stages and potential benefits related to the implementation of ABIs, and at keeping all the organisation (including the people not directly involved in the ABI) updated about the scope and benefits of the initiative. This is crucial in order to shape an organisational culture that recognises the potential benefits of the arts and facilitates the adoption of ABIs and ultimately the creation of value. Indeed ABIs, in order to be successful, require a receptive organisational context. This is due to their fundamental nature to catalyse and support emotional and energetic dynamics. In order for this to take place, it is fundamental that the organisation is receptive and the information flow about ABIs responds to this need.

Conclusion

The impact of ABIs on business performance is subordinated to their integration and alignment with the organisational operations and strategy. The accomplishment of business performance improvements is the result of the capability of the arts management team to define ABIs in such a way that they activate cause-and-effect chains that, by transforming organisational components, ultimately allow the achievement of operational and strategic objectives. For this reason, ABIs have to be properly managed to ensure that they meet the organisations' wants and needs. The management cycle of ABIs identifies the fundamental stages to make sure that arts-management actions are combined with other management initiatives, and are incorporated into the organisational management system. It can be helpful for management to introduce ABIs in organisations and, when systematically adopted, it allows for the creation of a virtuous cycle facilitating the absorption of the arts in the organisational life and functions. The arts management team is the organisational function responsible for the planning, designing, implementation, assessment and review of ABIs. It has to take into account that the arts have a general validity and a potential ability to generate value for business, but in practice their impact depends on the quality of the management process. Indeed, ABIs can turn into failures and produce detrimental effects rather than positive ones when they are not defined properly as addressing business issues. In this book, I have illustrated the principles and the tools to help organisations blend their rational-based management models with innovative managerial approaches that value and engage people's emotions and energy. By managing organisational aesthetic dimensions managers can handle emotional and energetic dynamics that foster the development of the capabilities that twenty-first century organisations need in order to face the challenges of the new business age.

A closing remark

This section closes the conceptual journey exploring *The Value of Arts for Business*. As a closing remark I would like to share the fundamental reflection that has inspired and animated my passion in writing this book. For this reason, dear reader, I would like to ask you to take a few moments to reflect on what your life would be if it was not enriched with the music, colours, scent and movements of the arts. *How would our life be without the arts?* The arts bring emotions and energy to human life. They represent a fundamental path to express, discover and develop people's emotions that ultimately contribute to the quality of our life.

In the last decade, while developing my research on the intangible factors that affect the performance of organisational systems, I have investigated the key knowledge-based value-drivers of the success of organisational systems. During my theoretical and empirical investigation, I have discovered that what makes the difference between good and excellent organisations is not only technical knowledge and know-how, but also very importantly what I label as emotive knowledge and know-feel, i.e., the ability to be in touch with and deploy emotions and energy to perform tasks and achieve objectives.

Organisations are not machine-like systems but are made up of people, and they work to create value for people. This means that to fully understand the factors that explain the success of an organisation, we cannot disregard the emotional and energetic traits of human life. Thus, executives need to understand how they can handle emotional and energetic dynamics within and around organisations. In the new millennium, leaders are challenged to shape and govern emotional and energetic organisations in which emotions and energy are recognised as key value-drivers affecting employees' engagement and the creation of intangible value incorporated into organisational infrastructure and products.

My thesis is that during the twentieth century, management has been creating organisations that are dominated by rational thinking. This has allowed the definition of organisational systems that are controllable and technically efficient. But we need to ask ourselves: *Do people love to work in efficient systems? Do people just like to experience products and activities without an emotional attachment? Can people allow their imagination to run free and put their passions into an efficient and rational 'machine-like organisation'?* People are very productive and creative when they are engaged in activities that spark and nourish positive emotions and energy. The arts have the power to shape organisational assets and activities so that they can incorporate aesthetic experiences and properties that will evoke emotional and energetic mechanisms both within and around organisations. My fundamental argument is that twenty-first century organisations have to evolve by distinguishing their techno-human nature and recognising people's emotions and energy as important resources and sources of value creation. The integration of the arts in management systems represents a crucial challenge to develop organisations that can face the complexity and unpredictability of the new business landscape. My purpose in writing *The Value of Arts for Business* has been to prepare the conceptual and managerial ground for exploring how managers can create organisations that value the centrality of human nature for wealth creation, and can enhance organisational value-creation capacity by implementing ABIs. I believe that today's organisations need to absorb and integrate the characteristics of the arts in their business models. This book represents a research contribution to bridge the existing gap between business and the arts.

Appendix
A fundamental assumption: the distinction between the rational and emotive mind

A fundamental hypothesis underlying the arguments of this book is that human knowledge is the result of a synergetic integration of two minds: the rational and the emotive mind. Although they can play a different role in human decision-making and actions, the recognition of their existence is a central issue to point out that emotions have a great relevance in shaping and affecting people and organisational life and activities.

In the last decade, many disciplines have highlighted that human mental life is affected by two semi-independent faculties related to emotive and rational abilities. As a consequence, two different minds can be recognised: the 'rational mind' and the 'emotive mind' (Ekman, 1992; Ekman and Davidson, 1994; Epstein, 1994). They affect people's behaviour, with the first driving thinking abilities, and the second influencing feelings. They represent two different ways of knowing that are strictly interwoven and functionally interrelated, together continuously interacting to construct individual reality. The two minds operate in close harmony, guiding one's ability to make sense of the world and take decisions, as well as to perform tasks. The rational and emotive minds usually operate in a coordinated manner, with feelings supporting the functioning mechanisms of the thinking mind, and the rational mind controlling the dynamics of emotions.

The two forms of mind are the result of millions of years of human beings' evolution and are related to different parts of the brain. In the last decade, neuroscience has investigated the brain's emotive centres revealing the interplay between the thalamus, the neo-cortex, the amygdale and the other brain's circuits (Damasio, 2006). The results of this research show that people's actions fundamentally come from the balanced integration and interaction of two parts of the brain, the neo-cortex and the amygdale. The first drives the rational mind affecting people's thinking and understanding processes, while the second operates as a storehouse for the emotions and influences people's feelings. The amygdale operates as a storehouse of emotive memory, without it people lose all recognition of feelings as well as any feeling about feelings (Ekman and Davidson, 1994). The amygdale occupies a critical position in the brain's architecture. It is an emotive sentinel, able to hijack the brain, as LeDoux's research has proved (2000). So people's actions are fundamentally the result of the interplay of understanding and feelings. Ordinarily the rational and emotive minds interact, affecting each other, driving our decisions, knowledge construction and learning capabilities. However, in some circumstances feelings can directly drive our actions. This happens when emotions swamp the rational mind in specific situations such as peril or emergency in which an instantaneous response is required. The amygdale is the result of mankind's biological evolution and provides the ability to respond quickly to unknown peril situations, which require fast reaction.

Figure A.1 shows schematically the working mechanisms of the human mind and their interplay in affecting decisions and actions. It shows the interdependence between feelings and thoughts in constructing people's knowledge for action. In a very schematic way this representation highlights that the sensory system is at the basis of information acquisition. The acquired information is elaborated by the rational and emotive mind that produces thoughts and feelings respectively. Their interplay and integration generates knowledge for action. Individual reasoning and acting capabilities depend on both the rational mind and the emotive one. Feelings are indispensable for effective and efficient thoughts in the same way as the rational mind plays an executive role in emotion regulation. The rational mind and the emotive one are interconnected and related. Indeed, it is common knowledge that anger, anxiety or depression causes difficulties in efficient information processing due to the reduction of the retention and elaboration capacity of the brain. This is due to the effect of the emotive mind on working memory and on the thinking mind. Consequently emotions play a crucial role in building people's competency for making wise decisions, in performing good quality actions and simply in reflecting clearly about the world. Thus people's knowledge system is an integrated combination of the rational mind and the emotive mind. The logic of the rational mind is causality and interpretation. At the basis of its working mechanisms there are the connections between cause and effect as well as the continuous renewal of cognitive maps.

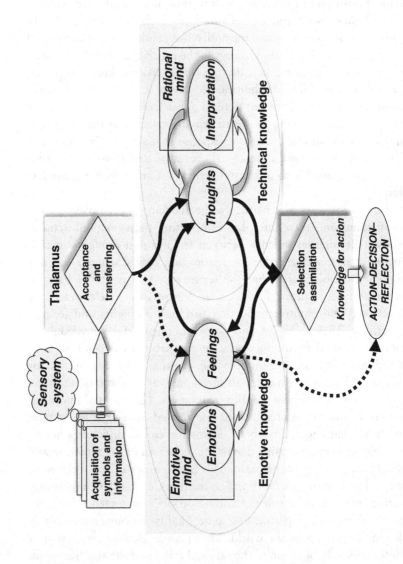

A.1 People's knowledge for action is based on a balanced integration of the emotive mind and the rational mind

The logic of the emotive mind is associative. The emotive mind is activated by metaphors, images and more generally by any element that symbolises a reality or triggers a memory of it. Accordingly, for managerial purposes in this book it is assumed that the knowledge affecting people and organisational behaviour can be conceptually interpreted as the integration of 'technical knowledge', i.e., knowledge related to rational faculties, and 'emotive knowledge', i.e., knowledge built by emotive abilities.

Notes

1 Why arts matter in management

1 Technologies need to become more intuitive, but also capable of incorporating human traits. In this regard, there are many efforts put into the development of technologies that are able to understand and respond to human emotions. For example, Hanson Robotics aims to develop robots that act and react virtually indistinguishably from people. The endeavour of integrating artificial intelligence, speech recognition and computer vision software with the ability to mimic and respond to human emotional expressions is gradually making huge leaps towards the development of technologies that are able to fully interact with people (see www. hansonrobotics.com).

2 The Global Workforce Study, an international employee survey conducted by the consulting company Towers Perrin, with the aim of understanding the level and drivers of employee engagement in midsize and large organisations, highlights the relevance of engaging people within organisations. The study shows that higher employee engagement levels reflect the employees' perception and belief that they can have an impact on business performance. Moreover, the analysis of the links between employee engagement and financial figures provides evidence of the existence of correlations between the variables. The investigation of fifty global companies over a one-year period indicates a positive correlation between employee engagement and the increase of operating income (19 per cent) and earnings per share (28 per cent), while companies with low levels of engagement had a drop in operating income (32 per cent) and a decline of earnings per share (11 per cent). For further information about the study see Towers Perrin, *Closing the Engagement Gap: a Road Map for Driving Superior Business Performance*. New York: Global Report, 2009.

3 Management constitutes a paradigm. As postulated by Kuhn (1962), a paradigm is characterised as a clear definition of the reality under investigation, of the fundamental problems to be addressed and of the principles and techniques adopted to solve the problems. Accordingly management

is a body of knowledge to investigate organisational systems for interpretative and normative purposes and the management theories, models and techniques developed throughout the twentieth century define a disciplinary arena animated by different research programmes.

4 Although management, as a practice to guide and affect the success of human actions and undertakings, is not new in the history of human civilisations, it has become a true discipline, starting from the beginning of the twentieth century. The formulation of a clear set of problems to be solved, along with the definition of a set of principles and the adoption of scientific-based methods for their investigation, laid the foundations for the formation of the modern management paradigm.

5 Although some scholars mark out a distinction between feelings and emotions, considering feelings as fundamentally private sensations while emotions denote feelings that are grounded in cultural rules and therefore are enacted in social situations (Sandelands, 1988; Rosemberg, 1990), it is possible to consider feelings and emotions as two interchangeable concepts. This is coherent with the organisational studies that have investigated the role of emotions in organisations (Fineman, 1985; Strongman, 1991).

6 The study of emotions has been a research issue in many disciplines, particularly in philosophy, psychology and evolutionary biology. More recently the fields of neuroscience and the economy have paid great attention to the investigation of emotions and to their role. In the last decades the adoption of innovative technologies, such as Positron Emission Tomography (PET) and functional Magnetic Resonance Imaging (fMRI), has allowed neurobiology not only to identify the activities of emotions in the human brain, but also to investigate the influence that emotions exercise upon people's actions and mental processes. Emotions affect all the different dimensions of human life. They influence the way in which and the quality of the perception and interpretation of the outer and inner reality of human beings; determining how people behave and acting as regulators of the individual and social energetic levels.

2 The arts into action: Arts-based Initiatives

1 The concept of 'artworld' is a fundamental trait of the conventionalist perspective recognising the position of institutions in defining what are artworks. It aims to denote the institutional environment in charge of deciding what is art and what is not. Its adoption is important because it provides interpretative dimensions to distinguish what stands for an artwork in the public domain.

2 At the basis of the adoption of theatrical forms in order to address management issues there is the reconstruction and simulation of real or supposed business realities. Participants are engaged in an experience in which they may play the role of either actors acting in different roles or spectators empathising with actors and vicariously experiencing the performance (Boal, 1985).

3 This is coherent with the results of the market research on consumers' propensity, which stress that repeated purchases are linked to the quality and level of satisfaction of the consumption experience (Gobe, 2001; Underhill, 1999).

4 These more practical interpretations are aligned with the general understanding of the energy concept. In this regard, the *Chambers English Dictionary* defines energy as 'the capacity for vigorous activity, liveliness or vitality', 'force or forcefulness', or 'the capacity to do work'. The focus of this definition is primarily on physical energy, however it provides a powerful analogy to interpret people's energy at work and supports an understanding of energy within organisations.

5 The physical wellbeing and capacity resides within three main processes: renovation, maintenance and development. At the individual level, these processes can be viewed as sleeping, correct nutrition and physical exercise (Loehr and Schwart, 2001).

6 The mind is related to cognitive abilities. Cognitive energy and capacity, like physical capacity, can be improved by training the 'mind muscle'. It is affected by cognitive processes, such as learning, engaging in problem-solving and using approaches to knowledge management. In addition, time management, positive and critical thinking, meditation and visualisation are useful approaches for renewing cognitive energy.

7 Feelings are the result of the combination of emotional and spiritual states. For the rationale of this work spirituality is considered as a dimension governed by emotions, though it can be acknowledged that they are two different realities. Emotions are mainly related to human physiological nature as explained by neuroscience (Williamson, 2002), while spirituality is connected to individuals' values, sense of purpose and beliefs (Loehr and Schwartz, 2003; Mitroff and Denton, 1999).

8 For simplicity's sake it is assumed that spiritual energy is an integrated component of emotional energy and spirituality is considered essentially as the set of beliefs and ethical codes that contribute to shape and affect people's behaviours and attitudes.

9 Energy in a relationship is affected by three orthogonal dimensions: emotion, i.e., the level of intimacy created between two or more people in the interaction; cognition, i.e., the decision of taking part in the interaction; and motivation, i.e., the reasons prompting the involvement in the interaction (Hassebrauck and Buhl, 1996).

10 Steers *et al.* (2004) highlight that all of the main definitions of motivation are primarily concerned with the factors that energise, channel and sustain human behaviour over time. In this context energy is a fundamental component of motivation. In one sense it can be considered as the engine of motivation. It affects both the direction in which a person chooses to act and the effort a person invests (Marks, 1977).

11 The studies on the imitation of facial movements provide important empirical evidence of the working mechanisms of the emotive communication process and particularly of the role and relevance of the emotions synchronisation during the transferring of an emotive state. Experiments on non-verbal communication highlight how emotive communication is characterised by the transferring of an emotive state from the source to the receiver (Zuckerman *et al.*, 1975).

12 Leadership plays a fundamental role in shaping and creating positive emotions and energy in organisations. It defines the conditions for generating, bundling and channelling organisational emotions and energy in order to accomplish targeted value goals. It is a leadership task to define an appropriate vision and strategy to enable the unleashing of organisational energy and marshalling people's emotive capacities in support of key strategic goals (Bruch and Ghoshal, 2003).

13 Among the management practices to regulate emotional and energetic dynamics, particularly important is the recruitment and selection processes as well as general human resource management practices. Organisations can seek and develop people who can bring positive emotions and energy to the organisation and spark emotional and energetic dynamics.

14 An organisation's culture defines the organisational values and purposes that affect emotional and energetic dynamics providing behavioural drivers for both individuals and teams. Greenfield (2004) identifies that when there is a disconnection between personal values and the perceived values of the organisation, employee disengagement is often the result and organisations may waste employee energy through a variety of disengaging behaviours.

15 Management systems represent an essential organisational dimension for affecting individual and organisational behaviours (Neely *et al.*, 2002). Their nature, contents and working mechanisms strongly affect emotional and energetic dynamics of individuals and groups.

3 The value of Arts-based Initiatives in business

1 According to Brown (2009: 60) play can be defined as: 'an absorbing, apparently purposeless activity that provides enjoyment and a suspension of self-consciousness and sense of time. It is also self-motivating and makes you want to do it again'. On the basis of this interpretation the

author considers the impulse to create art as the result of the play impulse and interprets the origin of many artistic expressions as rooted in play behaviour.

2 The notion of 'hot spots' was coined by Lynda Gratton (2007) to address the strategic importance for organisations to focus on and manage their energy. Gratton defines hot spots as: 'places and times where co-operation flourishes creating great energy, innovation, productivity and excitement' (Gratton, 2007: xi).

3 Boal (1985) stresses that the power of the arts to change how people see the world and behave is an issue that was already stressed by Aristotle when he said that the purpose of drama was to harness the transformation of people.

4 The World Health Organisation defines health as a state of complete physical, mental and social wellbeing and not merely the absence of disease (Staricoff, 2004). Health depends on physical and mental functioning and the degree to which these functions are in equilibrium with the physical, biological and social environment (Lock et al., 2001). Arts can play a fundamental role in achieving this equilibrium (Jamison, 1996).

5 Staricoff (2004) through an in-depth review of the medical literature has highlighted that the arts have a wide range of beneficial outcomes for patients and staff in healthcare settings. Reviewing the literature, Staricoff provides strong evidence supporting the relevance of arts-based experiences. The arts can have a positive impact on clinical outcomes, such as: cancer care, in which case arts-based experiences contribute to reducing anxiety and depression; cardiovascular, where in particular the use of music can have positive effects on blood pressure, heart rate and demand of myocardial oxygen; intensive care, supporting a reduction of the length of stay in hospital; medical procedures, in which case the use of arts-based interventions has proved to be useful to increase the level of comfort; pain management, in which case music seems to play a critical role in the reduction of medication to decrease pain after surgery, and particularly music and visual arts appear to be very effective in the post-operative recovery period with a reduction of sedative use.

6 Different modes of arts involvement can be adopted as therapeutic means. There are two main types of arts therapies: the hands-on versus the hands-off approach. The therapies can involve different forms of artistic activities. The most common are: music activities that involve either listening to music to induce relaxation or singing to develop vocal control or to express emotions; dance activities involving rhythmic movements to foster physical and emotional development; visual arts activities such as painting and sculpture; and theatre activities involving creative expression in which patients role-play in real-life or structured situations.

7 Enel Contemporanea is a growing ABI that is gradually enlarging and involving the development of partnerships between Enel Group and important cultural institutions, such as the Museum of Contemporary Art of Rome (MACRO). For further information, see: www. enelcontemporanea.it.

8 Today, the Vitra Design Museum is an internationally recognised museum devoted to the research and popular dissemination of design, presenting works of art on design and culture, with a focus on furniture and interior design. For further information, see: www.design-museum.de.

9 It is recognised that there is a deep difference between the decorative arts and the use of fine arts for decorative purposes. However, with the purpose of aesthetically qualifying organisation office spaces in this research work I have not made this distinction. Therefore, I have assumed the perspective that managers implementing ABIs focus on 'environment' as an organisational value-driver. This means that fine arts and decorative arts can be considered as equivalent for this purpose. Of course, this becomes an issue if managers are looking not only to the aesthetic value of the works of art, but also their value as investments, in which case the selection of the artistic artefacts has to focus on artworks that are recognised as such in the public artworld.

10 This quote was taken from an interview with Andrea Illy reported in the Italian magazine *L'impresa*, n. 3, 2007.

11 Art is a universal language. Thousands of years ago, early man told his stories through pictures drawn on cave walls. Through the ages, artists told us their history through drawings, paintings, architecture and sculptures. Joy, sorrow, anger, peace and the emotions and experiences of the artists are shared in a sketched line or a splash of colour.

12 A communication based on a work of art has a twofold nature. It is a rational-cognitive communication concerning information processing and interpretation characterising the rational mind as well as an empathetic communication involving symbols, messages and cues that are able to speak directly to the emotive mind, stimulating and arousing feelings.

13 The real name has been changed because the company wants to remain anonymous.

14 From the final evaluation report produced by Ci: Creative intelligence.

4 Arts-based Initiatives and business performance

1 The concepts of competencies and capabilities denote two different realities, though they are strictly related and interwoven. The distinctions and relationships between the two concepts have been largely explored in the management literature. As a working interpretation it is possible to

consider a competence as the ability to perform a specific set of activities in order to achieve a task or deliver an output; and a capability as the way of combining and deploying organisational resources and the capacity to renew competencies. In this perspective competencies can be considered as a specific form of organisational resources. Hill and Jones (1992) and Hitt *et al*. (1999) distinguish between resources and capabilities by suggesting that resources are an organisation's financial, individual and organisational capital attributes, while capabilities are those attributes of an organisation that enable the exploitation of resources in implementing strategies. Thus, organisational resources can be interpreted as stocks of available factors that are owned or controlled by the organisation, while capabilities represent the way of using resources. Hence, capabilities are more dynamic and complex entities and should be treated independently to resources (Amit and Schoemaker, 1993).

2 The distinctions between the following concepts are implicitly adopted: resource, asset and capital. Any tangible or intangible factor that an organisation uses in its value-creation processes is considered as a resource. Asset stands for an organisational resource that is strategically relevant to sustain and affect the organisational value-creation capacity. Capital indicates a stock of assets that is attributed to an organisation and defines the competencies and capabilities of an organisation.

3 Dealing with the concept of knowledge it is necessary to distinguish between simple information and information that has undergone an interpretation process. Information is the structural dimension of knowledge, as data is the building block of information. Focusing on personal knowledge, it is possible to conceptualise knowledge as the result of an interpretation process, carried out by a cognitive system, of a set of information acquired through experience and meditation on the experience itself, that is able to provide its owner with an ability (Johnson-Laird, 1993; Kim, 1993; Kolb, 1984; Polanyi, 1962, 1966).

4 The attempt to make knowledge an operative entity has been the subject of a number of scholarly contributions. Different concepts have been proposed such as invisible assets (Itami and Roehl, 1987), intangible assets (Hall, 1992, 1993), intangible elements (Carmeli and Tishler, 2004) and knowledge resources (Spender and Grant, 1996; Teece, 1998; Winter, 1987). More recently great attention has been paid to the concept of intellectual capital. This conceptual category was initially introduced by practitioners to distinguish knowledge-based resources from tangible and financial ones (Stewart, 1997; Sveiby, 1997). It has inspired the definition of a number of frameworks for classifying organisational knowledge resources (Marr and Schiuma, 2001). The conceptualisations adopted in this book gather insights from the review of these models.

However, a further conceptual category is adopted. In particular, tangible knowledge assets as an organisational knowledge category is considered, denoting the tangible assets incorporating strategic knowledge that must be considered when analysing the knowledge domains at the basis of organisational competencies.

5 Organisational resources are distinguished in the management literature on the basis of their physical substance in the tangible and intangible (Helfat and Peteraf, 2003). On the one hand, tangible resources refer to the fixed and current assets of an organisation, e.g., plant, equipment, land and other capital goods. On the other hand, intangible resources include intellectual property rights, organisational know-how and culture. Most of the knowledge-based analysis of organisational resources has identified knowledge assets as intangible resources. This view is restrictive because, although the tangible resources that correspond to natural resources cannot be considered knowledge assets, all the other tangible assets embed knowledge and, as such, on the basis of the strategic relevance of the incorporated knowledge, can be considered as knowledge assets.

6 It is worth highlighting that this question does not aim to disclose how ABIs act at individual levels developing the emotive knowledge. The issue is not to discover the mechanisms grounding people's know-feel. Although this is a valuable issue, it appears mainly as an interesting research problem, rather than the focus of management's interest in the use of ABIs. Nevertheless, an understanding of this issue can shed light on the individual psychological mechanisms activated by ABIs and this would also provide important managerial insights.

7 For further information about Pret A Manger, see: www.pret.com. For more information about the ABI implemented at Pret A Manger, see: www.peoplemanagement.co.uk.

8 In the economic and management literature, several classifications of the knowledge resources have been proposed. Many of them are based on dichotomy taxonomies distinguishing knowledge assets on the basis of two opposite dimensions. Some of the main criteria adopted to classify knowledge resources are: the level of codification, the degree of control, the transferability and the intrinsic nature. They can be considered as the managerial purposes for the classification process.

9 This interpretation is consistent with the performance measurement literature. Neely (1998) defines the measurement process as a quantitative and/or qualitative evaluation of the efficiency and effectiveness of a specific organisation's action.

10 The definition of performance targets is not an easy task. It is even more challenging when it concerns the identification of targets for the

development of knowledge assets. Kaplan and Norton (2008) address the challenge of defining performance targets and provide useful managerial implications to drive managers in this task.

11 Examples are the analytic hierarchy process (AHP) and the analytic network process (ANP) methodology to support the practical definition of maps for the assessment of knowledge assets (Carlucci and Schiuma, 2009).

References

Adajian, T. 2009. 'The definition of art', in E. N. Zalta (ed.), *The Stanford Encyclopedia of Philosophy* (online encyclopedia: http://plato.stanford. edu/entries/art-definition/).

Adler, N. J. 2006. 'The arts and leadership: now that we can do anything, what will we do?', *Academy of Management Learning and Education*, 5: 486–99.

 2010. 'Going beyond the dehydrated language of management: leadership insight', *Journal of Business Strategy*, 31, 4: 90–9.

Adler, P. S. and Kwon, S. W. 2002. 'Social capital: prospects for a new concept', *Academy of Management Review*, 27: 17–40.

Adner, R. and Helfat, C. E. 2003. 'Corporate effects and dynamic managerial capabilities', *Strategic Management Journal*, 24: 1,011–25.

Afuah, A. 2000. 'How much do your competitors' capabilities matter in the face of technological change?', *Strategic Management Journal*, 21: 387–404.

Ambrosini, V. and Bowman, C. 2001. 'Tacit knowledge: some suggestions for operationalisation', *Journal of Management Studies*, 38: 811–29.

Amis, J., Slack, T. and Hinings, C. R. 2004. 'The pace, sequence and linearity of radical change', *Academy of Management Journal*, 47: 15–39.

Amit, R. and Schoemaker, P. J. 1993. 'Strategic assets and organizational rent', *Strategic Management Journal*, 14: 33–46.

Anand, V., Glick, W. H. and Manz, C. C. 2002. 'Thriving on the knowledge of outsiders: tapping organisational social capital', *Academy of Management Executive*, 16: 87–101.

Aragon-Correa, J. A. and Sharma, S. 2003. 'A contingent resource-based view of proactive corporate environmental strategy', *Academy of Management Review*, 28: 71–88.

Argyris, C. 1964. *Integrating the Individual and the Organisation*. New York: John Wiley.

Argyris, C. and Schön, D. 1996. *Organisational Learning: Theory, Method and Practice*. Reading, MA: Addison-Wesley.

Arkes, H. R., Herren, L. T. and Isen, A. M. 1988. 'The role of potential loss in the influence of affect on risk-taking behaviour', *Organisational Behaviour and Human Decision Processes*, **42**: 181–93.

Austin, R. D. 2008. 'Aesthetic coherence and the hunt for big margins', *Harvard Business Review*, January: 18–20.

Austin, R. D. and Devin, L. 2003. *Artful Making: What Managers Need to Know About How Artists Work*. Upper Saddle River, NJ: Prentice Hall.

Axelrod, R. and Cohen, M. D. 2000. *Harnessing Complexity*. New York: Basic Books.

Bain, J. S. 1956. *Barriers to New Competition*. Cambridge, MA: Harvard University Press.

Baker, W. 1990. 'Market networks and corporate behaviour', *American Journal of Sociology*, **96**: 589–625.

Bangle, C. 2001. 'The ultimate creativity machine: how BMW turns art into profit', *Harvard Business Review*, January: 47–55.

Barney, J. B. 1991. 'Firm resources and sustained competitive advantage', *Journal of Management*, **17**: 99–120.

  2001. 'Is the resource-based "view" a useful perspective for strategic management research? Yes', *Academy of Management Review*, **26**: 41–56.

Barrett, F. J. 1998. 'Managing and improvising: lessons from jazz', *Career Development International*, **3**: 283–6.

  2000. 'Cultivating an aesthetic of unfolding: jazz improvisation as a self-organising system', in S. Linstead and H. Höpfl (eds.), *The Aesthetics of Organisation*. London: Sage Publications.

Barry, D. 1994. 'Making the invisible visible: using analogically based methods to surface the organizational unconscious', *Organizational Development Journal*, **12**: 37–48.

Baumgarten, A. G. 1750. *Aesthetica*. Hildesheim, Germany: Olms.

Beardsley M. 1982. *The Aesthetic Point of View*. Ithaca, NY: Cornell University Press.

Becker, G. S. 1964. *Human Capital*. New York: National Bureau of Economic Research.

Beckwith, A. 2003. 'Improving business performance: the potential of arts in training', *Industrial and Commercial Training*, **35**: 207–9.

Benedict, S. 1991. *Public Money and the Muse: Essays on Government Funding for the Arts*. New York: W. W. Norton.

Berg, I. 1969. *Education and Jobs: the Great Training Robbery*. New York: Praeger Publishers.

Berkeley, G. 2008(1710). *A Treatise Concerning the Principles of Human Knowledge*. Dublin: Aaron Rhames for Jeremy Pepyat.

Berman, M. 1984. *The Reenchantment of the World*. New York: Bantam Books.

Bianchini, F. 1993. 'Remaking European cities: the role of cultural policies', in F. Bianchini and M. Parkinson (eds.), *Cultural Policy and Urban Regeneration*. New York: Manchester University Press, 1–20.

Boal, A. 1985. *Theatre of the Oppressed*. New York: Theatre Communication Group.

Boisot, M. H. 1998. *Knowledge Assets: Securing Competitive Advantage in the Information Economy*. Oxford: Oxford University Press.

Bolino, M. C., Turnley, W. H. and Bloodgood, J. M. 2002. 'Citizenship behaviour and the creation of social capital in organisation', *Academy of Management Review*, 27: 505–22.

Bontis, N. 1998. 'Intellectual capital: an explanatory study that develops measures and models', *Management Decision*, 36: 63–76.

Bourne, M. (ed.) 2001. *Handbook of Performance Measurement*. London: GEE Publishing Ltd.

Boyatzis, R., McKee, A. and Goleman, D. 2002. 'Reawakening your passion for work', *Harvard Business Review*, April: 87–94.

Boyle, M. and Ottensmeyer, E. 2005. 'Solving business problems through the creative power of the arts: catalyzing change at Unilever', *Journal of Business Strategy*, 26, 5: 14–21.

Brehm, J. W. and Self, E. A. 1989. 'The intensity of motivation', *Annual Review of Psychology*, 40: 109–31.

Brooks, A. C. and Kushner, R. J. 2001. 'Cultural policy and urban development', *International Journal of Arts Management*, 3: 4–15.

Brown, S. L. and Eisenhardt, K. M. 1995. 'Product development: past research, present findings, and future directions', *Academy of Management Review*, 20: 343–78.

Brown, S. M. 2009. *Play*. London: Penguin Group.

Bruch, H. and Ghoshal, S. 2003. 'Unleashing organizational energy', *MIT Sloan Management Review*, 45: 45–51.

Budd, M. 1995. *Values of Art*. London: Penguin Books.

Burgi, P., Jacobs, C. and Roos, J. 2005. 'From metaphor to practice in the crafting of strategy', *Journal of Management Inquiry*, 14, 1: 78–94.

Burnham, J., Augustine, N. and Adelman, K. 2001. *Shakespeare in Charge: the Bard's Guide to Learning and Succeeding on the Business Stage*. New York: Hyperion.

Burns, T. and Stalker, G. M. 1961. *The Management of Innovation*. London: Tavistock.

Burt, G. 1992. *Structural Holes. The Social Structure of Competition*. Cambridge, MA: Harvard University Press.

Burt, R. S. 1997. 'The contingent value of social capital', *Administrative Science Quarterly*, **42**: 339–65.

Callahan, E. 1988. *The Role of Emotion in Ethical Decision Making*. Cambridge University Press.

Carlucci, D., Marr, B. and Schiuma, G. 2004. 'The knowledge value chain: how intellectual capital impacts business performance', *International Journal of Technology Management*, **27**: 575–90.

Carlucci, D. and Schiuma, G. 2007. 'Assessing and managing knowledge assets for company value creation', in C. Yoosuf (ed.), *Knowledge Management Integrated*. Heidelberg, Germany: Heidelberg Press, 27–46.

2009. 'Applying the analytic network process to disclose knowledge assets value creation dynamics', *Expert Systems With Applications*, **36**, 4: 7,687–94.

2010. 'Determining key performance indicators: an analytical network approach', in A. Gunasekaran and M. Sandhu (eds.), *Handbook on Business Information Systems*. Abingdon: World Scientific Publishing.

Carmeli, A. and Tishler, A. 2004. 'The relationships between intangible organizational elements and organizational performance', *Strategic Management Journal*, **25**: 1,257–78.

Carter, P. and Jackson, N. 2000. 'An-aesthetics', in S. Linstead and H. Höpfl (eds.), *The Aesthetics of Organisation*. London: Sage Publications.

Caves, R. E. and Porter, M. E. 1977. 'From competitive entry barriers to mobility barriers: conjectural decisions and contrived deterrence to new competition', *Quarterly Journal of Economics*, **91**: 241–62.

Champoux, J. E. 1999. 'Film as a teaching resource', *Journal of Management Inquiry*, **8**: 206–17.

Chung, S., Singh, H. and Lee, K. 2000. 'Complementarity, status similarity and social capital as drivers of alliance formation', *Strategic Management Journal*, **21**: 1–22.

Clegg, S., Kornberger, M. and Pitsis, T. 2005. *Managing and Organisations*. London: Sage Publications.

Cockburn, I. M., Henderson, R. M. and Stern, S. 2000. 'Untangling the origins of competitive advantage', *Strategic Management Journal*, **21**: 1,123–45.

Coleman, J. S. 1990. *Foundations of Social Theory*. Cambridge, MA: Harvard University Press.

Collins, R. 1981. 'On the micro-foundations of macrosociology', *American Journal of Sociology*, **8**: 984–1,014.

1993. 'Emotional energy as the common denominator of rational action', *Rationality and Society*, **5**: 203–230.

Collis, D. J. 1991. 'A resource-based analysis of global competition: the case of the bearings industry', *Strategic Management Journal*, 12: 49–68.

Conner, K. R. 1991. 'A historical comparison of resource-based theory and five schools of thought within industrial organization economics: do we have a new theory of the firm?', *Journal of Management*, 17: 121–54.

Corrigan, P. 1999. *Shakespeare on Management: Leadership Lessons for Today's Managers*. London: Kogan Page.

Corsun, D. L., Young, C. A., McManus, A. and Erdem, M. 2006. 'Overcoming managers' perceptual shortcuts through improvisational theater games', *Journal of Management Development*, 25: 298–315.

Cross, R., Baker, W. and Parker, A. 2003. 'What creates energy in organizations?' *MIT Sloan Management Review*, **Summer**: 51–6.

Crossan, M. 1997. 'Improvise and innovate', *Ivey Business Quarterly*, Autumn: 1–6.

Csikszentmihalyi, M. 1990. *Flow. The Psychology of Optimal Experience*. New York: Harper & Row.

Csikszentmihalyi, M. and Robinson, M. 1991. *Art of Seeing. The Interpretation of Aesthetic Encounter*. New York: Oxford University Press.

Damasio, A. 2006. *Descartes' Error*. London: Vintage.

Danto, A. 1981. *The Transfiguration of the Commonplace*. Cambridge, MA: Harvard University Press.

Darsø, L. 2004. *Artful Creation: Learning-tales of Arts-in-Business*. Gylling, Denmark: Narayana Press.

Davemport, S. L. and Beers, M. C. 1996. 'Improving knowledge work processes', *Sloan Management Review*, 37: 53–65.

Davemport, T. H. and Prusak, L. 1998. *Working Knowledge: How Organizations Manage What They Know*. Cambridge, MA: Harvard Business School Press.

Davemport, T. H., Thomas, R. J. and Cantrell, S. 2002. 'The mysterious art and science of knowledge-worker performance', *MIT Sloan Management Review*, 43, 3: 23–30.

Davies, S. 1991. *Definitions of Art*. Ithaca, NY: Cornell University Press.

Deasy, R. (ed.), 2002. *Critical Links: Learning in the Arts and Student Academic and Social Development*. Washington, DC: Arts Education Partnership.

Deasy, R. 2004. *The Arts and Education: New Opportunities for Research*. Washington, DC: Arts Education Partnership.

DeFilippi, R. J. and Arthur, M. B. 1998. 'Paradox in project based enterprise', *California Management Review*, 40: 125–39.

Denhardt, R. B. and Denhardt, J. V. 2006. *The Dance of Leadership: The Art of Leading in Business, Government, and Society.* Armonk, NY: M. E. Sharpe.

de Sousa, R. 2009. 'Emotions', in E. N. Zalta (ed.), *The Stanford Encyclopedia of Philosophy* (online encyclopedia: http://plato.stanford.edu/entries/conceptual-art/).

Dess, G. G. and Picken, J. C. 2000. 'Changing roles: leadership in the 21st century', *Organizational Dynamics,* 29: 18–34.

Dick, R. 1995. *Artful Work. Awakening, Joy, Meaning, and Commitment in the Workplace.* San Francisco, CA: Berrett-Koehler.

Dickie, G. 1984. *The Art Circle.* New York: Haven.

Dierickx, I. and Cool, K. 1989. 'Asset stock accumulation and sustainability of competitive advantage', *Management Science,* 35: 1,504–11.

Dissanayake, E. 1990. *What is Art For?* Seattle, WA: University of Washington Press.

2000. *Art and Intimacy: How the Arts Began.* Seattle, WA: University of Washington Press.

Dolev, J. C., Friedlaender, F., Krohner, L. and Braverman, I. M. 2001. 'Use of art to enhance visual diagnostic skills', *Journal of the American Medical Association,* 286: 1,020–1.

Donaldson, T. and Preston, L. E. 1995. 'The stakeholder theory of the corporation: concepts, evidences and implications', *Academy of Management Review,* 20: 65–91.

Dosi, G., Nelson, R. R. and Winter, S. G. (eds.), 2000. *The Nature and Dynamics of Organizational Capabilities.* Oxford: Oxford University Press.

Dow, A. W., Leong, D., Anderson, A. and Wenzel, R. 2007. 'Using theater to teach clinical empathy: a pilot study', *Journal of General Internal Medicine,* 22: 1,114–18.

Drucker, P. F. 1999. *Management Challenges of the 21st Century.* New York: Harper Business.

Dutta, S., Bergen, M., Levy, D., Ritson, M. and Zbaracki, M. 2002. 'Pricing a strategic capability', *MIT Sloan Management Review,* 43: 61–6.

Eisner, E. W. 2002. *The Arts and the Creation of Mind.* New Haven, CT: Yale University Press.

Ekman, P. 1992. 'An argument for basic emotions', *Cognition and Emotion,* 6: 169–200.

Ekman, P. and Davidson, R. J. 1994. *The Nature of Emotion: Fundamental Questions.* Oxford: Oxford University Press.

Epstein, S. 1994. 'Integration of the cognitive and the psychodynamic unconscious', *American Psychologist,* 49: 709–24.

Fineman, S. 1985. *Social Work Stress and Intervention.* Aldershot: Gower.

Fischer, H. M. and Pollock, T. G. 2004. 'Effects of social capital and power on surviving transformational change: the case of initial public offering', *Academy of Management Journal*, 47: 463–81.

Fiske, E. (ed.), 1999. *Champions of Change: the Impact of the Arts on Learning*. Arts Education Partnership and President's Committee on the Arts and the Humanities (www.aep-arts.org/files/publications/ ChampsReport.pdf).

Flam, H. 1993. 'Fear, loyalty and greedy organisations', in S. Fineman (ed.), *Emotion in Organisations*. London: Sage Publications, 58–75.

Florida, R. 2004. *The Rise of the Creative Class*. New York: Basic Books.

Frank, R. H. 1988. *Passions within Reason: the Strategic Role of the Emotions*. New York: W. W. Norton.

Friedman, T. L. 2005. *The World is Flat: a Brief History of the 21st Century*. New York: Farrar, Straus and Giroux.

Frijda, N. H. 1988. 'The laws of emotion', *American Psychologist*, 43: 349–58.

Frost, P. J., Moore, L. F., Louis, M. R., Lundberg, C. C. and Martin, J. 1985. *Organisational Culture*. London: Sage Publications.

Gallos, J. 2009. 'Artful teaching: using visual, creative and performing arts in contemporary management education', in S. Armstrong and C. Fukami (eds.), *Handbook of Management Learning, Education and Development*. Thousand Oaks, CA: Sage Publishing.

Gaut, B. 2000. 'The cluster account of art', in N. Carroll (ed.), *Theories of Art Today*. Madison, WI: University of Wisconsin Press, 25–45.

Giacalone, R. A. and Rosenfeld, P. R. 1991. *Applied Impression Management*. London: Sage Publications.

Gibb, S. 2004. 'Arts-based training in management development: the use of improvisational theatre', *Journal of Management Development*, 23: 741–50.

Gobe, M. 2001. *Emotional Branding: the New Paradigm for Connecting Brands to People*. New York: Acworth Press.

Goldman, A. H. 1995. *Aesthetic Value*. Boulder, CO: Westview Press.

Goleman, D. 1995. *Emotional Intelligence*. London: Bloomsbury Publishing.

Grant, R. M. 1991. 'The resource-based theory of competitive advantage: implications for strategy formulation', *California Management Review*, 33: 114–35.

    1996a. 'Prospering in dynamically competitive environments: organizational capability as knowledge integration', *Organization Science*, 7: 375–87.

    1996b. 'Toward a knowledge-based theory of the firm', *Strategic Management Journal*, 17: 109–22.

1997. 'The knowledge-based view of the firm: implications for management practice', *Long Range Planning*, 30: 450–4.

Gratton, L. 2007. *Hot Spots*. London: FT Prentice Hall.

Green, M. 2001. *Variations on Blu Guitar*. New York: The Lincoln Center Institute Lectures on Aesthetic Education, Teachers' College, Columbia University.

Greenfield, W. M. 2004. 'Decision making and employee engagement', *Employment Relations Today*, Summer: 13–24.

Griffiths, R. 1993. 'The politics of cultural policy in urban regeneration strategies', *Policy and Politics*, 21: 39–46.

Grisham, T. 2006. 'Metaphor, poetry, storytelling and cross-cultural leadership', *Management Decision*, 44: 486–503.

Guss, D. M. 1989. *To Weave and Sing. Arts, Symbol and Narrative in the South American Rain Forest*. Berkeley, CA: University of California Press.

Hakim, D. 2004. 'GM executive preaches: sweat the smallest details', *New York Times*, 5 January.

Hall, R. 1992. 'The strategic analysis of intangible resources', *Strategic Management Journal*, 13: 135–44.

1993. 'A framework linking intangible resources and capabilities to sustainable competitive advantage', *Strategic Management Journal*, 14: 607–18.

Hamel, G. 2000. *Leading the Revolution*. Cambridge, MA: Harvard Business School Press.

2007. *The Future of Management*. Cambridge, MA: Harvard Business School Press.

2009. 'Moon shots for management', *Harvard Business Review*, 87: 91–8.

Hassebrauck, M. and Buhl, T. 1996. 'Three dimensional love', *Journal of Social Psychology*, 136: 121–2.

Heber, L. 1993. 'Dance movement: a therapeutic program for psychiatric clients', *Perspectives in Psychiatric Care*, 29 2: 22–9.

Held, D., McGrew, A., Goldblatt, D. and Perraton, J. 1999. *Global Transformations*. Palo Alto, CA: Stanford University Press.

Helfat, C. E. and Peteraf, M. A. 2003. 'The dynamic resource-based view: capability lifecycles', *Strategic Management Journal*, 24: 997–1,010.

Helfat, C. E. and Raubitschek, R. S. 2000. 'Product sequencing: co-evolution of knowledge, capabilities and products', *Strategic Management Journal*, 21: 961–79.

Henderson, R. and Cockburn, I. 1994. 'Measuring competence? Exploring firm effects in pharmaceutical research', *Strategic Management Journal*, 15: 63–84.

Hess, D. 2009. 'Art as a mirror of our time', *Hess Art Collection Catalogue*. Stuttgart, Germany: Hatje Cantz.

Hill, C. W. L. and Jones, G. R. 1992. *Strategic Management Theory: an Integrated Approach*. Boston, MA: Houghton Mifflin.

Hilpinen, R. 2004. 'Artifact', in E. N. Zalta (ed.), *The Stanford Encyclopedia of Philosophy* (see: plato.stanford.edu/entries/artifact/).

Hitt, M. A., Ireland, R. D. and Hoskisson, R. E. 1999. *Strategic Management: Competitiveness and Globalisation*. Cincinnati, OH: South-Western College Publishing.

Hochschild, A. R. 1983. *The Managed Heart*. Berkeley, CA: University of California Press.

Iansiti, M. and Clark, K. B. 1994. 'Integration and dynamic capability: evidence from product development in automobiles and mainframe computers', *Industrial and Corporate Change*, 3: 557–605.

Ireland, R. D., Hitt, M. A. and Vaidyanath, D. 2002. 'Alliance management as a source of competitive advantage', *Journal of Management*, 28: 413–46.

Itami, H. and Roehl, T. 1987. *Mobilizing Invisible Assets*. Cambridge, MA: Harvard University Press.

Jackson, M. R. 1998 'Arts and culture indicators in community building: project update', *Journal of Arts Management Law and Society*, 28: 201–05.

Jacobs, J. 1961. *The Death and Life of Great American Cities*. New York: Random House.

Jacobson, M. 1993. *Arts and Business*. Singapore: Thames and Hudson.

Jamison, K. R. 1996. *Touched with Fire*. New York: The Free Press.

Jawahar, I. M. and McLaughlin, G. L. 2001. 'Toward a descriptive stakeholder theory: an organisational life cycle approach', *Academy of Management Review*, 26: 397–414.

Jeffrey, D., Jeffrey, P., Jones, D. and Owen, R. 2001. 'An innovative, practical course in medical humanities', *European Journal of Palliative Medicine*, 8: 203–06.

Jensen, J. 2002. *Is Art Good for Us? Beliefs About High Culture in American Life*. Lanham, MD: Rowman and Littlefield.

Johnson-Laird, P. N. 1993. *The Computer and the Mind. An Introduction to Cognitive Science*. London: William Collins.

Kaplan, R. S. and Norton, D. P. 1992. 'The balanced scorecard: measures that drive performance', *Harvard Business Review*, 70, 1: 71–9.

1996. 'Using the balanced scorecard as a strategic management system', *Harvard Business Review*, 74, 1: 75–85.

2000. 'Having trouble with your strategy? Then map it', *Harvard Business Review*, Sep-Oct: 167–76.

2003. *Strategy Maps: Converting Intangible Assets into Tangible Outcomes*. Cambridge, MA: Harvard Business School Press.

2008. *The Execution Premium*. Cambridge, MA: Harvard Business School Press.

Kim, H. 1993. 'The link between individual and organizational learning', *Sloan Management Review*, 35: 37–50.

Kim, W. C. and Mauborgne, R. 2005. *Blue Ocean Strategy: How to Create Uncontested Market Space and Make the Competition Irrelevant*. Cambridge, MA: Harvard Business School Press.

Kivy, P. 1997. *Philosophies of the Arts*. Cambridge University Press.

Klamer, A. 1996. *The Value of Culture: on the Relationship between Economics and Arts*. Amsterdam University Press.

Kogut, B. and Zander, U. 1992. 'Knowledge of the firm, combinative capabilities, and the replication of technology', *Organization Science*, 3: 383–97.

Koka, B. R. and Prescott, J. E. 2002. 'Strategic alliances as social capital: a multidimensional view', *Strategic Management Journal*, 23: 795–816.

Kolb, D. 1984. *Experimental Learning: Experience as the Source of Learning and Development*. Englewood Cliffs, NJ: Prentice Hall.

Konlaan, B. B., Bjorby, N., Weissglas, G., Karlsson, L. G. and Widmark, M. 2000. 'Attendance at cultural events and physical exercise and health: a randomised controlled study', *Public Health*, 114: 316–19.

Kottow, M. and Kottow, A. 2002. 'Literary narrative in medical practice', *Medical Humanities*, 28: 41–4.

Kuhn, T. S. 1962. *The Structure of Scientific Revolutions*. Chicago, IL: University of Chicago Press.

Langer, S. K. 1942. *Philosophy in a New Key*. Cambridge, MA: Harvard University Press.

Leana, C. R. and Van Buren III, H. 1999. 'Organisational social capital and employment practices', *Academy of Management Review*, 24: 538–55.

LeDoux, J. E. 2000. 'Emotion circuits in the brain', *Annual Review of Neuroscience*, 23: 155–84.

Lei, D., Hitt, M. A. and Bettis, R. 1996. 'Dynamic core competences through meta-learning and strategic context', *Journal of Management*, 22: 549–69.

Leonard-Barton, D. 1995. *Wellsprings of Knowledge*. Cambridge, MA: Harvard Business School Press.

Levinson, J. 1990. *Music, Art, and Metaphysics*. Ithaca, NY: Cornell University Press.

1996. *The Pleasures of Aesthetics: Philosophical Essays*. Ithaca, NY: Cornell University Press.

Likert, R. 1961. *New Patterns of Management*. New York: McGraw-Hill.

Linstead, S. and Höpfl H. (eds.), 2000. *The Aesthetics of Organisation*. London: Sage Publications.

Lock, S., Last, J. M., and Dunea G. (eds.), 2001. *The Oxford Illustrated Companion to Medicine*. Oxford: Oxford University Press.

Loehr, J. and Schwartz, T. 2001. 'The making of a corporate athlete', *Harvard Business Review*, January: 120–8.

2003. *The Power of Full Engagement*. New York: The Free Press.

Loermans, J. 2002. 'Synergizing the learning organization and knowledge management', *Journal of Knowledge Management*, 6: 285–94.

Lorenzoni, G. and Lipparini, A. 1999. 'The leveraging of interfirm relationships as a distinctive organizational capability: a longitudinal study', *Strategic Management Journal*, 20: 317–38.

Lounsbury, J. W., Gibson, L. W. and Hamrick, F. L. 2004. 'The development and validation of a personological measure of work drive', *Journal of Business and Psychology*, 18: 427–51.

Loury, G. C. 1977. 'A dynamic theory of social income differences', in P. A. Wallace and A. M. La Monde (eds.), *Women, Minorities and Employment Discrimination*. Lexington, MA: Lexington Books, 153–86.

Lowe, S. S. 2000. 'Creating community art for community development', *Journal of Contemporary Ethnography*, 29: 357–86.

Marks, S. R. 1977. 'Multiple roles and role strain: some notes on human energy, time, and commitment', *American Sociological Review*, 42: 921–36.

Marr, B. and Schiuma, G. 2001. 'Measuring and managing intellectual capital and knowledge assets in new economy organisations', in M. Bourne (ed.), *Performance Measurement Handbook*. London: GEE Publishing.

Marwick, C. 2000. 'Music therapists chime in with data on medical results', *Journal of the American Medical Association*, 283: 731–3.

Maslow, A. 1954. *Motivation and Personality*. New York: Harper and Row.

Mau, B. and The Institute Without Boundaries. 2004. *Massive Change*. London: Phaidon Press, Ltd.

Mayo, E. 1930. 'Changing methods in industry', *Personnel Journal*, 8: 326–32.

McCarthy, K. F. and Kimberly, J. 2001. *A New Framework for Building Participation in the Arts*. Santa Monica, CA: Rand Corporation.

McCarthy, K. F., Ondaatje, E. H., Zakaras, L. and Brooks, A. 2004. *Gifts of the Muse: Reframing the Debate About the Benefits of the Arts*. Santa Monica, CA: Rand Corporation.

McGrath, R. G., MacMillan, I. C. and Venkataraman, S. 1995. 'Defining and developing competence: a strategic process paradigm', *Strategic Management Journal*, 16: 251–75.

McGrath, R. G., Tsui, M. H., Venkataraman, S. and MacMillan, I. C. 1996. 'Innovation, competitive advantage and rent: a model and test', *Management Science*, **42**: 389–403.

Menzies-Lythe, I. 1988. *Containing Anxiety in Institutions. Selected Essays*. London: Free Association Books.

Meredith, R. 2007. *The Elephant and the Dragon: the Rise of India and China and What it Means for All of Us*. New York: W. W. Norton.

Miller, D. 2003. 'An asymmetry-based view of advantage: towards an attainable sustainability', *Strategic Management Journal*, **24**: 961–76.

Miller, J. B. and Stiver, I. 1997. *The Healing Connection*. Boston, MA: Beacon Press.

Mintzberg, H. 1985. 'The organisation as a political arena', *Journal of Management Studies*, **22**: 133–54.

Mitroff, I. I. and Denton, E. A. 1999. 'A study of spirituality in the workplace', *MIT Sloan Management Review*, **40**: 83–92.

Mol, M. J. and Birkinshaw, J. 2008. *Giant Steps in Management*. London: FT Prentice Hall.

Monks, K., Barker, P. and Mhanachain, A. N. 2001. 'Drama as an opportunity for learning and development', *Journal of Management Development*, **20**: 414–23.

Montealegre, R. 2002. 'A process model of capability development: lessons from the electronic commerce strategy at Bolsa de Valores de Guayaquil', *Organization Science*, **13**: 514–31.

Morris, B. 2008. 'What makes Apple golden?', *Fortune*, 17 March, 40–4.

Myerscough, J. 1988. *The Economic Importance of the Arts in Great Britain*. London: Policy Studies Institute.

Nahapiet, J. and Ghoshal, S. 1998. 'Social capital, intellectual capital, and the organizational advantage', *Academy of Management Review*, **23**: 242–66.

Neely, A. 1998. *Performance Measurement – Why, What and How*. London: Economist Books.

Neely, A., Adams, C. and Kennerley, M. 2002. *The Performance Prism: the Scorecard for Measuring and Managing Business Success*. London: FT Prentice Hall.

Neely, A., Mills, J., Gregory, M., Richards, H., Platts, K. and Bourne, M. 1996. *Getting the Measure of Your Business*. Cambridge University Press.

Nelson, R. R. and Winter, S. G. 1982. *An Evolutionary Theory of Economic Change*. Cambridge, MA: Harvard University Press.

Neu, A. J. 2000. *A Tear is an Intellectual Thing: the Meaning of Emotions*. New York: Oxford University Press.

Newton, T., Handy, J. and Fineman, S. 1993. *Stress at Work: Alternative Perspectives*. London: Sage Publications.

Nissley, N. 2002. 'Art-based learning in management education', in B. DeFillippi and C. Wankel (eds.), *Rethinking Management Education in the 21st Century*. Greenwich: Information Age Press, 27–61.

2008. 'Framing arts-based learning as an intersectional innovation in continuing management education: the intersection of arts and business and the innovation of arts-based learning', in C. Wankel and R. DeFillippi (eds.), *University and Corporate Innovations in Lifelong Learning*. Charlotte, NC: Information Age Publishing, 187–211.

2010. 'Arts-based learning at work: economic downturns, innovation upturns, and the eminent practicality of arts in business', *Journal of Business Strategy*, 31, 4: 8–20.

Nonaka, I. 1991. 'The knowledge-creating company', *Harvard Business Review*, 69: 96–104.

1994. 'A dynamic theory of organizational knowledge creation', *Organization Science*, 5: 14–37.

Nonaka, I. and Takeuchi, H. 1995. *The Knowledge-creating Company: How Japanese Companies Create the Dynamics of Innovation*. Oxford: Oxford University Press.

Nonaka, I., Toyama, R. and Konno, N. 2000a. 'SECI, Ba and leadership: a unified model of dynamic knowledge creation', *Long Range Planning*, 33: 5–34.

Nonaka, I., Toyama, R. and Nagata, A. 2000b. 'A firm as a knowledge-creating entity: a new perspective on the theory of the firm', *Industrial and Corporate Change*, 9: 1–20.

Nussbaum, M. 2001. *Upheavals of Thought: The Intelligence of Emotions*. Cambridge University Press.

Oakley, J. 1992. *Morality and the Emotions*. London: Oxford University Press.

Pehrsson, A. 2000. 'Strategy competence: a key profitability driver', *Strategic Change*, 9: 89–102.

Pennings, J. M., Lee, K. and Van Witteloostuijn, A. 1998. 'Human capital, social capital, and firm dissolution', *Academy of Management Journal*, 41: 425–40.

Perkins, D. N. 1994. *The Intelligent Eye: Learning to Think by Looking at Art*. Santa Monica, CA: The Getty Center for Education in the Arts.

Peteraf, M. A. 1993. 'The cornerstones of competitive advantage: a resource-based view', *Strategic Management Journal*, 14: 179–88.

Peteraf, M. A. and Bergen, M. E. 2003. 'Scanning dynamic competitive landscapes: a market-based and resource-based framework', *Strategic Management Journal*, 24: 1,027–1,041.

Petroski, H. 1992. *The Evolution of Useful Things*. New York: Random House.

Pfeffer, J. 1981. *Power in Organisations*. Marshfield, MA: Pitman.

Pinard, M. C. and Allio, R. J. 2005. 'Improving the creativity of MBA students', *Strategy and Leadership*, 33: 49–51.

Polanyi, M. 1962. *Personal Knowledge: Towards a Post-Critical Philosophy*. London: Routledge and Kegan Paul.

1966. *The Tacit Dimension*. Garden City, NY: Anchor Books.

Porter, M. E. 1985. *Competitive Strategy*. New York: Free Press.

1996. 'What is strategy?', *Harvard Business Review*, 74: 61–78.

Post, J., Preston, L., and Sachs, S. 2002. *Redefining the Corporation, Stakeholder Management and Organisational Wealth*. Palo Alto, CA: Stanford University Press.

Prahalad, C. K. and Hamel, G. 1990. 'The core competence of the corporation', *Harvard Business Review*, 68: 79–91.

Putnam, R. D. 1993. *Making Democracy Work. Civic Traditions in Modern Italy*. Princeton, NJ: Princeton University Press.

1995. 'Bowling alone: America's declining social capital', *The Journal of Democracy*, 6: 65–78.

Quinn, R. W. and Dutton, J. E. 2005. 'Coordination as energy-in-conversation', *Academy of Management Review*, 30: 36–57.

Radich, A. J. 1992. *Twenty Years of Economic Impact Studies of the Arts: A Review*. Washington, DC: National Endowment for the Arts.

Rafaeli, A. and Sutton, R. I. 1987. 'Expression of emotion as part of the work role', *Academy of Management Review*, 12: 23–37.

1988. 'Untangling the relationship between displayed emotions and organisational sales: the case of convenience stores', *Academy of Management Review*, 31: 461–87.

1990. 'Busy stores and demanding customers: how do they affect the display of positive emotion?', *Academy of Management Review*, 33: 623–37.

1991. 'Emotive contrast strategies as means of social influence: lessons from criminal interrogators and bill collectors', *Academy of Management Review*, 34: 749–75.

Richards, D. 1995. *Artful Work: Awakening Joy, Meaning, and Commitment in the Workplace*. San Francisco, CA: Berrett-Koehler.

Richards, M. C. 1989. *Centering: in Pottery; Poetry; and the Person*. Middletown, CT: Wesleyan University Press.

Rindova, V. P. and Kotha, S. 2001. 'Continuous "morphing": competing through dynamic capabilities, form, and function', *Academy of Management Journal*, 44: 1,263–1,280.

Rob, R. 2002. 'Social capital, corporate culture, and incentive intensity', *Rand Journal of Economics*, 33: 243–57.

Roethlisberger, F. G. and Dickson, W. J. 1939. *Management and the Worker*. Cambridge, MA: Harvard University Press.

Roos, G. and Roos, J. 1997. 'Measuring your company's intellectual performance', *Long Range Planning*, 30: 413–26.

Roos, J., Victor, B. and Statler, M. 2004. 'Playing seriously with strategy', *Long Range Planning*, 37, 6: 549–68.

Rosemberg, M. 1990. 'Reflexivity and emotions', *Social Psychology Quarterly*, 53: 3–12.

Rouse, M. J. and Daellenbach, U. S. 2002. 'More thinking on research methods for the resource-based perspective', *Strategic Management Journal*, 23: 963–7.

Rumelt, R. P. 1984. 'Towards a strategic theory of the firm', in R. B. Lamb (ed.), *Competitive Strategic Management*. Englewood Cliffs, NJ: Prentice Hall, 556–70.

Ryan, R. M. and Frederick, C. 1997. 'On energy, personality, and health: subjective vitality as a dynamic reflection of wellbeing', *Journal of Personality*, 65: 529–66.

Sandelands, L. E. 1988. 'The concept of work feeling', *Journal for the Theory of Social Behaviour*, 18: 437–57.

Scharmer, C. O. 2009. *Theory U: Leading from the Future as it Emerges: the Social Technology of Presencing*. San Francisco, CA: Berrett-Koehler.

Scharmer, C. O. and Kaeufer, K. 2010. 'In front of the blank canvas: sensing emerging futures', *Journal of Business Strategy*, 31, 4: 21–9.

Scheff, T. J. 1988. 'Shame and conformity: the deference-emotion system', *American Sociological Review*, 53: 395–406.

Schellekens, E. 2009. 'Conceptual art', in E. N. Zalta (ed.), *The Stanford Encyclopedia of Philosophy* (online encyclopedia: http://plato.stanford.edu/entries/conceptual-art/).

Schiuma, G., De Pablos, P. O. and Spender, J. C. 2007a. 'Intellectual capital and company's value creation dynamics', *Learning and Intellectual Capital*, 4: 331–41.

Schiuma, G., Lerro, A. and Carlucci, D. 2008a. 'The knoware tree and the regional intellectual capital index: an assessment within Italy', *Journal of Intellectual Capital*, 9: 283–300.

Schiuma, G., Lerro, A. and Sanitate, D. 2008b. 'Intellectual capital dimensions of Ducati's turnaround: exploring knowledge assets grounding a change management program', *International Journal of Innovation Management*, 12: 161–93.

Schiuma, G., Mason, S. and Kennerley, M. 2007b. 'Assessing energy within organisations', *Measuring Business Excellence*, 11, 3: 69–78.

Schroeder, R. G., Bates, K. A. and Junttila, M. A. 2002. 'A resource-based view of manufacturing strategy and the relationship to manufacturing performance', *Strategic Management Journal*, 23: 105–17.

Schultz, T. W. 1961. 'Investment in human capital', *American Economic Review*, 51: 1–17.

Seifter, H. and Buswick, T. 2005. 'Arts-based learning for business', *Journal of Business Strategy*, 26: 5.

Senge, P. M. 1990. *The Fifth Discipline – The Art and Practice of The Learning Organisation*. London: Century Business.

Senge, P. M., Roberts, C., Ross, R., Roth, G., Smith, B. and Kleiner, A. 1999. *The Dance of Change: the Challenges to Sustaining Momentum in Learning Organizations*. New York: Doubleday.

Shafritz, J. 1999. *Shakespeare on Management: Wise Business Counsel from the Bard*. New York: Harper Collins.

Shusterman, R. 2002. *Pragmatic Aesthetics: Living Beauty, Rethinking Art*, 2nd edn. Lanham, MD: Rowman and Littlefield.

Simon, H. 1996. *The Sciences of the Artificial*, 3rd edn. Cambridge, MA: MIT Press.

Skelton, J. R., Macleod, J. A. A. and Thomas, C. P. 2000. 'Teaching literature and medicine to medical students, part II: why literature and medicine?', *The Lancet*, 356: 2,001–3.

Solomon, R. 1990. 'Emotions and choice', in R. Solomon (ed.), *Explaining Emotions*. Oxford: Oxford University Press.

Spender, J. C. 1996. 'Making knowledge the basis of a dynamic theory of the firm', *Strategic Management Journal*, 17: 45–62.

Spender, J. C. and Grant, R. M. 1996. 'Knowledge and the firm: overview', *Strategic Management Journal*, 17: 5–9.

Stalk, G., Evans, P. and Shulman, L. E. 1992. 'Competing on capabilities: the new rule of corporate strategy', *Harvard Business Review*, 70: 57–69.

Staricoff, R. L. 2004. *Arts in Health: a Review of the Medical Literature*. London: Arts Council England.

Stearns, P. N. 1989. 'Suppressing unpleasant emotions: the development of a twentieth-century America', in A. E. Barnes and P. N. Stearns (eds.), *Social History and Issues in Human Consciousness*. New York: New York University Press.

Stecker, R. 1997. *ArtWorks: Definition, Meaning, Value*. Pennsylvania State University Press.

Steers, R. M., Mowday, R. T. and Shapiro, D. L. 2004. 'The future of work motivation theory', *Academy of Management Review*, 29: 379–87.

Stern, M. J. 2000. 'Arts, culture, and quality of life', *Social Impacts of the Arts Project (SIAP)*, University of Pennsylvania.

Stern, M. J. and Seifert, S. C. 2000. 'Re-presenting the city: arts, culture, and diversity in Philadelphia', in G. Bradford, M. Gary and G. Wallach (eds.), *The Politics of Culture*. New York: The New Press.

Stewart, T. A. 1997. *Intellectual Capital: the New Wealth of Organisations*. London: Nicholas Brealey.

Stone, A. 1997. *The Arts and Prosocial Impact Study: an Examination of Best Practices*. Santa Monica, CA: Rand Corporation.

Stone, A., McArthur, D., Law, S. and Moini, J. 1999. *The Arts and Prosocial Impact Study: Program Characteristics and Prosocial Effects*. Santa Monica, CA: Rand Corporation.

Strati, A. 1992. 'Aesthetic understanding of organisational life', *Academy of Management Review*, 17: 568–81.

2000a. 'Aesthetic theory', in S. Linstead and H. Höpfl (eds.), *The Aesthetics of Organisation*. London: Sage Publications.

2000b. *Theory and Method in Organisation Studies*. London: Sage Publications.

Strauss, C. L. 1962. *The Savage Mind*. Chicago, IL: University of Chicago Press. (Translated from French, *La Pensèe Savage*. Paris: Lybrarie Plon.)

Strongman, K. T. (ed.), 1991. *International Review of Studies on Emotion*, Vol. I. New York: Wiley.

Sullivan, J. J. 1986. 'Human nature, organisations, and management theory', *Academy of Management Review*, 11: 534–49.

Sveiby, K. E. 1997. *The New Organisational Wealth: Managing and Measuring Knowledge Based Assets*. San Francisco, CA: Berret–Koehler.

Taylor, F. W. 1911. *The Principles of Scientific Management*. New York: Harper and Row.

Taylor, S. S. 2003. 'Knowing in your gut and in your head: doing theater and the underlying epistemology of communication', *Management Communication Quarterly*, 17: 272–9.

Taylor, S. S. and Hansen, H. 2005. 'Finding form: looking at the field of organizational aesthetics', *Journal of Management Studies*, 42, 6: 1,211–31.

Taylor, S. S. and Ladkin, D. 2009. 'Understanding arts-based methods in managerial development', *Academy of Management Learning and Education*, 8: 55–69.

Teece, D. J. 2007. 'Explicating dynamic capabilities: the nature and microfoundations of (sustainable) enterprise performance', *Strategic Management Journal*, 28: 1,319–50.

1998. 'Capturing value from knowledge assets: the new economy, markets for know-how, and intangible assets', *California Management Review*, 40: 55–79.

2000. 'Strategies for managing knowledge assets: the role of firm structure and industrial context', *Long Range Planning*, 33: 35–54.

Teece, D. J., Pisano, G. and Shuen, A. 1997. 'Dynamic capabilities and strategic management', *Strategic Management Journal*, 18: 509–33.

Thayer, R. E. 1989. *The Biopsychology of Mood and Arousal*. New York: Oxford University Press.

Tsai, W. 2000. 'Social capital, strategic relatedness and the formation of intraorganizational linkages', *Strategic Management Journal*, 21: 925–39.

Turner, B. 1990. *Organisational Symbolism*. Berlin: De Gruyter.

Underhill, P. 1999. *Why We Buy: The Science of Shopping*. New York: Simon and Schuster.

Vaill, P. B. 1989. *Managing as a Performing Art*. San Francisco, CA: Jossey-Bass.

Verganti, R. 2006. 'Innovating through design', *Harvard Business Review*, December: 114–22.

Verghese, J. *et al.* 2003. 'Leisure activities and the risk of dementia in the elderly', *New England Journal of Medicine*, 348: 2,508–16.

Verona, G. 1999. 'A resource-based view of product development', *Academy of Management Review*, 24: 132–42.

Vico, G. 1968. 'The new science of Giambattista Vico', in T. G. Bergin and M. H. Fisch (eds.), *The Autobiography of Giambattista Vico*. Ithaca, NY: Cornell University Press.

Vroom, V. H. 1964. *Work and Motivation*. New York: Wiley.

Waldron, V. R. and Krone, K. J. 1991. 'The experience and expression of emotion in the workplace: a study of a corrections organisation', *Management Communication Quarterly*, 4: 287–309.

Watson, D., Clarck, L. A. and Tellengen, A. 1988. 'Development and validation of brief measures of positive and negative affect: the PANAS scales', *Journal of Personality and Social Psychology*, 54: 1,063–70.

Weitz, M. 1956. 'The role of theory in aesthetics', *Journal of Aesthetics*, 15: 27–35.

Wernerfelt, B. 1984. 'A resource-based view of the firm', *Strategic Management Journal*, 5: 171–80.

Wheatley, M. J. 1999. *Leadership and the New Science*. California, CA: Berrett-Koehler.

Whitney, J. and Packer, T. 2000. *Power Plays: Shakespeare's Lessons in Leadership and Management*. New York: Simon and Schuster.

Wiggins, R. R. and Ruefli, T. W. 2002. 'Sustained competitive advantage: temporal dynamics and the incidence and persistence of superior economic performance', *Organization Science*, 13: 82–105.

Williamson, M. 2002. 'Emotions, reason and behaviour: a research for the truth', *Journal of Consumer Behaviour*, 2: 196–202.

Winter, S. G. 1987. 'Knowledge and competence as strategic assets', in D. J. Teece (ed.), *The Competitve Challenge: Strategies for Industrial Innovation and Renewal*. Cambridge, MA: Ballinger, 159–84.

2000. 'The satisfying principle in capability learning', *Strategic Management Journal*, 21: 981–96.

2003. 'Understanding dynamic capabilities', *Strategic Management Journal*, 24: 991–5.

Wittgenstein, L. 1968. *Philosophical Investigations*. Oxford: Blackwell.

Wollheim, R. 1980. *Art and its Objects*. Cambridge University Press.

Youndt, M. A., Subramaniam, M. and Snell, S. A. 2004. 'Intellectual capital profiles: an examination of investments and returns', *Journal of Management Studies*, 41: 335–61.

Zander, U. and Kogut, B. 1995. 'Knowledge and the speed of the transfer and imitation of organizational capabilities: an empirical test', *Organization Science*, 6: 76–92.

Zollo, M. and Winter, S. G. 2002. 'Deliberate learning and the evolution of dynamic capabilities', *Organization Science*, 13: 339–51.

Zuckerman, M., Lipets, M. S., Koivumaki, J. H. and Rosenthal, R. 1975. 'Encoding and decoding nonverbal cues of emotion', *Journal of Personality and Social Psychology*, 32: 1,068–76.

Index

Printed in the United States
by Baker & Taylor Publisher Services